C000216159

The Main Lines
of
EAST ANGLIA

The Main Lines
of
EAST ANGLIA

John Brodribb

OPC

An imprint of
Ian Allan Publishing

Contents

First published 2009

ISBN 978 0 86093 629 9

All rights reserved. No part of this book may be reproduced or transmitted in any form or by any means, electronic or mechanical, including photocopying, recording, scanning or by any information storage and retrieval system, on the internet or elsewhere, without permission from the Publisher in writing.

© Ian Allan Publishing Ltd 2009

Published by Oxford Publishing Co
an imprint of Ian Allan Publishing Ltd, Hersham, Surrey KT12 4RG.
Printed in England by Ian Allan Printing Ltd, Hersham, Surrey KT12 4RG.

Code: 0910/B

Visit the Ian Allan Publishing website at www.ianallanpublishing.com

Copyright
Illegal copying and selling of publications deprives authors, publishers and booksellers of income, without which there would be no investment in new publications. Unauthorised versions of publications are also likely to be inferior in quality and contain incorrect information. You can help by reporting copyright infringements and acts of piracy to the Publisher or the UK Copyright Service.

Half-title: A Great Eastern express leaves Liverpool Street in the charge of Class D15 4-4-0 No 1888. *Ian Allan Library*

Title pages: No 70013 *Oliver Cromwell* waits at Norwich Thorpe before going on shed as a DMU on a local working creeps in behind. *John C. Baker*

Above: The M&GN locomotive shed at Cromer Beach, probably in the early years of the 20th century, with No 18, a Class C Sharp Stewart of 1894, and No 43, a Class C rebuild. *Ian Allan Library*

Introduction

This book does not pretend or attempt to record a complete history of the main lines of East Anglia — to do so would be impossible without the number of volumes resembling a complete set of the *Encyclopædia Britannica*. There is also much yet to be discovered. History continues to be written, of course, and at the time of writing the country is going through a severe economic downturn which is having its impact on the railway. The forthcoming Olympic Games, based largely on former railway land at Stratford, has already radically changed the face of the area and will continue to do so. There will continue to be the usual incremental changes at local level.

In this book, I have left spellings of place names and stations as they were at the time, whilst trying to say when they changed. Britain's railways were mostly built in Imperial units and paid for in pounds, shillings and pence. Speeds were calculated in miles per hour, and the timetable was written with the 12-hour clock; of course, the universal adoption of 'Railway Time' was yet another of the benefits brought by the iron horse. Modern equivalents are not given in the text; were they to be, a good half of it would be in brackets or appear as footnotes. For this reason, a summary of these systems is given below; readers above a certain age may elect to skip this section!

Money: the United Kingdom went decimal in February 1971. Before that the pound (£) was divided into 20 shillings (s), each shilling containing 12 pennies, or pence (d). Note that three pence (3d) was *never* 'three dee', more like 'thrupp'nce', and similarly for other amounts. A penny could be divided into two halfpennies (ha'p'nce, ½d) or four farthings (¼d). Silver coins before World War 1 were made of silver: there were the threepenny bit (later to become a 12-sided brass coin), sixpence (6d), shilling (1s), two shillings or florin, and half crown (2s 6d). Crowns (5s) had all but gone by the turn of the century. The sovereign (£1) and half sovereign (10s) were gold coins, but because of the demands of wartime, started to be replaced by notes from about 1914. Coins were much bigger than they are today: at decimalisation the shilling turned into 5p, and the florin into 10p. Both have since shrunk greatly in size and value. The sixpence, which remained briefly in circulation, was worth 2½p.

It matters more what these coins would buy. It probably isn't much use to say that in 1900 one could get a gallon of 10-year old Scotch whisky for 23s 6d (often written 23/6), or that W. Drake's 'Perfect Shirt' cost 4/6 each, or six for 26/-. A railway-carriage washer in 1911 earned 21s for a seven-day week. After all their other expenses had been met, 8s 1d was left over for the family's food: there was the man and his wife and three children. Eleven loaves of bread cost 2s 7d. Half a pound of butter cost 6d, a pound of jam 3d, two pounds of sugar 4d, and tin of milk 4d. They also spent 4d on cocoa and 2d on suet. By the 1930s a very substantial new three-bedroom semi-detached house in Beccles — way out in deepest Suffolk — would cost about £400, just about within the reach of the better-paid railway grades, many of whom had housing provided by the company.

Wages and hours improved slowly. In 1891 a newly hired engine cleaner could expect to earn 5s per week, working five days of 12-hour shifts and a half day on Saturday. The top rate might be as much as 2s 6d a day, while a top-link engine driver would be getting something like 8s a day — and that was really good money. In the 1930s a job in a factory paid about 30s per week, while the railway offered 45s for permanent way men. It would take a full social history to go through all the changes in attitude and circumstances that have taken place, and it can be well worth pursuing this.

Weights and measures do not generally come into the picture quite as much. Weight on the old Imperial system was generally measured in ounces (oz) and pounds (lb), 16oz being equal to 1lb. The stone contained 14lb, and hundredweight (cwt) was 112lb. There were 20cwt to the ton. In terms of metric equivalents there are about 454 grams to the pound — the jar of jam, and a kilogram (a bag of sugar) is about 2lb 3oz. The Imperial ton and metric tonne are actually very similar in size. Length on the Imperial system was complex, especially as the railways were originally surveyed and built long before many more modern simplifications. The mile is straightforward enough, and five miles are roughly equivalent to eight kilometres. The mile could be simply divided into halves and quarters, which is what the railways showed on their lineside posts, but could also be divided into 8 furlongs, or 80 chains (so 10 chains to the furlong), or 320 rods, or 1,760 yards, or 5,280 feet. In surveying, the other relevant measurement was that there were 100 links to the chain. In metric equivalent, a metre is just over a yard, or about 39 inches. In terms of area the old and new units are the acre and hectare: the hectare, at 2.471 acres, is much larger, 1 acre measuring 0.405 hectares.

The main lines of East Anglia are very much working railways, so do get out and use them. There remains a great deal of interest, and as both passenger and freight traffic are generally still on the increase there are many good things to come. Who knows — we may even get some new sections of line, or get some of the old bits back again. Watch out for Crossrail, which will have a huge effect on the main line between Shenfield and Liverpool Street, and for the Olympic Games. Electrification is back on the cards, so the cross-country routes, notably Felixstowe–Ipswich–Ely–Peterborough and onwards, may benefit. Take pictures, record what is happening today, and, above all, get out and enjoy our railways.

Acknowledgements

A book such as this cannot be written without the help of a great many people, and in particular the staff of the National Archives at Kew and the Cambridge, Essex, Hertfordshire, Norfolk and Suffolk Record Offices have been superb. Ken Barton and Derek Harrison have been particularly helpful, as have many current and former railway staff; thankyou to everyone, and apologies to anyone who I have inadvertently missed. I must also thank my wife Wendy, for her support, encouragement and forbearance while the book was being written. Finally, I should be delighted to hear from anyone who has further information to add about the lines, and can be contacted via the publisher.

John Brodribb
Beccles
August 2009

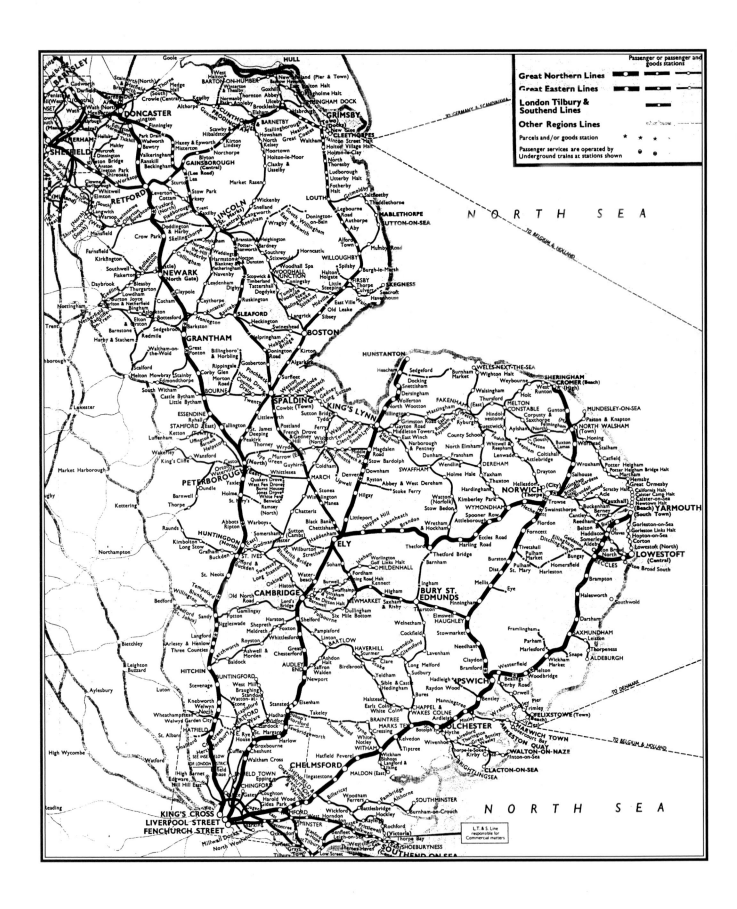

A Brief History of the Lines

London to Norwich via Ipswich

The present main line to Norwich via Ipswich is now widely known as the 'Great Eastern main line', which overlooks the fact that the route via Cambridge was also part of the Great Eastern and of similar status for most of its existence. The origins and development of both routes are closely interwoven throughout their length, although they share only two very short stretches of line, between Liverpool Street and Bethnal Green, and Trowse Lower Junction and Norwich Thorpe station. The London terminus was not there at the start, of course, and did not open fully until November 1875.

Today's Great Eastern main line can reasonably be said to have its origins back in 1834, when a prospectus for the 'Grand Eastern Counties Railway' was issued, although the 'Grand' was soon dropped. It was to have a London terminus somewhere in the Shoreditch or Whitechapel area and would have followed the present line more or less exactly to Ipswich and thence by a more easterly route to Norwich. Had it been built small, quiet towns such as Debenham, Eye and Harleston might now seethe with commuters for London, rather than Stowmarket and Diss. The Bill received the Royal Assent on 4 July 1836, on the same day as that for the Northern & Eastern Railway, which proposed to build to Cambridge, with a branch serving Thetford, Norwich and Yarmouth. At a very early stage this company approached the Eastern Counties with a view to sharing its Shoreditch terminus.

The ECR made rapid progress east of Stratford, and this was the first part to be opened, between Mile End and Romford, on 18 June 1839, which made Mile End the first London terminus for East Anglian services, albeit briefly. The section between Stratford and London was marshy, especially around Bow and later gave much trouble for Stratford depot. Much of the line had also to be carried on raised viaducts, which were costly to build. The opening to Shoreditch took

Below: Class T19 2-4-0 No 743 heads an up express away from Ipswich station in GER days. The train is a mixture of six-wheel and bogie stock. *Ian Allan Library*

place on 1 July 1840, whilst at the same time it was extended to Brentwood at the country end. Colchester was not reached until almost three years later, opening on 29 March 1843. It is a curious thing that the Eastern Counties initially built to a track gauge of 5ft, the Great Western having chosen 7ft 0¼in. The Eastern Counties and Northern & Eastern were converted to the standard gauge of 4ft 8½in in 1849.

The extension had not been without its problems, and the company was in serious financial difficulties, being rescued by a call upon its shareholders. The Essex clay and excessive rainfall in 1841 seriously delayed construction, and the track on these parts of the main line needs far more maintenance than most to this day because of the geology of the area. Costs had been greatly in excess of those originally allowed. Associated lines were being opened in the London area, and suburban traffic was already growing rapidly. By 1845 surveying had reached Ardleigh for a proposed extension from Colchester to Harwich, but parliamentary permission was refused. However, on 30 July 1845 the Northern & Eastern line, now taken over by the Eastern Counties, was extended from Bishop's Stortford to Newport and Brandon, and the Norfolk Railway simultaneously opened its line from Trowse, just outside Norwich, to connect with it. There was then the problem of crossing the River Wensum to get into Norwich, and this was done by means of a single-track swing bridge, the connection between Trowse and Thorpe Junction (the line from Yarmouth Vauxhall via Reedham had opened in May 1844) opening on 15 December 1845. The first route to Norwich and Norfolk (and indeed Suffolk) was thus the one via Cambridge.

By the start of 1841 it had become obvious that the Eastern Counties was not going to start on the construction of its Norwich–Yarmouth section, as had been promised, and that there would be rather a large gap between Norwich and Colchester. However, the line between Norwich and Yarmouth was promoted as an independent entity, although with the collusion of the Eastern Counties Railway, and after amalgamation with the Norwich & Brandon it became the Norfolk Railway. It was worked from May 1848 by the Eastern Counties.

The complete absence of Ipswich from the story so far had not gone unnoticed by the inhabitants of that town, who were aggrieved that arch-rival Norwich would soon have its own access to London, whilst they had none. Accordingly the Eastern Union Railway was formed with the backing of the influential Cobbold family, obtaining its Act for a line from Colchester to Ipswich on 19 July 1844. This intersected the proposed Eastern Counties line about 2 miles from Colchester, and, the ECR's powers of construction not having lapsed, the Eastern Union would only build its own line if the ECR did not, compensating the latter if this happened. An Act permitting this was passed on 26 June 1846. A

junction was intended with the Eastern Counties to the west of its station, which became the Colchester North of later years, and the EUR would have had its own station still further to the north on the Nayland Road. As it was, the EUR was eventually brought into the existing station, and this perpetuated the sharply curved approach from the London end which was only finally eliminated with the 1960 rebuilding.

The route to Ipswich crossed three watersheds, the summits being near Parsons Heath, Ardleigh and Bentley, and at Manningtree it crossed the Stour estuary by two short viaducts, where a plan to put a quay between the two did not materialise. At the Ipswich end a terminal station was built on the southern outskirts overlooking the River Orwell, being well-placed for extension of the line round the east side of Stoke Hill. The building was a long timber structure with the roof overhanging on each side to cover the platform and entrance. An engine shed and other buildings were also provided, and the line duly opened on 15 June 1846 with all the usual ceremony. A special train had left Ipswich for Colchester, where it met another which had come from London, the two being joined for the return to Ipswich. There was much rejoicing generally; the directors had a sumptuous lunch at the Assembly Rooms, whilst the junior officers of the railway had to be content with dinner at the Golden Lion. The workmen had their meal at the Railway Tavern, with the sub-contractors at the Coach & Horses: there was a nicely observed hierarchy in these eating arrangements. Goods traffic had been working over the line since 1 June, using locomotives that had arrived by sea from Sharp Bros. Excursion traffic also started soon after, including one giving a connection for Rotterdam at Ipswich, and such traffic remained a feature of the line.

On 21 July 1845 the Ipswich & Bury St Edmunds Railway obtained its Act; although nominally independent, it was closely connected with the Eastern Union. The Act provided for the abandonment of the original Ipswich station and the building of one on the present site, north-east of Stoke Hill, together with the tunnel to connect the two lines. Construction of the line was relatively easy, and intermediate stations were provided at Bramford, Blakenham (later Claydon), Needham, Stowmarket, Haughley, Elmswell and Thurston. The line opened on 7 December 1846, though all the stations were not ready, including the new one at Ipswich, so trains from the north had to pass Halifax Junction, where the new and old lines met, and reverse into the old station. The new one north of the tunnel lasted until 1860, when it was replaced by the present up-side platform and buildings, the long single face accommodating traffic in both directions. The island platform giving separate facilities for down trains was opened in 1883.

Meantime, the Ipswich & Bury had leased the Stowmarket Navigation, as the River Gipping had become, this taking effect in June 1846. On 1 January 1847 the Eastern Union and Ipswich &

Bury Railways concluded an agreement whereby the former worked the latter, and they were amalgamated on 9 July 1847. The Hadleigh branch was opened from its junction at Bentley on 21 August 1847, again by a nominally independent company which was soon taken over by the Eastern Union. The next major event was the extension to Norwich. An Act for this was obtained by the Ipswich & Bury even before amalgamation with the Eastern Union, and it included provision for the purchase of all the parts by the EUR. The Eastern Counties, which had taken over the Norfolk Railway, feared abstraction of its traffic to London by the new route and so would not permit the new line into its terminus at Thorpe. This obliged the EUR to construct its own station in Victoria Street, but the line from Ely had to be crossed to reach it. Because of the likely increase in traffic, a bridge — Lakenham (or Harford) Viaduct — was required rather than a crossing on the level, though it was also proposed to build a branch at Trowse to connect with the Eastern Counties line. Construction started at Norwich on 25 February 1847, again with much celebration, for the new line offered Norwich a more direct route to London. Work also started between Haughley and Stowmarket; when the new line opened Haughley Junction station replaced the original, which was closed.

The new line opened in sections: to Finningham on 7 June 1848 and Burston on 2 July 1849, through passengers being taken on to Norwich by road. The line having at last been completed, the official opening was set for 7 November 1849. The day appears to have been cold and wet, with sleet and a biting wind. A train started from Norwich at about 11.15am, carrying more than 500 people and a band. The intention had been for the train from Ipswich to meet that from Norwich at Stowmarket, where lunch had been arranged, but the Ipswich train arrived earlier and many of its passengers had already eaten by the time the northern contingent arrived. The ensuing scenes were apparently not edifying! The trains from Ipswich and Norwich were then combined at Stowmarket and taken to Norwich with both the locomotives, where a feast had been laid on at St Andrews Hall. Public passenger traffic did not start until 12 December, and goods traffic about two weeks later.

Mark's Tey became a junction on 2 July 1849, with the line to Sudbury opening at the same time as one from Colchester to The Hythe. Both were leased to the Ipswich & Bury company and later taken over by the Eastern Union. Work on the connecting line between the EUR line and the older Eastern Counties route began in the autumn of 1850 and was mostly on a gradient of 1 in 84, falling towards Thorpe, 75 chains in length — just under a mile. The line between Trowse Upper and Lower junctions was first used in September 1851 for excursion trains to Yarmouth races but was not advertised for regular traffic until 1 October. However, the Eastern Counties insisted that Eastern Union locomotives hauling exchange traffic should not enter on the ECR line, and so they had to run round their trains and propel their stock onto the main line. Other obstructive policies arose from the fact that the ECR was reluctant to see traffic diverted away from its route via Cambridge and so embarked on a rate-cutting war, as well as generally putting obstacles in the way of through traffic: the service between Norwich and London via Ipswich was so bad as to be almost unusable. During 1852 and early 1853 the EUR provided a steamer service between Ipswich and Blackwall, where passengers caught a train to Fenchurch Street. However, the Eastern Counties took over the working of the Eastern Union and associated lines from 1 January 1854, the arrangement being legalised in an Act of 7 August. This continued until 1 July 1862 when both were incorporated into the new Great Eastern Railway.

The need for a separate station at Victoria had now passed, though its continued use for passengers was enforced by a clause inserted by Norwich Corporation into the ECR's 1854 Act allowing the takeover of the EUR. Matters improved somewhat, and the GER gradually developed a reputation for smartness and efficiency with its blue-liveried locomotives and varnished-wood coaches, though it was never able to make the investments in service improvements of some of its more prosperous contemporaries. An important opening on 27 May 1872 was between Bethnal Green and Stoke Newington, the line to Edmonton Junction being available from 22 July. When the connection between Hackney Downs and Copper Mill Junction opened on 22 June, it meant that the new route to Cambridge was available for traffic, avoiding Stratford and making Bethnal Green the important junction that it is today. It was a momentous year: Bethnal Green to Bishopsgate Low Level opened on 4 November, though the remaining portion into the new Liverpool Street terminus had to wait until 1874. Also in that year the line opened between Whitlingham Junction and North Walsham, a direct connection being made five years later between Trowse Swing Bridge Junction and Wensum Junction, thus allowing through trains to the north Norfolk coast to avoid Norwich. Wensum Junction signalbox is preserved in full working order on the North Norfolk Railway at Sheringham.

With the system almost complete, there were few additions after this, although a line from Forncett to Wymondham opened in 1861. Ipswich station was enlarged in 1883, and the new Norwich Thorpe station opened on 3 May 1886. Shenfield acquired new significance on 19 November 1888 when the line thence to Wickford opened, extended to Southend on 1 October of the following year. The connection with the London, Tilbury & Southend's Upminster branch was made at Romford in 1893, and the following year saw the opening of the east side of Liverpool Street station, on 2 April. The last two new pieces of route to impinge on the main line came in 1903 and 1904 respectively, when the Fairlop loop opened between Ilford and Woodford, followed by the Kelvedon–Tollesbury section of the famous light railway. Other significant dates included the 'Radical Alterations' timetable of 1914 and the effects of the Great War, followed almost immediately by the 1923 Grouping, when the Great Eastern became part of the London & North Eastern Railway. Its lines were then put together for administrative purposes with those of the Great Northern and Great Central, forming the LNER's Southern Area, though a bill for the amalgamation of those very companies had been rejected by Parliament as recently as 1909. The Norwich line via Ipswich had vied for supremacy with the Cambridge route for most of this period, though the former was the clear winner by the start of World War 2, the 'East Anglian' perhaps giving the clearest indication of policy. The faster and straighter exit from London was a powerful factor, and the quadrupling west of Shenfield made a significant difference.

The Great Eastern pulled out all the stops for the Royal Agricultural Show when it came to Norwich in 1911. It was held in parkland at Crown Point, and the GER constructed a complete station for the occasion. There were two platforms on the double-track Wensum Curve and terminal platforms in the goods yard, where the loading and unloading of most of the livestock and other exhibits took place. Two temporary bridges were provided over the railway, and another over the River Yare, which had two lifting flaps giving a 25ft space for the passage of boats. The show ran for five days, from 26 to 30 June, up to 75,000 passengers arriving per day and needing around 80 special livestock trains. An additional passenger platform and other facilities were also provided at Trowse station. The GER had extensive stands at the show and provided dormitory accommodation and refreshment facilities for about 100 of its staff.

During the 20th century the demands on the main line increased steadily. The relentless march of suburban housing led to the opening of more stations at greater distances from London, so that Seven Kings, Goodmayes and Squirrels' Heath & Gidea Park opened within a 10-year period around the turn of the century. The Fairlop loop added further pressure, although it eased train operation by allowing trains to Ilford to continue on to Woodford and back to London without reversal. The line was quadruple-tracked as far as Romford Junction, about half a mile short of the station, the latter being at the start of the double-track section and having only two through platforms. In 1929 proposals were brought forward for quadrupling between Romford Junction and Gidea Park — a total distance of 1 mile 26 chains — and for the complete rebuilding of Romford station to a modern four-platform layout with new buildings. Additional goods sidings were also to be provided, and the contract was placed with Robert McAlpine & Co Ltd. Considerable earth-moving and bridge reconstruction were needed, and the

new tracks were placed on each side of the existing running lines. In 1931, before the Gidea Park scheme had been completed, the LNER announced its intention to extend the widening to Shenfield, the stations at Harold Wood, Brentwood and Shenfield being enlarged and improved. A new burrowing junction was to be provided at Shenfield to take Southend trains under the main line, and the scheme was to be funded by a government grant for unemployment relief.

The first part of the scheme, as far as Gidea Park, was brought into use late in 1931. The main lines had formerly passed between the two island platforms, their outer faces being used for local services. The tracks were now arranged so that the main lines passed either side of the southern platform, the local lines using the north. Heavy engineering work was needed on Brentwood Bank, with well over half a million cubic yards of earth having to be excavated. The banks were provided with heavy concrete retaining walls up to 20ft high and some 2½ miles long. Brentwood and Harold Wood were rebuilt to have four platform faces, with new offices provided at Shenfield, on the north side. The trailing connection between the down Southend line and the connection from the main line used the then-novel idea of spring points, with no connection to the signalbox. New searchlight signalling was provided from Gidea Park to just beyond Shenfield on the main line and Billericay on the Southend line. A number of signalboxes were abolished under the scheme, including Harold Wood, Brentwood Yard and Ingrave, while a new 'box at Romford took over from the former Junction and Station 'boxes. The widening allowed a number of long distance trains to be speeded up and extra suburban services to be provided. The whole scheme was completed at the end of 1933, with the train service improvements taking place from 1 January 1934.

The Great Eastern lines generally had a good safety record but were not immune from accident, and one instance which sadly has to be noted occurred on 7 March 1950. The up Peterborough postal overran signals at Rivenhall, between Witham and Kelvedon, and collided at speed with the rear of a Whitemoor–Witham goods. The accident occurred at 3.11am in conditions of poor visibility, and the fireman of the postal and the guard of the goods were killed. Additionally, the driver of the express was seriously injured and was unable to give evidence for 11 weeks after the accident happened. The freight train, hauled by a 2-8-0 and with 34 loose-coupled open and closed wagons, plus brake, had been moving very slowly, being about to enter the loop at Witham. The postal was hauled by Class B1 4-6-0 No 61057, an Ipswich locomotive, and consisted of a four-wheel van, three passenger coaches, two brake and two mail vans, plus two more passenger coaches. It appears that it was running fast, and the driver, trying to make up time because of earlier delays in station working, missed seeing signals at

Rivenhall. The 'B1' was heavily damaged and was scrapped as a result; the first four vehicles were also severely damaged, though the rear four remained upright and on the rails: steel frames and buckeye couplings doubtless helped. The report on the crash described the brake van and the last seven wagons as being 'demolished'; their remains could not even be located on the plan of the accident site.

Visibility had been getting worse during the night, and fog signalmen were on the point of being called out. At that time double-block working should have been introduced in the event of poor visibility if fog signalmen had not been put in position, but this had not been done, although the rulebook was somewhat ambiguous on the procedure. One of the problems noted by Brigadier C. A. Langley in his report was that the signalmen did not have a clear set of markers to allow them to judge the density of fog; nor was there any automatic train control, as used on the former Great Western and London, Tilbury & Southend lines. Brig Langley concluded that the blame rested on the driver of the postal, for his failure to observe the signals at Rivenhall, and that he was travelling too fast for the prevailing conditions. However, the signalman there also bore some responsibility because he had been slow in calling out fog signalmen and had not instituted double-block working; moreover he did not operate his detonator placer, which might have alerted the driver of the postal.

London to Norwich via Cambridge

The main line to Cambridge and Norwich originated with the Northern & Eastern Railway, whose bill received Royal Assent on 4 July 1836, on the same day as that for the Eastern Counties Railway. It proposed to build to Cambridge, with a branch serving Thetford, Norwich, and Yarmouth. At a very early stage the N&E approached the Eastern Counties with a view to sharing the latter's Shoreditch terminus.

The original Northern & Eastern scheme had been for a much grander railway from London, following the valley of the River Lea, and then going on to Ware, Cambridge, Peterborough, Lincoln and York, with a branch from Cambridge to Norwich. The London & Birmingham, Midland Counties and York & North Midland Counties Railways between them had a route to York, albeit longer than the Northern & Eastern's, but their opposition ensured that the N&E bill was thrown out in the 1835 session. The Northern & Eastern stated that there was insufficient time for it to prepare plans and sections for the line to York in order to present a bill to Parliament for the 1836 session, so the bill was therefore confined to the London–Cambridge section, with the extension through Newmarket, Thetford and Attleburgh (sic) to Norwich and Yarmouth, the capital needed for this being only £2 million. Applications for shares had already been invited, and powers were to be sought in the following year's session for the extension to York. At the same time the Great Northern Railway was also promoting a bill for essentially the same line, serving Cambridge and Norwich, and starting from a London terminus in Whitechapel, about ¼ mile south-east of the present Liverpool Street station.

Public meetings in Norfolk produced strong support, especially for a link between Norwich and Yarmouth. Cambridge also strongly supported the new line, seeing it as a means of getting agricultural produce to the capital. There was considerable ill-feeling between the Northern & Eastern and the Great Northern, a war of words being conducted via local newspapers such as the *Cambridge Chronicle*, but it was the Northern & Eastern's bill for the shortened line that was duly passed. This had the consequence of abandonment of a separate London terminus, and in 1839 arrangements were made with the Eastern Counties to use its line between Stratford and Shoreditch, at a rental of £7,000 per annum. The ECR, itself strapped for cash, cut back its ambitions north of Ipswich.

Construction of the line between Stratford and Bishop's Stortford proceeded apace, the engineer being Robert Stephenson, and it was originally built to the 5ft gauge. Rail was in 12 or 15ft lengths, in chaired larch sleepers 9ft long. Gradients were very favourable, the worst being about half a mile of 1 in 210 at Ponders End. Curves were gentle — nothing less than 35 chains' radius — and earthworks few. The line opened in stages, the first section, from Stratford to Broxbourne, on 15 September 1840, that to Harlow on 9 August 1841 and that to Bishop's Stortford on 16 May 1842. In February 1843 a special meeting of the company determined that the line should be extended to Newport and Cambridge. Later that year, on 25 October, a joint meeting of the shareholders of the Northern & Eastern and Eastern Counties railways agreed to amalgamate the two companies, and to press forward with the extension. The Eastern Counties agreed to extend the line to Ely and Brandon — there to meet the Norfolk Railway — and also for a branch to Peterborough, the line to Lincoln being dropped. The branch from Broxbourne Junction to Ware and Hertford, a distance of 5¾ miles, was opened for public use on 4 November 1843.

Eventually, by an Act of 1844, the Northern & Eastern was leased to the Eastern Counties for 999 years, the company finally being vested in the Great Eastern on 1 July 1902. The extensions were being pushed ahead rapidly, and on 30 July 1845 the line was extended from Bishop's Stortford to Newport and Brandon. The Norfolk Railway simultaneously opened its line from Trowse, just outside Norwich, to connect with it.

There had been much speculation about the state of the earthworks on the new line, and instabilities north of Ely had delayed the opening. During his official inspection of the line Gen Pasley, of the Board of Trade, paused at

Prickwillow for half an hour on his return and lunched at the Lamb Inn at Ely with a party of contractors, including Messrs Grissell and Peto. In its report of the opening the *Cambridge Chronicle* complained about Cambridge station, which it described as presenting a 'handsome arched front to the visitor, who will probably admire it as an extensive and tasteful stone erection ...' whilst going on to say that it was a flimsy affair, convenient in some respects, but not adequate for any considerable amount of business. Even before it opened the paper wanted it extended!

The directors of the railway companies involved invited a large number of people to travel on the first train from London, including the editors of some of the most important national papers including *The Times, The Morning Chronicle, The Morning Post* and the *Morning Herald*. The train was due out at 8.30am, although it did not leave until 8.53am — perhaps not a good omen for future timekeeping. It consisted of 16 First-class carriages and one Third-class, this last being for the 36-strong band of the Coldstream Guards. The train was double-headed by two new locomotives, one of them called *Wildfire*. After pausing for 19 minutes at Wenden — later Audley End — the train continued to Cambridge, there to await the arrival of that from Norwich. Passengers were able to partake of lunch while they passed the time, those from the east having broken their journey at Ely for the same purpose.

The usual magnificent collation — a sumptuous banquet — was laid on at Cambridge, the many courses including soups, fish, entrées, salads, chickens, a wide selection of tropical fruits and a selection of alcoholic drinks including champagne and turtle punch. The band of the Coldstream Guards played, cannons roared, flags flew, and everything was decked with bunting. There were a great many speeches by a great many of the great and the good, and the railway was welcomed with great fervour here and at stations along the line. While all this was happening the contractors had laid on a dinner for upwards of 400 labourers in the 'luggage-house' at Cambridge, with a 'good band of music'. Ely station was described as being a 'temporary erection', with a substantial building promised. The gardens in front were laid out and planted on Monday for the opening on Tuesday!

Things did not go smoothly in the weeks following the opening. On Monday 5 August 1845, just two weeks after the opening of the line, there was a fatal accident about a mile south of Chesterford and just north of Littlebury Tunnel. The train, the 11.30am from Shoreditch, had called at Wenden and cleared the tunnels, and there was some doubt as to whether it was exceeding the usual 30mph speed. The locomotive derailed as the line crossed an embankment over a steep dip, careered across the up line and eventually buried itself in the bank at the side of the track, at which point the carriages piled up behind it. Although many were hurt no passengers were killed, but one of the guards, sitting on top of

a Second-class coach, died later of his injuries. A trainee fireman on the footplate, on his first trip on the line, was killed instantly when the locomotive turned over on top of him. After much deliberation by Gen Pasley, the cause of the derailment was deemed to have been faulty track, exacerbated by excessive speed on the new section of line north of Bishop's Stortford.

More was to come. On Tuesday 20 August the same train, the 11.30am from Shoreditch, reached Cambridge, where it stopped for water and refreshments — this was long before the days of on-train catering. It had cleared Waterbeach and was passing Milepost 64½ when the locomotive left the track on the left-hand side and dragged the tender, luggage van and three coaches into the ditch. There had been prolonged heavy rain, so the ground was soft, and although the locomotive turned on its side the carriages did not. The locomotive crew were thrown clear, and there were no fatalities.

Complaints continued about poor management at Cambridge station, the facilities being completely inadequate for the crowds wishing to buy tickets. Poor timekeeping seemed to be endemic on the Eastern Counties' lines, and the layout of Cambridge station, with its single platform, caused problems. Up and down trains both needing to use the platform led to one or more being delayed, often within sight of it, for 15 minutes. Major extensions were effected in 1863, when the Great Eastern lengthened the main platform and provided a new booking office.

None of this stopped the Norfolk Railway advertising that it was now open for passenger traffic between Yarmouth and London, with down trains leaving Shoreditch at 8.0 and 11.30am, 8.15pm and the mail at 8.40pm. What it failed to mention was that there was no rail connection between the Yarmouth–Norwich and Trowse–Ely lines, there being the problem of crossing the River Wensum to reach Norwich. This was achieved by means of a single-track swing bridge, and the connection between Trowse and Thorpe Junction opened on 15 December 1845. The Norwich & Yarmouth Railway's Thorpe station had been erected in 1844 and was enlarged to accommodate the Norwich & Brandon trains; it lasted until 1886, when the present Thorpe station was built adjacent to it on the east side, the old one becoming a goods depot.

The half-yearly meeting of the Eastern Counties Railway in August 1845 reported on events to date and noted that the 26-mile line between Ely and Peterborough was not yet open. The line between Ely and Brandon was not showing any return. The Act had been obtained for the line between Ely and Lynn, which was expected to open within 12 months.

Agitation continued for the ECR to run excursion trains from Cambridge, and eventually some were run from London and Hertford to Cambridge during August 1845. Complaints were made about the low level of discounts on day tickets and the refusal of the company to offer season tickets. Shareholders began to be concerned at the sight of their deteriorating assets. Meanwhile the Ipswich & Bury Railway was pressing ahead, and had gained parliamentary approval for the line between Ipswich and Bury, thus extending the Eastern Counties' route from Colchester. It now sought to extend it to Cambridge. The Newmarket & Chesterford also issued its prospectus in early October, proposing a direct line between the two places, with a branch from Newmarket to Cambridge, a total length of 24 miles.

Problems with the permanent way were perhaps to be explained by serious skimping on standards when the line was being built. At the Eastern Counties' board meeting in June 1847 the directors learned that the track on the Newport–Brandon line had only four sleepers to one yard of 75lb rail, and question M. A. Borthwick, who had worked as assistant to Robert Stephenson on the line. Peto also attended as the contractor. The board agreed to lay a fifth sleeper in each yard at a cost of £16,377, with the ECR to carry out the work. At the same time plans were approved for alterations at Cambridge station costing £10,000.

The route from Shoreditch and Stratford to Cambridge had been duly completed by the Eastern Counties Railway, successor to the Northern & Eastern; the latter was not finally vested in the Great Eastern until 1 July 1902. The line between Norwich and Brandon was built by the Norfolk Railway, as noted earlier. This company had its origins in the Yarmouth & Norwich Railway, whose bill received the Royal Assent on 18 June 1842. Work on the line via Reedham proceeded rapidly under the guidance of its chairman, George Stephenson, and his son Robert, who was the engineer. The line opened on 30 April 1844 with all the usual music and feasting, the Norwich terminus being at Thorpe. The Norwich & Brandon Railway's bill received Royal Assent on 10 May 1844, it being now obvious that there was far more prospect of linking Norwich with the outside world via Cambridge than via the seemingly moribund Ipswich route. Messrs Grissell and Peto were awarded the contract for the line, having already built the one from Yarmouth. Construction was rapid, although the crossing of the navigable River Wensum caused problems. They were solved by the design and construction of the first of the characteristic swing bridges at Trowse, but this was not ready until 15 December 1845. The Trowse–Brandon line opened on 30 July 1845, but, perhaps with an eye to two lots of feasting, the celebrations for the opening took place the day before. Wymondham soon became a junction, the opening of the line to Dereham on 7 December 1846 being followed on 2 May 1881 by the line from Forncett. This was intended to be a main line, allowing trains to run fast from the Ipswich line to Dereham and Wells, and was laid out accordingly, but it never carried significant traffic.

Ely to King's Lynn and Peterborough

The line between Ely and King's Lynn was authorised in two stages by the Lynn & Ely Railway's Act of 30 June 1845, which had the support of the Eastern Counties. This authorised the line from Ely, the branch to Lynn Harbour, and another branch from Watlington to Wisbech. The terrain was easy for railway building, although construction did not start for nearly a year after the Act was passed. It then proceeded quickly, so that the line was opened between Lynn and Downham on 27 October 1847. South of here the Bedford Level Corporation, which controlled the waterways of the area, imposed conditions which required the construction of viaducts over the River Ouse. The ground conditions proved difficult in the extreme and swallowed seemingly endless amounts of material before a solid trackbed could be achieved. The viaducts, including one over the River Wissey, were constructed entirely of timber. At last, on 25 October 1847, the line was opened throughout between Lynn and Ely. In the meantime, on 22 July 1847, the Lynn & Ely, the Lynn & Dereham and the Ely & Huntingdon railways had amalgamated to form the East Anglian Railway, which in turn became one of the constituents of the Great Eastern upon its formation in 1862.

Peterborough was also receiving the attention of railway promoters. The first successful Act received assent on 4 July 1843 and was promoted by the London & Birmingham for a line from Northampton, following the Nene valley; this line later became part of the London & North Western. There was much support for it, but opposition from Cambridgeshire and Huntingdonshire, where the extension of the Northern & Eastern from Cambridge was seen as more advantageous. Meanwhile the Eastern Counties had proposed its branch from Ely, the Act receiving Royal Assent on 4 July 1844. There was a proposal for a joint station between the L&B and ECR, but this fell through, and the Eastern Counties agreed to let its station — later Peterborough East — be used by the trains from Northampton. It opened for public passenger traffic on 2 June 1845 and for goods on 15 December.

The Eastern Counties was now in the curious position of having its station in Peterborough open without yet having opened its railway, apart from the short connection to the London & Birmingham's route. The contractor, Samuel Morton Peto, pushed ahead rapidly and was able to report the line completed by October 1846, although the ECR directors had expected it to open in September. In the event goods traffic started on 10 December, and passenger on 14 January 1847. A separate bill for a deviation at Whittlesea had been necessary in 1845. Buoyed by all these developments, the Eastern Counties' traffic revenue for the first six months of 1846 showed a healthy 7% increase over 1845, up to £86,718.

Cromer

Cromer was relatively late in becoming connected to the railway system. A start was finally made by the East Norfolk Railway on the line from Whitlingham to North Walsham as late as 1865, but there were many problems, and construction was slow. Long before the Cromer line came to fruition the company proposed building extensions westwards. With its line to North Walsham already authorised, it sought powers in the 1864/5 session to build a branch from its main line just south of Wroxham to Aylsham. Nothing came of this proposal. An extension to Cromer was projected, and North Walsham was reached in 1874 and — at long last — Cromer in 1877, where the Great Eastern's inconveniently sited station later became Cromer High. The line was widened in two stages, from Whitlingham to Wroxham in 1890, and from Wroxham to North Walsham in 1897. The section from Norwich to Whitlingham had been doubled in 1874 and was awaiting Board of Trade inspection when, on the night of 10 September, there occurred a disastrous head-on collision. Twenty-five people were killed, including both locomotive crews, and 73 injured.

Further improvements were made in 1879, when the direct line between Trowse Swing Bridge Junction and Wensum Junction — also known as the Wensum Curve — was opened, allowing trains to run from the south directly towards North Walsham and Cromer. It had been authorised in the GER Act of 1875.

East Suffolk

The East Suffolk between Ipswich and Yarmouth South Town was the main line for many years, also providing Lowestoft with its main outlet to the south. Its sawtooth gradient profile and, in later years, increasing locomotive power together ensured that trains could cover the longer route to Yarmouth Vauxhall in less time, and the East Suffolk declined in importance until the section between Beccles and South Town closed in November 1959.

The East Suffolk had started life as the Halesworth, Beccles & Haddiscoe, building its line southwards from a junction with the Lowestoft–Norwich line. It opened on Monday 4 December 1854, with a temporary terminus at Halesworth. It was renamed the East Suffolk Railway before it opened, by which time plans were already in hand to extend northwards to Yarmouth and south towards Ipswich. Yarmouth was keen to have another rail route to London and took a jaundiced view of the Eastern Counties' services. The new line would form an end-on link with the Eastern Union's line between Ipswich and Woodbridge, and branches to Lowestoft, Framlingham, Snape and Leiston were also proposed, the first-named being by far the most important in traffic terms. Construction stretched over nearly five years and involved closure of the original line for 15 months for doubling. There was already one swing bridge over the River Waveney, between Aldeby and Beccles, and another was needed at St Olaves. There were considerable delays caused by the need to get the earthworks between Bealings and Westerfield into a sufficiently stable condition to allow the line to open, and it did not do so until 1 June 1859. The Eastern Counties worked the lines from the outset, and the East Suffolk became a constituent of the Great Eastern when it was formed.

Harwich

Harwich has long been recognised as an important port. The Eastern Union & Harwich Railway & Pier Company obtained its Act in July 1847, and the line between Manningtree and Harwich (now Harwich Town) was completed by the Eastern Union in 1853. There were further delays and it was not officially opened by the Eastern Counties until 15 August 1854. The passenger station was in George Street, and the line continued along by the harbour. Increasing traffic quickly necessitated the building of the New Pier, which was rail-served from the start, although the earlier lines to the harbour remained in use. The passenger station was rebuilt on a new site, still in George Street, as a terminus, and the site of the old one became part of the goods yard. The Great Eastern ran boat trains between London and Harwich to connect with the Continental steamers, although passengers had to make their own way between the quay and the railway station.

By the end of the 1860s the levels of traffic on offer were leading to the need for expansion. Ships were getting bigger, and plans were drawn up to reclaim the large area of mudflats and create a new deep-water quay using Ray Island, which became Parkeston Quay. This was authorised by an Act of 1874, and the work was done from about 1879 onwards. Parkeston Quay station, built wholly of wood, opened in 1882, and was named after the then chairman of the Great Eastern, Charles H. Parkes. The railway line was re-routed between Wrabness and Dovercourt so that it served the new station, the old alignment being abandoned, and the track lifted.

Further improvements followed after World War 1. Through its subsidiary Great Eastern Train Ferries Ltd the railway bought the redundant train-ferry berth at Southampton, for re-erection at Harwich. It also bought from the Government three train-ferry boats, built in 1917 by Armstrong Whitworth and the Fairfield Shipbuilding & Engineering Co, and together with corresponding improvements at Zeebrugge in Belgium, the new train-ferry service was inaugurated on 24 April 1924 by HRH Prince George (later the Duke of Kent). The new ferries used the New Quay at Harwich and offered transit between Great Britain and the Continent without the need for trans-shipment. The last remaining intermodal service, the train ferry to Zeebrugge, was withdrawn by

British Rail's Railfreight Distribution prior to the opening of the Channel Tunnel, the last day of operation being 29 April 1994.

Midland & Great Northern

The Midland & Great Northern Joint Railway was the only serious competitor to the Great Eastern in East Anglia, and although there were a number of minor independent lines such as the Colne Valley & Halstead, the Mid-Suffolk Light and the narrow-gauge Southwold, none can remotely be considered as a main line, despite any possible early pretensions. The M&GN did have such pretensions, and was seen by its parent companies as providing the means to reach the coast of Norfolk and Suffolk, and tap into the burgeoning holiday traffic.

The system eventually came to consist of a number of lines based on Melton Constable, in rural Norfolk. One originated just to the west of Bourne, in Lincolnshire, where it made an end-on junction with the Midland Railway near Castle Bytham, and then went via Spalding to Sutton Bridge and King's Lynn to Melton Constable. The other western arm started in Peterborough and went across to Wisbech, joining the other route at Sutton Bridge. From Melton the main line meandered through Fakenham and North Walsham to Yarmouth Beach, whilst there were also lines from Melton to Sheringham and Cromer and to Norwich City.

The lines were opened in stages by a series of small companies, starting with the Holbeach–Spalding section in 1858. The companies themselves were subjected to amalgamations, takeovers and changes of name, but by the end of 1866 the lines between Bourne, Peterborough and King's Lynn had been opened, although opening eastward did not start until 1879. Meanwhile the Great Yarmouth & Stalham company opened as far as Ormesby in August 1877, and the Lynn & Fakenham reached Norwich in 1882. The Melton–North Walsham section was opened in 1883 by the Eastern & Midlands, and this finally created the link from west to east. At last, in 1887, the Eastern & Midlands reached Cromer, by extending its line from Holt. The system was completed in 1894 when the Midland and M&GN opened the line between Saxby and Bourne.

The Eastern & Midlands company, successor to the string of smaller concerns, was formed by amalgamation in 1883, and relations with the Great Northern and Midland were often strained; both operated services over its lines, and both harboured ambitions to reach further into Norfolk. However, its financial situation was precarious, and in 1883 the Great Northern and Midland took joint ownership of the western section, west of Sutton Bridge. This precipitated a further financial crisis on the eastern section, where there had been no returns for shareholders for several years. Finally, in 1893, they gained control of the whole of the Eastern & Midlands, and this was vested in the Midland & Great Northern Joint Committee. Most of its lines were single-track, and almost all were duplicated by competing Great Eastern routes.

At the Grouping in 1923 the Great Eastern and Great Northern became parts of the London & North Eastern Railway, whilst the Midland was a constituent of the London, Midland & Scottish. The M&GN therefore remained a joint concern, separately managed, with its offices in King's Lynn and its works at Melton Constable. However, in 1936 the LNER took over responsibility for the whole management of the system, and it effectively ceased to be a joint concern, although the initials 'M&GN' remained in use until closure of most of the system in 1959.

Today East Anglia's main lines retain a distinctive identity, even after being modernised. The architectural legacy of the stations at Ipswich, Needham, Stowmarket, Norwich Thorpe and Cambridge is particularly fine, and there is much else still to savour. The creation in April 1988 of British Rail's new Anglia Region, embracing most of the remaining Great Eastern lines, continued the feeling that had been evident 30 years earlier, when No D200 carried its 'Progress ... by Great Eastern' headboard on its first run. BR subsequently abolished the regions in favour of business sectors, but East Anglia managed to feature in at least four: InterCity, Network SouthEast, Regional Railways and Railfreight. At privatisation in the 1990s infrastructure and operation were separated, with the creation of Railtrack (and, later, Network Rail). Anglia Railways took over operation of longer-distance passenger services on the main line between Liverpool Street, Ipswich and Norwich, together with the rural routes of Norfolk and Suffolk, whilst Great Eastern operated the suburban services. West Anglia Great Northern was awarded the franchise for routes out of Liverpool Street to Cambridge and Ely, as well as those from King's Cross to Cambridge and King's Lynn. Services from Norwich and Cambridge to the Midlands were awarded to Central Trains, Ipswich and Harwich having lost through running beyond Peterborough.

Further upheavals in 2004 changed the picture so that all services out of Liverpool Street on both main lines were taken over by National Express, initially trading as 'one Railway'. However, First Capital Connect took over the King's Cross services, so train operation at Cambridge regained some of its complexity. The 2005 Railways Act removed any autonomy from the passenger-train operators, the Department for Transport now having direct responsibility for timetabling and service provision. Cross-country services were altered in November 2007, so that East Midlands Trains (Stagecoach) took over the Norwich services, and Cross Country (Arriva) the Cambridge and Stansted Airport routes.

Steam may be long gone from the East Anglian main lines, but there remains a great deal of interest, and they face an intriguing future.

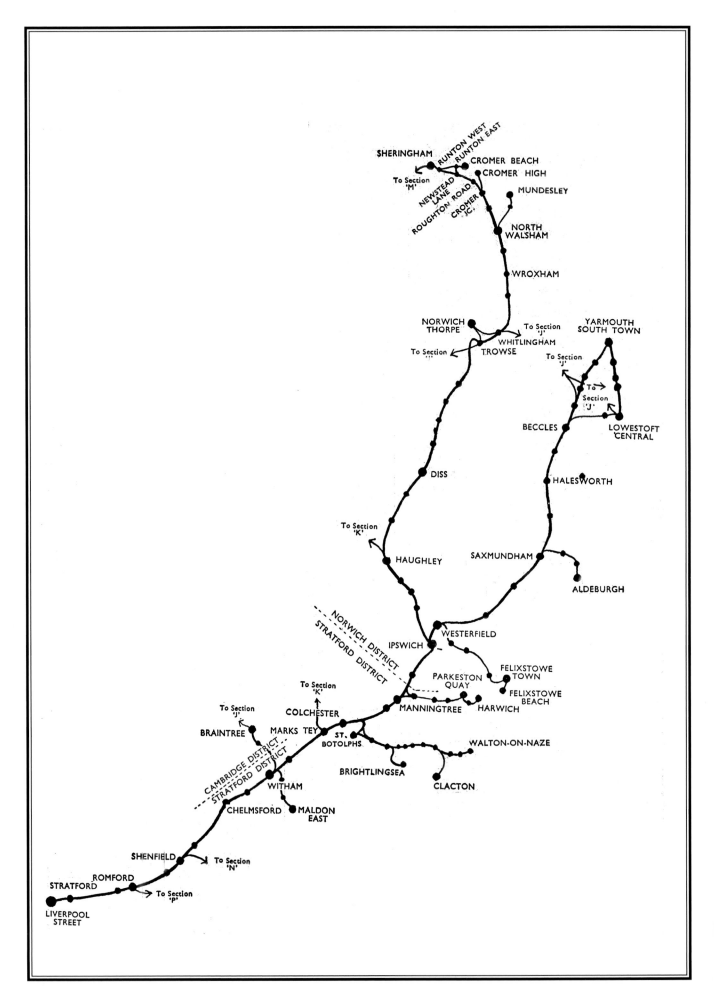

SHERINGHAM
RUNTON WEST
RUNTON EAST
CROMER BEACH
CROMER HIGH
To Section 'M'
NEWSTEAD LANE
ROUGHTON ROAD
CROMER JC.
MUNDESLEY
NORTH WALSHAM
WROXHAM
NORWICH THORPE
To Section 'J'
WHITLINGHAM
TROWSE
To Section 'I'
YARMOUTH SOUTH TOWN
To Section 'J'
To Section 'J'
BECCLES
LOWESTOFT CENTRAL
DISS
HALESWORTH
To Section 'K'
HAUGHLEY
SAXMUNDHAM
ALDEBURGH
NORWICH DISTRICT
STRATFORD DISTRICT
IPSWICH
WESTERFIELD
PARKESTON QUAY
FELIXSTOWE TOWN
FELIXSTOWE BEACH
To Section 'K'
COLCHESTER
MANNINGTREE
HARWICH
To Section 'J'
BRAINTREE
MARKS TEY
ST. BOTOLPHS
WALTON-ON-NAZE
CAMBRIDGE DISTRICT
STRATFORD DISTRICT
BRIGHTLINGSEA
WITHAM
CLACTON
CHELMSFORD
MALDON EAST
SHENFIELD
To Section 'N'
STRATFORD
ROMFORD
To Section 'P'
LIVERPOOL STREET

The Route via Ipswich

Although there have been many ways to reach East Anglia by train from London, Liverpool Street station has been the real gateway since it opened in 1874. Together with the Great Eastern Hotel its frontage occupied much the greater part of the north side of Liverpool Street, EC2, sharing it only with the North London Railway's Broad Street terminus. Across the road was the main entrance of the Metropolitan Railway's station, reached also by subway from the main line. Many a journey into East Anglia has begun with the traveller rattling into the eastbound Metropolitan platform, and then struggling with a mountain of luggage through the tortuous narrow passage that gave access to the surface. There was the bother of finding the Underground ticket and handing it to the collector whilst keeping moving through the throng of people relentlessly headed in the same upward direction. Turning sharp left and bearing upwards the traveller emerged from the gloom of the Underground into ... the gloom of Liverpool Street main-line station.

Liverpool Street was built by the Great Eastern Railway at a low level to replace the former Eastern Counties terminus of Shoreditch, later to become Bishopsgate goods station. This near-subterranean site contributed greatly to its perpetually dark atmosphere, for although the trainsheds were lofty, the streets that flanked them were high up by comparison. The term 'gloom' is perhaps a little unfair: 'haze' or 'fog' or even 'smog' might better have described it, certainly in the days of steam. The atmosphere owed much to the intensity of the suburban service, which demanded that large numbers of tank engines be continually arriving, released and awaiting the next inward service so that they could back on and be away. Not until the glass was cleaned or replaced in the rebuilding of the 1980s did the light really flood in.

There had been many plans to electrify the lines that it served, dating right back to the days of the Great Eastern, but for various reasons, due largely to the chronic lack of finance and the intervention of war, the first part was not inaugurated until it had passed into the hands of British Railways. The Great Eastern proudly boasted that it operated the most intensive steam service in the world — the famous 'Jazz' trains — and the London & North Eastern continued the tradition. It certainly made for a unique atmosphere in every sense of the word, but one that was gradually dispelled from 1949 when the first stage of the suburban electrification was opened to Shenfield. Thereafter the march of the wires became relentless, public electric services reaching Chelmsford on 11 June 1956 and Southend Victoria on 31 December of that year, and culminating in the electrification to Norwich in 1987.

Trains on the main line might be destined for a number of places apart from Norwich Thorpe station. The first short section of the route, as far as Bethnal Green, was shared with all the suburban and Cambridge-line services, including those to Norwich via Ely. Numerous workings to the likes of Chingford, Enfield Town and Hertford East pounded up the suburban lines through Bishopsgate Tunnel, whilst the longer-distance services to Bishop's Stortford, King's Lynn and named trains such as the celebrated 'Fenman' to Hunstanton used the main lines, diverging at Bethnal Green East Junction. The Southend and suburban services operated over the local lines, which later became the 'electric lines' when the new service to Shenfield was inaugurated. Before the Central Line of the Underground encroached on former Great Eastern territory these also included the branch to Ongar and the Fairlop loop.

The throat at Liverpool Street was sharply curved and had hitherto been controlled by East and West signalboxes. On 9 November 1949 the new electric signalling was commissioned, controlled by a single 'box, itself replaced by the new power 'box at Worship Street during Easter 1989. The suburban lines — in other words the pair on the down or left side for trains leaving the station — burrowed through Bishopsgate Tunnel and under the high-level line into the goods station. Great care had to be taken by firemen in the terminus not to make smoke, and there were inspectors watching out for this. Only a few hundred yards from the buffer stops, East London Junction was passed on the up side, the connection to the East London line and Shoreditch station being clearly visible. At one time a joint concern controlled by the Great Eastern, Metropolitan, South Eastern & Chatham and London, Brighton & South Coast companies, it became an offshoot of London Transport's Metropolitan Line and for many years was one of the important links across the Thames, especially for freight coming off the Southern via New Cross Gate. Until fairly recently such trains, in either direction, worked into Liverpool Street at night for the purposes of reversal.

The incline, a gradient that was one of the steepest on the Great Eastern system, started within a fairly short distance of the platform ends,

Above: 'B12' No 1505 has steam to spare departing Liverpool Street with an express in GER days. *Ian Allan Library*

Right: Mail is loaded onto the 17.30 departure for Great Yarmouth as it stands at Liverpool Street's Platform 9 on Saturday 7 August 1982. At the head of the train was Class 47/4 No 47 585 *County of Cambridgeshire*. *Richard Lyndsell*

Right: On 14 June 1958 the 10.35am from Yarmouth South Town to Liverpool Street passes East London Junction behind 'B17' 4-6-0 No 61670 *City of London*, formerly streamlined. Note the London Transport East London Line train in the station at Shoreditch (far right). *R. E. Vincent*

and provided a stern test of the driving and firing skills of men on both the express and the equally heavy suburban trains hauled by their often-diminutive tank engines. Trains ground up the sinuous grade, bounded by the grimy retaining walls with Bishopsgate Goods above and Spitalfields on the right. Having climbed back to the level of the original route the line was now on a series of brick viaducts, six tracks overlooking the backs of East London terraced houses. At this point the 'new' line from Liverpool Street joined the original ECR route from Bishopsgate at Bethnal Green West Junction, Spitalfields goods station being slightly towards London on the old line, and giving access to Spitalfields coal depot, also on the up side.

Bethnal Green station (1 mile 10 chains) had three platforms in the 1930s, two side and one island, giving four faces. The tracks were organised respectively (north to south: the line here went in a more or less easterly direction) as the suburban, local and through lines. Only the suburban lines had a straight run through, and even they curved sharply to the left at the East Junction to take the route via Hackney Downs. As today, six running roads out of Liverpool Street became four to Hackney Downs and four to Stratford at Bethnal Green East Junction, a sure recipe for congestion as trains funnelled in to the terminus. The local and through lines were reorganised when the Ilford flyover was opened in 1947 and their functions were reversed, and what had been the up local platform was abolished. This allowed the newly named main lines to be realigned, and the speed limit to be raised by 10mph to 40mph. As part of the general resignalling the old East and West Junction signalboxes were replaced by a single new brick-built structure, in the LNER's standard style, at the west end of the main platform. For many years this was the point at which trains to and from Norwich via either main line converged or diverged, usually working by one route and back via the other.

The Norwich line continued, still largely on viaducts. One prominent landmark, two miles from Liverpool Street, was the huge red-brick edifice of Bryant & May, makers of matches, which stood on the down side of the line and had a large blue British Railways sign proclaiming 'LONDON 2 MILES', with a large arrow pointing the way. The line then crossed over the Grand Union Canal, past Coborn Road station (2¼ miles) which finally closed in 1946, and over the North London's line to Devons Road (Bow), Poplar and the docks. At Bow Junction, controlled latterly by another of the LNER-designed standard brick 'boxes, the line from Fenchurch Street and Stepney trailed in on the up side. Between Bow Junction and Stratford there were nine running roads, which were (from left to right looking towards Stratford) the down and up goods, down and up Cambridge, down and up main, down and up electric and the Fenchurch Street single line. The goods roads were worked on the 'no block'

system and were thus not available for passenger use, and the Fenchurch Street line has now been taken over by the Docklands Light Railway.

The next junction — Carpenters Road South — marked the approach to the maze that was Stratford. As the largest steam shed in the country it was unmistakable, with a pall of smoke often hanging over it, worse on Monday mornings when more locomotives were being lit up from cold. Here was the real smell of steam and sulphur and hot oil which many now remember so fondly, but which at that concentration was a major pollutant and a killer from respiratory disease. Trains bearing off to the left at the junction passed Carpenters Road goods depot, not closed until 1964, and could then join either the North London line westbound, or the Great Eastern's Cambridge line at Loughton Branch Junction.

A little further along the main line Stratford Western Junction gave access for down trains to the North Woolwich line, and further still Stratford Central Junction completed the triangle with Carpenters Road. Central Junction East adjoined immediately, facing the opposite direction, and allowed down trains to pass directly to the original Northern & Eastern line to Cambridge via Chobham Farm Junction. Platforms 12 and 13 were available for down trains, and No 11 for those in the up direction. Stratford station itself (4 miles 3 chains) stood in the 'V' of Central Junction East, Platforms 10 and 12 forming the apex. In the rebuilding to accommodate the Central Line extension the new signalbox, called simply 'Stratford Station', was constructed at the London end of these platforms, fitting the spirit of the times with its austere brick lines and concrete roof, and sporting the LNER style of enamelled nameboard adopted by British Railways, of white Gill Sans letters on a dark blue ground. Exactly four miles from Liverpool Street, it controlled parts of the Stratford complex as well as the main line between Bow Junction and Forest Gate.

Having made their brief acquaintance with the Underground, trains on the surface curved under the Angel Lane bridge and on eastwards through the brick-lined cuttings towards Maryland and Forest Gate. The former (Maryland Point in Great Eastern and early LNER days) was only half a mile from Stratford, and set well below street level, with an island and two side platforms serving the four running lines, the station buildings fronting Windmill Lane, on the down side. Because of its subterranean position it was a gloomy place at the best of times, but received one of the most complete refurbishments under the postwar scheme, completed in 1948 as the precursor to the Shenfield electrification. Its new style typified the spirit of renewal after the war and better things to come. Internally, the booking office was completely refitted in light oak by a leading firm of shopfitters, and all the latest equipment for the storage and issue of tickets was provided, including a 'Rapid Ticket Printer' and a Bellmatic installation. The latter were familiar until the late 1980s on both British Rail and the

Above: Opened in 1947, Ilford flyover was built as part of the reorganisation of Liverpool Street station, the objective being to reduce the number of conflicting movements between local and main-line trains. Forming a service for Gidea Park, Class 315 EMU No 315 812, in BR blue and grey livery, comes off the flyover on 3 July 1982. *Michael J. Collins*

Underground, issuing tickets from a large roll of card at the press of a button. Fluorescent lighting made a stark contrast with the old single incandescent light bulbs. The cream and blue tiled décor in the public areas was applied to interior and exterior surfaces, and is still apparent at platform level, even after refurbishment. There were no goods facilities at Maryland; it was purely a station for the inner-suburban passenger traffic.

Forest Gate station (5 miles 21 chains) was a further three-quarters of a mile to the east. It was located in a shallow cutting, and in common with many of the larger inner-suburban stations on the main line had its principal buildings — and access from a road overbridge — here at the country end. There had also been access stairs at one time at the London end of what was latterly the up electric platform. The main building, in red brick, was unusual in having a fully hipped roof with red tiles and an ornate ridge. Enclosed stairways led from the building straight onto the platforms, these being arranged, as elsewhere, in the form of an island flanked by two side platforms. The track layout was a little unusual in that the main and electric lines both diverged to pass the island, whilst elsewhere only the pair provided by the widening tended to show this.

Forest Gate Junction was just over half a mile further on, and controlled by one of the older signalboxes — a Great Eastern wooden superstructure with brick to first-floor level. At this point the Tottenham & Forest Gate Joint line

(between the Midland and London, Tilbury & Southend) passed high over the Great Eastern at an acute angle, the junction allowing trains from Liverpool Street to gain direct access to the LT&S line to Barking. Forest Gate goods station was a little further to the east of the junction and had been the original passenger station, closing as early as 1843, although it soon reopened for goods and was not finally closed until December 1970.

The line continued, still in a shallow brick-lined cutting, with one of the most prominent features on the down side being Manor Park Cemetery and Crematorium. Its ornate buildings are clearly visible from the railway, together with some sumptuous monuments to the long-departed. Even past Manor Park station, a mile from Forest Gate, the cemetery continued to dominate the lineside until almost halfway to Ilford.

By Manor Park station (6 miles 19 chains) the lineside was beginning to open out somewhat. The down main-line platform was again on the north side, with an island forming the up main and down electric platforms. As with the other stations in the original electrification scheme 'next train' indicators were provided, consisting of double-sided metal boxes split internally into sections, each lit by a fluorescent tube. Station names were in white Gill Sans letters on a black ground, and covered all stops to Shenfield. The up platform was also an island, but only the inner face was used for up electric services, a goods line worked by permissive block running round the outside of this platform. The main building was again in red brick over the country end of the main lines, the roof this time fitting between the gable ends, which had a stone coping. Enclosed stairways again projected out onto the platforms, and extensive use was made of the buff and blue tiles, especially on the high wall which hid the goods line from the up electric platform. The coal yards at Manor Park closed for public use in 1968, although sidings were retained, access being controlled by a ground frame.

Between here and Ilford a flyover had been built which opened on 6 October 1947, taking the electric or suburban tracks over the main lines, thus removing a serious conflict between the two services. Here the railway crossed the Roding valley, and there were extensive sidings to the south just before it reached the river. Today a huge flyover carrying the A406 North Circular Road goes over everything at this point.

Ilford station (7 miles 28 chains) was altogether bigger and better appointed than the string of inner-suburban stations so far, with the notable exception of Stratford, and sported one of the LNER-style brick signalboxes some way from the London end of the up platform. The layout was essentially the same as with the other stations, with an island and two side platforms, and the main buildings on an overbridge at the country end. Additionally there was a London-facing bay on the down side of the down electric platform. Being much more heavily used than the smaller stations Ilford also had a series of red-brick buildings at platform level, incorporating toilets, offices and so on.

Drivers and motormen had to concentrate intensely on these inner-suburban parts of the line where the closeness of the stations and the curvature of the tracks as they snaked around the platforms made the line ahead look sinuous, especially at speed. Additionally the signals were densely and unevenly spaced, which made sighting more difficult, and this was the more so at Ilford and Gidea Park.

There then followed Ilford Car Sheds, with its signalbox on the down side, and Seven Kings station (8 miles 45 chains), again tiled in the postwar modernisation scheme; there had once been a triangular junction between here and Ilford which gave access to the Fairlop loop from both directions on the main line. This was controlled by 'boxes at Ilford Carriage Sidings Junction and Seven Kings West Junction, the apex being Newbury Park Junction. These connections were severed after the Central Line took over the services on the loop, and although through goods services continued for a time, little trace now remains. Ilford was the only passenger station serving the town for many years, but the Great Eastern's assiduous development of the traffic led to the opening of Seven Kings early in the 20th century, with Newbury Park — on the Fairlop loop — another addition.

At the western end of the triangle Ilford Car Sheds extended over the former junction, access

being controlled by another large brick signalbox, this time on the north side of the line. The car sheds were easily the most prominent railway landmark since passing Stratford, and provided servicing and stabling facilities for the rapidly growing fleet of electric multiple-units coming into use as the wires marched steadily onwards.

The main line then emerged into Goodmayes station (9 miles 23 chains), also opened early in the 20th century, which with its extensive siding complexes was the destination for a very large number of freight trains from all parts of East Anglia. There were marshalling yards on both sides, the down having a 70ft turntable. There were also up and down hump yards, where operations were controlled by colour-light signals installed in LNER days, supplemented by a hooter in the up yard for use in poor visibility. Much of the work done here was the reception of goods from the country areas for forwarding into London as soon as space became available. Bishopsgate and Spitalfields would send empty wagons back to Goodmayes for resorting and despatch back to rural East Anglia. The station itself followed the usual pattern, with the buildings this time over the London end of the railway. The signalbox, again of postwar brick pattern was about 200 yards from the end of the down electric platform, and beyond that an exceedingly long lattice footbridge spanned the running and yard tracks.

At Chadwell Heath (9 miles 79 chains) there were more sidings and another of the postwar brick signalboxes, although the more open character of the line remained apparent. One curiosity between Chadwell Heath and Romford was a tall granite obelisk which stood on the down side and which bore the inscription: 'ACT 24 of 25 VICT: CAP 42'. It was a relic from well over a century before, and related to legislation dating back even further. In 1694 Parliament had passed an Act allowing for the relief of orphans and other creditors of the City of London to be paid from duties on wine and coals brought into the City. These levies were clarified by another Act of 1861, which was also inter-related with the Metropolitan Police Act of 1829. The 1861 legislation provided for 'two several duties of one penny and twelve pence per ton' to be levied on the wine and coal by the Corporation of London, and to eliminate the chances of error the boundaries where they came into the Metropolitan Police District were clearly marked by these obelisks. The right to levy duty was abolished in 1889, but this example still stands beside the Great Eastern line well over a century after its function was removed.

The stations now started to become more widely separated. On the approach to Romford (12 miles 30 chains) prominent features included the Ind Coope brewery and the stadium; there were extensive sidings on the up side at the London end. Romford signalbox, together with Brentwood, was one where a panel had been grafted over a mechanical frame when the signalling was modernised prior to electrification.

Above: Heading a train for Felixstowe in the 1930s, LNER Class B17 No 2806 *Audley End* is pictured having just passed Romford, where the line to Upminster can be seen diverging in the left foreground.
Ian Allan Library

Right: Class 31/1 No 31 238 heads an up milk train near Gidea Park on 7 September 1981. This traffic, in earlier days carried in churns, was once a staple of the line.
Alex Dasi-Sutton

Right: In the 1930s the main line was widened between Romford, Gidea Park and Shenfield. Here Class N7/1 0-6-2T No 987 heads an up local near Brentwood in 1926. *Ian Allan Library*

The gasworks on the up side was almost opposite the signalbox. Romford station had been extensively rebuilt in connection with the quadrupling in the area in 1930, when the goods yard was improved and extra facilities were provided for locomotives and carriages at Romford Factory, beyond Gidea Park. The larger station was needed to serve an important and growing population centre, which also played host to the London, Tilbury & Southend branch to Upminster and Grays, accommodated at a wooden platform off the country end of the up main platform.

The station was on an embankment and so had subways for access, rather than footbridges, and these were tiled largely in white. The side platforms were backed by red brick walls, and all had buildings at this level in a similar style to those at Ilford. Passenger access was from the road which crossed under the line at the country end of the station, the LT&S platform being on the other side of this. The branch then ran parallel with the main line for about half a mile before curving away to the south-east. Numbers of semi-fast trains and even a few expresses called at Romford, and it formed an interchange with the suburban services, latterly electrified, and which terminated at the next station.

Opened in December 1910 as Squirrels Heath & Gidea Park, Gidea Park & Squirrels Heath (13 miles 41 chains), to give it its full designation (carried between 1913 and 1969), was just over a mile from Romford, and was the terminus for the inner-suburban trains of the 'Jazz' service. Here Stratford crews once paused to clean the tubes of their hard-working locomotives before returning to Liverpool Street, whilst the majority of trains sped past without stopping. The station was in a deep cutting, and although having the usual pattern of platforms the buildings were quite different, because the station had opened after most others on the line. The booking office was at the top of the cutting wall on the up side, and the high lattice footbridge emerged from its side. There were small simple buildings on each platform, brick for the lower three feet or so, and concrete block above that. The canopies — in complete contrast to other older stations — attached only to these buildings and were thus of limited extent. As with many other stations on this section of the line the suburban lines curved away from the main lines in order to reach the platforms, reflecting the procedure adopted in quadrupling of the tracks. There were rail-served factories on the up side of the track, whilst on the north side carriage sidings (beyond a road overbridge) were later adapted for the stabling of electric multiple-unit stock.

Harold Wood station (14 miles 76 chains) was about 1¼ mile further on and marked the start of the celebrated Brentwood Bank, although the line had been climbing steadily all the way from Ilford. Starting gradually, with two miles of 1 in 103 just after Milepost 16 and increasing to 1 in 85 at Brentwood station (18 miles 16 chains), it

eased to 1 in 155 just before Ingrave Summit. Brentwood had been renamed 'Brentwood & Warley' in 1882 and reverted to its original title in 1969. It lost its goods facilities, which had been on the down side at the London end of the station, in 1970. Although the station was at ground level the uneven slope of the surrounding land meant that a road bridge crossed the line at the London end. The main building was on the down side by this bridge, and was of two storeys, passenger access from the street being at first-floor level. It was a fine red-brick structure with two gabled roof sections at right-angles to the line. A steel-plate footbridge connected it to the platforms, shelter being provided by an elliptical corrugated iron roof. Red-brick buildings on all platforms were of unusual design, having stone quoins, plinths and the like, and 'gothic' arches to the doorways. Unusually they had steeply pitched slate roofs.

Brentwood had had a locomotive depot whose purpose had been to supply locomotives for the local service between Shenfield and Liverpool Street. About six locomotives had been shedded here, but with electrification this need disappeared. Access to the depot had been possible through a wicket gate in the down electric platform, with the turntable being just off the end of the station. Its site is still clearly visible because of the circular wall let into the bank. For trains out on the line this was a place to have a good fire built up, and there were occasions when an old driver, who might not have too much confidence in his young and inexperienced fireman, would urge him to 'put plenty on'. Having done just that, and piled on the coal for all he was worth, the result was often far too much fire for the long descent to Chelmsford!

There had also been a banker shedded at Brentwood, and local instructions had required agreement between the signalmen at Shenfield and Brentwood prior to any move being made, and for a 'competent person' from Brentwood to ride on the assisting locomotive and authorise it to pass the automatic signals that had already been set back to danger by the train engine. Assisting had to stop at Milepost 19¼, which marked Ingrave Summit, halfway between Brentwood and Shenfield stations, the locomotive stopping at the next signal and awaiting permission to go on to Shenfield (20 miles 16 chains). There were several sets of trap points in the down lines so that a train that became stopped on the bank could not set back and restart: rear-end assistance was required. The line having been quadrupled, concrete retaining walls became necessary in the cutting, though it continued to be a spectacular and scenic location beloved of photographers. In steam days the lineside here was kept much clearer of trees and undergrowth by the platelayers, which reduced the problems with autumn leaf-fall and also lessened the risk of lineside fires. With modern electric traction it is difficult nowadays to appreciate quite what it was like to slog up Brentwood Bank with one of

Above: Class B17/6 4-6-0 No 61663 *Everton* heads a Butlins special to Clacton on 24 May 1958. The concrete retaining walls of the cutting at Brentwood Bank demonstrate how the extra width was achieved when the line was quadrupled in the 1930s. *S. Creer*

the 4-6-0s — or even a 'Claud' — in charge of a heavily loaded express.

Shenfield's main claim to fame was as the junction for Southend Victoria — this line opening in 1889 — and celebrated bottleneck. Quadrupling towards London eased the problem and allowed the introduction of a more intensive passenger service, and the building of the burrowing junction, brought into use at the very start of January 1934, aided traffic flow further. With the flyover at Ilford the Southend lines were now the pair on the north side thence to Shenfield, though they combined into a single track to pass under the Norwich lines, and a pair of tracks continued on the old alignment to join the main line on the up side. A further rather sinuous connection which threaded its way through carriage sidings to the east of the station allowed a Norwich train diverted over the electric lines to regain its proper course. The station itself occupied a sloping site so that the London end was in a cutting whilst the country end was on a bank, where the main public entrance was from the road passing underneath. Access to the one side and two island platforms was via a white-tiled subway. The platform buildings were again in red brick and were quite extensive. A memorial stone on the side of the Platform 3 building bore the following inscription:

THIS TABLET IS ERECTED BY THE TRAFFIC AND ENGINEERS STAFF OF THIS STATION IN PROUD MEMORY OF THEIR FIVE COLLEAGUES WHO MADE THE SUPREME SACRIFICE FOR KING AND COUNTRY IN THE 1914-18 WAR AND WHOSE NAMES ARE INSCRIBED BELOW.

BAILES S.
PEACOCK W.
SAVILL G.
TURNER A. L.
WOOD W.

Left: Class 47/4 No 47 588 *Carlisle Currock* heads a short van train from Thornton Fields to Colchester up Brentwood Bank on 25 August 1988.
Michael J. Collins

Below: A view of Shenfield & Hutton station in early LNER days, with what appears to be a Great Eastern 4-4-0 at the head of a down train.
Author's collection

Left: Class J20/1 0-6-0 No 64677 works a pick-up freight near Shenfield on a dull 10 April 1952.
P. Ransome-Wallis

Stock sidings were located on the down side at the London end, whilst the goods yard was on the up side.

Once beyond Shenfield (Shenfield & Hutton until 1969) the Norwich main line reverted to two tracks, and the feeling of being out in the country began at last. It is difficult now to believe that the Eastern Counties station had closed in 1850 because of its rural location and low traffic potential, and that Shenfield & Hutton Junction did not open until 1887 on the same site, in anticipation of the opening of the new route to Southend. The main line was carried on a bank which in recent years became heavily wooded, but from which rolling open country could at last be seen. Postwar the overall line speed limit was 80mph between Liverpool Street and Norwich, with a maximum as far as Shenfield of 60mph, except for a stretch at 70mph between Ilford and Gidea Park. Trains were extremely unlikely to approach these heights on the ascent of Brentwood Bank, but from Shenfield to Chelmsford, just under 10 miles, there was the chance to open out to the limit, helped at last by a favourable gradient. By the mid-1950s non-stop 'Britannia'-hauled trains such as the 'Easterling' were allowed 9 minutes to cover the 9½ miles before having to slow to 45mph for the restriction through the curved platforms at Chelmsford.

Although there had briefly been a workmen's platform at Margaretting after World War 1, the only intermediate station on this section was Ingatestone (23 miles 50 chains) where the site

was somewhat cramped. The side platforms were narrow and to the north of the level crossing, while the up and down loops were to the south. The level crossing gates were operated by a wheel in the signalbox, which retained its levers into the late 1980s, and which continues to supervise the crossing. The station buildings were in a quite uncharacteristic Tudor style with slate roofs, red brick with inlaid diamond patterns in blues, stone mullions and ornate windows, and were reputed to have been thus at the insistence of Lord Petre, a prominent local landowner resident at Ingatestone Hall, and who had extracted as much as possible from the Eastern Counties Railway when the line was first built. The line fell generally from Ingrave towards Chelmsford and Witham, and then undulated to Colchester, with minor peaks just past Hatfield Peverel and Stanway. Between many of the stations on the double-track section north of Shenfield there were intermediate signalboxes and refuges, breaking up the longer sections and helping the regulation of trains. Examples included Hylands and Crompton's sidings, between Ingatestone and Chelmsford, the latter also serving the factory. New Hall and Chantry were between Chelmsford and Hatfield Peverel, Blunt's Hall being in the next section towards Witham. Rivenhall was about 1¾ miles outside Kelvedon, Hill House being on the Colchester side.

Chelmsford (29 miles 65 chains) was approached from the London direction past the factories of Crompton's and Marconi, the town

Below: A scene that is no more than a distant memory. Notwithstanding the Class D (express freight) headlamps, Class K3/2 No 61949 heads a special train of empty cattle vans between Shenfield and Ingatestone on 12 May 1951. *R. E. Vincent*

Above: With its rambling roses and sylvan setting, Ingatestone, barely 20 miles from Liverpool Street, embodies the rural idyll. In this view a suburban service calls at the up platform, out of sight on the left. *Lens of Sutton Association*

Left: A view of Ingatestone station familiar to many travellers, recorded on Sunday 23 February 1969 from the 12.30 Liverpool Street–Norwich, headed by Class 47 No D1567. Train 1F53, the 11.52 Clacton–Liverpool Street, waits to continue its journey on the down line, necessitated by engineering work. The art of single-line working seems now to have been forgotten. *G. R. Mortimer*

having become an important centre for light industry and communications in the inter-war years. It had, of course, been the home of the famous pioneer radio station 2LO. The line ran out onto an embankment and then over the impressive viaduct which curved sharply through Admiral's Park, the tracks being fitted with guide rails in case of derailment. It then swept through the station platforms, themselves being elevated above Duke Street and overlooking the Eastern National bus station and depot. There had once also been a third track between the platforms, in effect an elongated crossover, which was removed in the 1960s. The station had been rebuilt in 1856 in solid grey brick, though the site was very restricted, which led to a number of unusual features. The signalbox was on the down side and so on the outside of the curve, and was perched high above the platform buildings. The goods

yard, at the country end and on the down side, was approached via a facing connection to a steep incline; on the right leaving the station could be seen the new cattle market. Here lay the key to Chelmsford's early prosperity as a market town of great importance: it lay in the centre of a fertile agricultural region, its affluence and geographical location making it a natural choice as county town. Chelmsford enjoyed an excellent train service, since many of the Norwich expresses called, together with the Clacton interval trains, and it also enjoyed the electric suburban service from 1956. Today it generates a remarkably high rate of income for the network, and an extensive rebuild was finished in 1989.

North of Chelmsford the main line plunged into a deep cutting, the start of which was marked by a large borrow pit from which material had been extracted to form embankments. A good

Right: The view southwards at Chelmsford station in GER days, showing clearly the through siding between the main lines. The signalbox, overlooking the other buildings, has since been made redundant by re-signalling but survives thanks to its listed status. *Lens of Sutton Association*

Right: An Edwardian postcard view of the front of Chelmsford station. Note the bell tower and the Great Eastern buses, the latter operating some of the earliest routes in the country. *Lens of Sutton Association*

Right: According to the notes with the photograph, a Great Eastern 2-4-0, No 727, heads an up semi-fast near Chelmsford. Any further information would be most welcome! *H. Gordon Tidey*

28

Left: Hauled by a Class 37 locomotive, the 14.40 Yarmouth–Liverpool Street has just crossed the viaduct as it leaves Chelmsford on 7 June 1975. *Stanley Creer*

Left: A 1956 electrification scene at Chelmsford. The train, formed of three of the 1,500V DC units (later Class 306), is part of the service which had just been extended from Shenfield. *Ian Allan Library*

Left: Headed by Class 47/0 No 47 052, a well-loaded Freightliner from Stratford to Felixstowe approaches Chelmsford on 1 March 1984. *Michael J. Collins*

Right: For many years diesels operated under the wires. Heading the 12.30 Liverpool Street–Norwich through Chelmsford on 11 December 1984, Class 47/4 No 47 574 *Lloyds List* had been so named prior to departure, in commemoration of the institution's 250th anniversary.
Michael J. Collins

Right: Photographed on the same day, Class 86/3 No 86 316 *Wigan Pier* heads through Chelmsford with train 5T02, the 11.02 Thornton Fields–Colchester crew-training run, in preparation for the introduction of electric haulage to Ipswich.
Michael J. Collins

Right: 'Britannia' Pacific No 70003 *John Bunyan* hustles a down express past Chantry signalbox, between Chelmsford and Hatfield Peverel, on 17 August 1952.
J. E. Garrett

Above: Witham Junction, probably in GER days, with a line of northbound commuters awaiting their train. Connecting services have arrived at the Maldon and Braintree platforms. *Lens of Sutton Association*

Left: Witham station looking towards Colchester before lengthening of the platforms. Although difficult to make out, the platform staff are lined up beside the bookstall. *Lens of Sutton Association*

Below: Class B17/4 No 61660 *Hull City* calls at Witham with an up Clacton service on a wintry day around 1959. *Author's collection*

Above: Class B12/3 No 61516 passes Witham on an up express on 17 September 1949. The signalbox and water tank are prominent, while the Maldon branch can be seen curving off to the right. *R. E. Vincent*

alignment through Springfield — now a suburb of Chelmsford and suggested as a site for a new station — again gave the opportunity for high speeds to be attained. New Hall, where there was an intermediate signalbox just under 2½ miles from Chelmsford, was particularly noted for this. The section northwards towards Witham was always a difficult and expensive one to maintain because of the geology of the area, much of it soft and unstable clay, although today it is mostly cleared for 100mph between Chelmsford and Colchester. The countryside is again open and undulating, although the view from the train has been spoiled by the 'improved' A12 trunk road which now runs close by for much of the distance between Brentwood and Colchester.

Hatfield Peverel station (35 miles 74 chains) was a simple two-platform affair about six miles on from Chelmsford and was served by relatively few trains, but has seen considerable growth since electrification with an increase in commuting to London. Although down trains faced a short rising gradient here, the line started to fall soon after the station until just beyond Witham, so that up trains faced a stiff climb between the two. It had opened originally as Hatfield in 1844 but was soon destroyed by fire and disappeared from the timetable after 1849. The current station opened as Hatfield Peverel in 1878.

Witham (38 miles 48 chains) was the next major station, and the junction for the Maldon and Braintree branches. The layout was spacious, with two wide island platforms, the main lines serving the inner faces, and the branches the outer ones. Fast trains were checked to 75mph through the platforms, and there was a curious restriction of 8mph for the curve onto the Maldon branch. Witham also had its own turntable, 42ft in diameter, fitted with lengthening irons, but even so was not much use to main-line locomotives. The principal station buildings were on the down side and built out over the platform, as the approach road was along the top of a bank. There had been a Station signalbox at the London end, whilst Witham Junction 'box was on the down side at the Colchester end of the station, and was an extremely tall wooden structure. In connection with electrification it was replaced by a modern flat-roofed brick building (on the up side) which also took over control of the line from New Hall, Chantry, Hatfield Peverel, Blunt's Hall, Rivenhall and Hill House 'boxes.

Both branches curved away sharply almost at the ends of their respective platforms, although they had been conceived as a through route linking Maldon and Braintree. For a time they were worked by the diminutive German-built diesel railbuses, but while the Braintree branch was the object of a determined and successful local campaign to boost its traffic and future prospects, the Maldon branch languished and closed to passengers in 1964. Witham had a good service of both fast and stopping trains on the main line, a few expresses to both Yarmouth and Norwich also

Left: Having been pressed into passenger service, Class K3 No 61863 restarts from Witham with the 9.56am Liverpool Street–Felixstowe on 2 August 1958. The height of the signalbox is well illustrated here. *K. L. Cook*

Left: The 1.45pm Norwich–Liverpool Street, hauled by English Electric Type 4 No D283, approaches Witham on 7 November 1960. The branch to Braintree can be seen on the left of the picture, and that to Maldon on the right. Extensions to both up and down platforms are in progress. *M. Edwards*

Left: Having arrived at a wintry Witham station with the 10.14 from Braintree, the driver of Class 308 EMU No 308 139 walks to the other end of the train in readiness for the 11.36 return working on 2 January 1979. *Michael J. Collins*

Above: The 17.30 Harwich Parkeston Quay–Halewood train for the Ford Motor Co is hurried through Witham on 1 July 1979 by ex-works '47/0' No 47 056.
Michael J. Collins

calling, together with the Clacton 'interval' trains and the semi-fasts to Ipswich.

The end of a era was reached at Witham on 1 April 1954 with the retirement of Snowy and Tiny. They were the last of a long line of shunting horses at the station, which had first been introduced in 1870, and of which there had been six at the busiest time. The stationmaster commented that the changes and decline in traffic had made them uneconomic for the job.

About 3½ miles further on was Kelvedon (42 miles 21 chains) where there were prominent seed warehouses close to the line. Just before the station Church Street level crossing gave steam drivers severe sighting difficulties. The station itself was unremarkable, with buildings in red brick and the usual two side platforms, and had a relatively sparse passenger service to London, although in earlier years it had handled the extensive agricultural and horticultural traffic characteristic of the area. In railway terms its main claim to fame was as the junction with the light railway to Tollesbury, which joined the up main line via a steep incline on the Colchester side of the station. Some of its coaching stock had been acquired from the Wisbech & Upwell Tramway when that line lost its passenger services, and was not allowed out on the main line unless out-of-gauge parts such as footboards were removed. Passenger traffic succumbed to road competition in May 1951, but it remained open for goods — of

which jam was an important constituent — as far as Tudwick Road siding, just beyond Tiptree, until 1962.

A feature which survived from the earliest days of the railway was a platform gong worked by a lever in the signalbox. This would be rung when a stopping train was approaching, and was also protection for the staff. It was made of brass and was 12 inches in diameter with a large plunger, the whole apparatus being mechanically worked. Its wooden housing was still there when the station buildings were demolished overnight in April 1989. Kelvedon signalbox was abolished when the new one at Witham opened.

Progress to Mark's Tey (46 miles 49 chains) continued to be good, the line being relatively straight and easily graded. Between Shenfield and Colchester it undulated gently, the only significant grades being at Blunts Hall (just over a mile on the London side of Witham) where it fell towards Witham at 1 in 150, at Kelvedon — rising at 1 in 193 towards Colchester — and at Stanway, falling at 1 in 160 towards Colchester. Marks Tey was the junction for the Stour Valley line to Long Melford, where trains could go either to Bury St Edmunds or Cambridge, and there was the alternative Colne Valley route as well from Chappel & Wakes Colne. It was thus an important operational point, and although passenger services over the branches were never heavy there were some interesting through workings, especially on summer

Left: An immaculate Class 47/4, 47 819, like its train in full InterCity livery, passes Witham with the 'Pathfinder Executive' of 12 September 1992.
John C. Baker

Below: For many years the warehouses of King's Seeds have stood alongside the main line at Kelvedon. For enthusiasts it the junction for Tollesbury, but the main-line station has always been a busy one. This was the view towards London in 1950.
Ian Allan Library

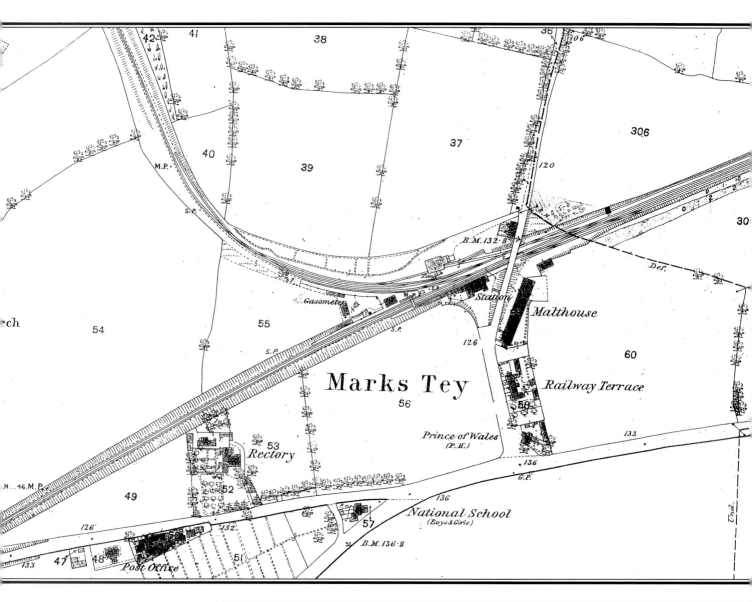

Right: Mark's Tey on
21 March 1959, as
'Britannia' No 70010
Owen Glendower speeds
through with the 3.45pm
Norwich–Liverpool Street;
re-signalling and platform
extension are yet to come.
Michael Mensing

Left: A fine view of Mark's Tey in the up direction, recorded on 30 July 1958. Class J15 No 65456 stands at the branch platform with a train from the Colne Valley line. Water is available, but only with a complex manœuvre. *Frank Church*

Saturdays. The surrounding area generated much horticultural produce, being noted for seed-growing, rose bushes and cut flowers, as well as livestock. An unusual traffic was the thousands of parcels of railway uniforms despatched to stations all over the system, which were made locally.

The branch and down main platforms formed a triangle, in the apex of the junction, and it had once been intended to lay track on all three sides, although in the end the junction faced Colchester. The main buildings and public access to the station were on the up platform, with the stationmaster's house also on this side. This was an impressive building with high, moulded ceilings, since this was a post on a par with those at Witham and Colchester. When the new A12 road was built it proved impossible to get road access to empty the cesspit and so the fine old house was condemned.

The goods yard and other station facilities were largely on the down side and were thus directly accessible to both branch and main line, the connections being controlled by the Yard 'box. There was a water tank next to the wooden goods shed which could be used only by locomotives in the yard, the only water for main-line trains between Shenfield and Colchester being at Chelmsford and Witham. In the early days — and certainly in the early 1950s — many long-distance trains called at Mark's Tey for the branch connections, and some, such as the 12.30pm Liverpool Street–Cromer in the 1951/2 winter timetable, did not then call at Colchester. With the accelerations brought about by the 'Britannias' the Mark's Tey stops were restricted to the Clacton and Walton trains, Sudbury and Cambridge passengers having to change at Colchester or additionally at Chelmsford.

In the suburban areas most of the signalboxes were located at or very near to stations, but this was not so out in the country. In many places the stations were too widely separated, so the sections needed breaking up, or a siding needed to be worked. One such was just over two miles on from Mark's Tey at Stanway, where the 'box and refuge were on the down side with sidings on the up, used for many years for the storage of rolling stock for scrapping. A signalman at a station had all the facilities available to him: not so out in the country. Stanway had no mains water and was fed from a spring (in the bank behind the 'box) whose beautifully pure water ran into a gully. At Hill House, just north of Kelvedon, there was no spring and no piped water, but the adjacent crossing cottage had a well in the garden. Parsons Heath, the first 'box north of Colchester on the main line, did not have a water supply at any time in its existence, and it all had to be brought in churns from Ardleigh. Sanitary facilities out in the country were quite another matter! There was also once a 'box a Lexden, about halfway between Stanway and Colchester.

Down trains approaching Colchester (51 miles 52 chains) were aided by the gradient, though the old North station had a speed limit of 40mph because of the severe curvature on the approach and through the platforms. In its earlier form Colchester North had two side platforms which served all through trains, with a bay for the Clacton line. The major buildings were on the down side. The extensive locomotive depot was also on the down side at the country end of the station, and housed a considerable allocation of both tender and tank engines. After rebuilding the new station boasted the longest platform in Britain, although not with a single continuous face. The down was made into an island with the outer face served by Clacton trains, whilst at the same time the buildings were almost completely replaced. A new diesel depot was constructed on the down side at the London end, and the former main lines became goods avoiding lines. The speed limit was raised to 90mph, although ironically almost all trains now called there.

Right: Forming the 17.50 Clacton/Walton–Liverpool Street, a pair of Class 309 EMUs pass through Mark's Tey on 23 July 1980. Note that the the leading unit, No 309 611, retains its original wraparound front windows. *Michael J. Collins*

Right: The view towards Chelmsford at Mark's Tey in the 1960s, the Sudbury line being out of shot to the right. *Lens of Sutton Association*

Below: In preparation for the launch of electric haulage to Ipswich the Mk 2d coaches in use on the main line were repainted in InterCity livery. Here Class 47/4 No 47 553 is in charge of the 10.30 Liverpool Street–Norwich, seen near Mark's Tey on 12 April 1985. *Michael J. Collins*

Left: Class 86/2 No 86 230 *The Duke of Wellington* heads the 09.30 Liverpool Street–Norwich past Mark's Tey on 12 February 1988. Only the locomotive retains Rail blue. *Michael J. Collins*

Left: Displaying an express headcode, LNER Class L1 2-6-4T No 9000 departs from Colchester with a train for Clacton. *C. W. Footer*

Left: Saturday 13 July 1957 was a fine sunny day in Colchester; here Class E4 2-4-0 No 62789 is ready to leave with the 3.44pm to Cambridge. The sharp curvature of the platforms is evident. *G. R. Mortimer*

Colchester to Clacton

Right: On 29 June 1980 Class 308 No 308 142 pauses at Alresford with the 09.37 Sundays-only local service from Colchester to Clacton. *John C. Baker*

Below: Class J39 0-6-0 No 64765 stands at Thorpe le Soken with a train for Walton. Clearly the crew are not yet ready to go. *M. E. Edwards*

Left: Thorpe le Soken was a typical small station but enjoyed a good through service to London by reason of being the junction for Walton and Clacton. The station building looks rather neglected in this photograph, taken on 4 August 1984. *John Rickard*

Below: Thorpe le Soken signalbox stood on the up platform and was of typical Great Eastern brick-and-timber construction. This photograph was taken on 4 August 1984. *John Rickard*

Above: Engineering work in the Colchester area necessitated locomotive haulage of trains to Clacton on Sundays over a six-week period in early 1982, as no overhead power was available. Class 47/0 No 47 005 arrives at Thorpe le Soken with the 08.30 Liverpool Street–Clacton on 7 March. *John D. Mann*

Right: A Summer Saturday service, the 14.10 to Leicester London Road, departs Clacton-on-Sea behind BR/Sulzer Type 2 No D5205 on 2 September 1967. *G. R. Mortimer*

Above: Prospective holidaymakers were able to visit the Essex 'Sunshine Coast' out of season. Class 37 No 37 075 stands at Clacton shortly after arriving with a 'Seaview Special' from Nelson, Lancashire, on 5 March 1977. *John D. Mann*

Left: A view over the buffers at Clacton on 19 May 1977, featuring Class 308/1 unit No 308 144 ready to depart as the 16.28 service to St Botolphs. *Brian Morrison*

Trains leaving Colchester northbound were faced with a relatively gentle climb towards Parsons Heath signalbox, about 2½ miles further on. Ardleigh (55 miles 71 chains) boasted a level crossing and a small country station whose single-storey buildings were unpretentious and in later years began to look rather down at heel. It was served almost entirely by stopping trains such as the Chelmsford–Ipswich all-stations, although later, after dieselisation had set in, some more exotic variations appeared such as through services between Ipswich and Haverhill or Sudbury. Although it lost its passenger services relatively late, on 6 November 1967, goods services had been withdrawn in 1964. Its signalbox survived until Colchester panel took over in the prelude to electrification in the 1980s.

Manningtree station (59 miles 35 chains) was a further 3½ miles from Ardleigh, with an intermediate signalbox at Dedham. In the 1950s the latter was open almost continuously, from 2.0am on Monday to 2.0am Sunday, but was also required to open for part of Sunday morning and evening. It shared this feature with a number of 'boxes on the line north of Hatfield Peverel, although those at main stations and junctions were open continuously. Dedham's water supply came from a spring, and another essential was coal.

Signalboxes were allowed a coal ration, depending on size. It was delivered in various ways according to the available access. A lorry might have been used, if it could get close to the 'box, or possibly a railway wagon. At Mark's Tey coal was delivered to the station coal store and then taken out to the 'box using a barrow. There was always a 'ready use' supply kept in buckets on the floor at the bottom of the stairs so that the night man never had to go out for coal. At Dedham coal could only be obtained from passing locomotives, which was strictly against the rules! The signalman on nights would have two cups of coffee ready for the down newspaper. At Manningtree this train detached two coaches for Harwich, which remained at the main platform for unloading by station staff. If the following goods train was less than 30 minutes behind the newspapers, it had to be held at Dedham, since the two coaches blocked the main line. The crew of the goods would be treated to tea or coffee in exchange for shovelsful of coal. Getting coal was not without its hazards, however. It would often be thrown off the footplate onto the ground by the 'box, and on at least one occasion at Dedham a large lump smashed vital signalling cranks and pulleys. Ingenuity, hand signals and a good deal of luck kept the trains running, and the damage was quietly repaired without management ever becoming aware of it or the rule-breaking. As with every other 'box the signalmen at Dedham observed the passage of every train, or in practice, nine out of 10, since not all of them would be fully visible. It was necessary to note, among other things, that the train was carrying a tail lamp to show that it had not accidentally become divided. A lookout was kept for anything else untoward such as an open door or hot boxes. On one occasion the signalman was watching an up train pass when he saw a woman waving a red handkerchief from the train, and looking at the signalbox. Thinking that something might be seriously amiss he called Ardleigh and had the train stop there. It turned out that she had been using the handkerchief to wrap her sandwiches and had been shaking out the crumbs!

Below: A fine view of 'K2' 2-6-0 No 61746 as it tackles the gradient from Colchester to Parsons Heath with a down goods on 18 June 1951. *C. W. Footer*

Manningtree station marked the furthest extremity of Essex, and was the busy and important junction for the Harwich branch. The line from London emerged into the upper reaches of the Stour Estuary and onto an embankment which afforded some superb views of Constable country, Flatford Mill being less than two miles away. The station itself had two side platforms, although the down was effectively an island, and there was also a bay on the up side for Harwich trains. The main buildings were on the up side and in red brick, and showed very obvious signs of the platforms' having been raised to modern levels. Interestingly, much of the glass in both the up and down side buildings is still the original etched material bearing legends such as 'Ladies Waiting Room' and suitably adorned with various embellishments.

There was a level crossing at the country end of the station, where the A137 road crossed the line, although it was bypassed by a very low bridge which allowed light vehicles to pass under the railway. Even so, considerable queues of traffic could build up, all watched over by Manningtree South Junction signalbox, which also controlled the North and East junctions. This triangular arrangement reflected the importance of the branch, which had been progressively developed by the Great Eastern and its successors. It was also the site of one of the LNER's first forays into power signalling, in 1928, when the South Junction 'box added the functions of East and North to its own, together with those of the station 'box, and Brantham. The goods yard was on the up side at the London end of the station, and as with so many has now been lifted and converted to a car park for commuters.

Above: The first signalbox on the Ipswich side of Colchester was Parsons Heath, where Class 31/1 No 31 193 was photographed hustling the 'Day Continental' (09.40 Liverpool Street–Harwich Parkeston Quay) on 30 June 1979. *Michael J. Collins*

Left: Single-line working due to engineering activity is almost unknown today. On Sunday 8 June 1980 Class 47/0 No 47 150 heads the 08.56 Great Yarmouth–Liverpool Street up the down line between Colchester and Ardleigh whilst in the background another '47' has charge of a ballast train. *G. R. Mortimer*

Above: Ardleigh station, between Colchester and Manningtree, closed to passengers in December 1967 but looks largely intact in this view, recorded on 30 June 1969. Class 47 No D1703 heads the 17.40 Norwich–Liverpool Street past the overgrown platforms. *G. R. Mortimer*

Right: Class 37s Nos 37 153 and 37 008 head the Willesden–Felixstowe Freightliner through Ardleigh on 29 May 1987. *Michael J. Collins*

Below: The up 'Norfolkman' climbs Dedham Bank on 12 June 1959 behind 'Britannia' Pacific No 70005 *John Milton*. *G. R. Mortimer*

Left: 'Britannia' No 70009
Alfred the Great on the
down main line between
Dedham 'box and
Manningtree on the
evening of 26 June 1954.
G. R. Mortimer

Below: Pictured just south of
the station, the Garston–
Felixstowe Freightliner,
headed by Class 37s
Nos 37 087 and 37 211,
approaches Manningtree on
20 August 1987.
Michael J. Collins

Right: Class 47/0 No 47 102 speeds through Manningtree with the 11.42 Norwich–Liverpool Street on 19 May 1977. The station is in the background, while the field to the left of the locomotive briefly served as a bus interchange in 2004, while the track in Ipswich Tunnel was being lowered.
Brian Morrison

Below: Class 37 No 37 052 runs into a busy Manningtree station on 27 May 1978 with the 10.24 relief train from Liverpool Street to Ipswich.
R. E. Ruffell

Above: Class 31/1 No 31 208 and an unidentified Class 47 pass at Manningtree on 19 May 1977, heading the 13.00 Parkeston Quay–Liverpool Street and 12.30 Liverpool Street–Norwich respectively.
Brian Morrison

Left: As yet unnamed (page 30 refers), '47/4' No 47 574 arrives at Manningtree on 6 March 1982 with the 07.43 Yarmouth–Liverpool Street. Re-signalling has taken place, but Manningtree 'box retains control.
John Glover

Above: A Liverpool Street–Ipswich train leaves Manningtree headed by Class K3 Mogul No 61880 on 12 May 1951. Meanwhile 'N7' 0-6-2T No 69677 sets back through the up platform onto its coaches, which will form a train for Dovercourt and Harwich.
W. Philip Conolly

Right: Manningtree South Junction signalbox watches over Class B1 No 61227 as it passes with a stopping service from Liverpool Street to Ipswich on 4 April 1954. Signalling at Manningtree had been concentrated on this 'box as far back as 1928.
B. K. B. Green

Left: BR/Sulzer Type 2 No D5048 passes Manningtree North Junction with the 18.45 Ipswich–Liverpool Street on 28 May 1966; the coaches are on the south viaduct. In the background is Brantham Works — a stark contrast with the Stour Estuary. *G. R. Mortimer*

Manningtree to Harwich

Right: An attractive view of Mistley, on the Harwich branch, in the 1950s, before modernisation started to take effect. *Lens of Sutton Association*

The route to Harwich branched from the main line at Manningtree station, although the latter is strictly in Lawford. Long an objective for railway builders, the Harwich branch was not especially challenging. When it was built all trains used what is now the south curve, diverging at Manningtree Junction, adjacent to the level crossing. This was joined by the north curve, which completed the triangle, when the new line via Parkeston Quay opened in September 1882. The curve, double-track from the start, connected Manningtree East and North junctions and allowed through carriages to start running between Doncaster and Harwich at that time. Finally, in May 1898, the Great Eastern secured a contract for the carriage of mails to the Netherlands.

Although the line hugs the south side of the Stour estuary throughout its length, it has to contend with some surprising gradients, the summit being at Wrabness (65 miles 3 chains), where it cut through the headland. At Mistley (61 miles 11 chains) the short quay branch was on the north side, and was steeply graded. Latterly connected only to the down line and requiring reversal to reach it, the branch had originally been reached from the up side and a connection which curved underneath the main line. The station had a number of sidings, many associated with the extensive maltings trade, but also Taylor & Butlers, timber merchants at Baltic Wharf. Bradfield (62 miles 40 chains) served the small village of that name half a mile inland, and closed in 1956. It had no goods facilities.

The line had once continued more or less straight between Wrabness and Dovercourt, but the new quay and station on reclaimed land at Parkeston, and the loop to serve it, opened in 1882 making the old one redundant. Hugging the edge of the new land, with mudflats on the seaward side, the new line was almost completely level, rising slightly to join the original route through Dovercourt (70 miles 19 chains) and Harwich town, the terminus being a little way beyond the level crossing and signalbox (70 miles 61 chains).

Parkeston Quay International station was impressive from the very start. In 1898 the quay was 1,800ft long and 100ft wide, with a depth of water of 28ft at high tide and 16ft at low water. It had cranes capable of lifting 30 tons, and berths for seven steamers. Very substantial warehouses were provided, with separate departments for wines and spirits, tobacco and dry goods, and there were large offices for Customs. Five miles of sidings were provided, and the new town springing up around the quay and station accommodated the people working for the Great Eastern and the associated activities. The GER had worked hard to build up a fleet of steamers for the continental services, which included ships to Rotterdam, Hook of Holland and Antwerp. The passenger station itself was also impressive, having a long single platform and extensive buildings, including the hotel. There was a short platform, initially wooden, at the Dovercourt end on the up side and reached by a footbridge, and the area was controlled by Parkeston West Junction 'box at one end, and Parkeston Goods Junction at the other.

On 1 September 1934 further extensions were opened by Admiral of the Fleet Sir Reginald Tyrwhitt. A reinforced concrete extension to the quay 1,120ft long and 146ft wide, had been built, with a new two-storey transit shed and passenger station, 900ft long. This was to be known as Parkeston Quay (West), and from the start the Flushing boat trains called there to serve the steamers using the new quay. It closed in 1972, having been out of use for some time. Parkeston Quay handled a sizeable tonnage of goods traffic, the main items in 1938 being bacon and hams (nearly 60,000 tons), eggs (over 21,000 tons), butter, cheese and lard (17,000 tons), grain and flour, potatoes, slates and machinery, together worth well over £120,000 to the LNER.

Above: Class 47/4 No 47 572 heads the down 'Day Continental' (09.40 Liverpool Street–Harwich Parkeston Quay) through Mistley on 15 December 1984. The Edme Malt Extract works remains rail-served. *Michael J. Collins*

Left: Headed by an unidentified Class 31, the 13.20 Harwich Parkeston Quay–Blackpool — the 'North West Dane' — approaches Mistley at about 13.30 on Monday 27 July 1987. The incline down to the quay can be seen on the left, but is very overgrown. *Richard Lyndsell*

Above: Class 37 No 37 031 heads a short Harwich Parkeston Quay–Mossend freight near Bradfield, on the Harwich branch, on 27 March 1984. Preparations for electrification are in progress. *Michael J. Collins*

Right: An early photograph of Wrabness, with the signalbox and goods shed in view. Typically, access to the yard was by a trailing connection. *Lens of Sutton Association*

Right: LNER 'B1' No 1135 passes Wrabness with a down BAOR leave train on 16 July 1947. *C. C. B. Herbert*

Above: Running wrong-line, Class 37 No 37 271 approaches Wrabness on 21 June 1983 with a special, the second vehicle being a high-speed recording coach. The up line, in the foreground, was blocked by electrification work.
G. R. Mortimer

Left: LNER Class B12 4-6-0 No 8532 stands at Harwich Parkeston Quay in the late 1920s with a short but varied train.
Ian Allan Library

Above: Class B17 4-6-0 No 61651 heads over the long wooden viaduct at Parkeston Quay West as it departs with a BAOR leave train in April 1954.
P. J. Lynch

Right: On Saturday 14 June 1984 Class 37 No 37 049 passes through the yard at Parkeston Quay with empty stock for the relief train to the 12.10 to Liverpool Street.
Gavin Morrison

Right: The train ferries plied the routes to the Continent for many years. Here is one of the terminals at Harwich in August 1953. *A. C. Mott*

Left: Class 37 No 37 021 waits to depart Harwich Town with a boat train for Liverpool Street on 30 May 1978. *J. C. Hillmer*

Below: Class 47/4 No 47 596 passes the container terminal at Parkeston Quay with the empty stock for a DFDS boat train to Liverpool Street on 25 March 1986. *Michael J. Collins*

Once past Manningtree North junction the line immediately ran onto the low Cattawade Viaduct over the Stour, which afforded remarkable views over the flats and salt marshes, whether the tide was in or out. It was a different matter for men working out on the line in winter, perhaps called out as fog signalmen, for it could be bitterly cold on the exposed east coast. The spectacle was rather ruined by the almost immediate appearance of chemical works on both sides of the line. They had their own sidings, served by trip workings from Manningtree, and took in coal and other raw materials, and generated a variety of outward chemical traffic.

Having cleared this industrial complex the line continued to climb gently towards Ipswich, a long, gradual left-hand curve through the deepening cutting at Brantham taking trains under the 'Manningtree Arches', a tall three-arch bridge carrying the A137 over the railway. For up trains the combination of the curve and falling gradient made stopping at Manningtree awkward, and there has always been a speed limit through the station and junctions.

The countryside in Suffolk is more rolling than that south of the Stour, although the character of the line was not seriously affected by this until it reached Belstead Bank, between Bentley and Ipswich, where there was a long stretch of 1 in 130 falling towards Ipswich. Bentley station (63 miles 8 chains) had a level crossing at the London end, with its signalbox off the Ipswich end of the down platform. The main station buildings were on the up side, as was the stationmaster's house, loading dock and cattle pens; long up and down refuges were provided. It was the junction for the Hadleigh branch, which latterly had its own single track from a bay platform in the station for a distance of about a mile before it diverged on the down side. The branch passenger service had succumbed as early as February 1932, but the station retained goods facilities until 1965. The junction had been intended as triangular, though only the south curve was laid, so that trains from

Ipswich had to reverse to get onto the branch. A curious feature of this, and a number of other potential triangular junctions was that the unused part of the formation was kept beautifully clear, as if awaiting the order to lay track tomorrow. Grain traffic was important here, as well as livestock, and there were a number of poultry farms in the area. Between Bentley and Halifax Junction (the last 'box before Ipswich station) was one of the few 'auto sections' on the line, where the former signalbox at Belstead had been replaced by automatic colour lights to break the long section.

Belstead Bank presented a test for up trains, and provided some stirring spectacles of locomotives working hard. Just beyond the foot, between 67 miles 48 chains and 67 miles 71 chains, were Ipswich Troughs, in use right up to the end of steam working on the line and important for the fast trains between Norwich and London, especially those running beyond to places such as Cromer. It was possible to get a 'Britannia' from Norwich to Liverpool Street without filling the tank, but this required careful driving, and it was customary to use the troughs. Speed was crucial when taking water by this method, 50-55mph being ideal; if it were too low water would not enter the tank, and if too high air would get in.

The line limit at this point was 60mph. On some occasions only half a tank might be needed, in which case the scoop would be lowered halfway along the troughs. If a fireman were too enthusiastic and lowered it too early the result would be a train and tender awash, as the scoop could not be retracted halfway along the trough. It was also necessary to get a clear run over the troughs, and standing instructions required drivers of up passenger trains starting from Platform 2 at Ipswich to inform the signalman at the Station 'box of their intention to take water at Belstead. They were discouraged from taking water from the station columns because of the potential delays. Goods trains not booked to call at Ipswich, such as the express fish, had to be held at Goods Junction 'box if a delay might be encountered at

Left: Class 47/4 No 47 457 heads the 13.46 Norwich–Liverpool Street across the River Stour at Manningtree on 17 December 1982. *Michael J. Collins*

Below: With electric traction now well established, Class 312/1 No 312 791 crosses the Stour north of Manningtree as the 10.10 from Ipswich. *John C. Baker*

Left: The honour of forming the first electric train to work into Suffolk under its own power, on 9 May 1985, fell to Class 305 EMUs Nos 305 505 and 305 510. Here they approach Brantham, north of Manningtree, on the return working of the second test run to Ipswich. *Ian Cowley*

59

Right: Bentley station on 23 August 1947, with LNER Class B17/4 No 1668 *Bradford City* passing at the head of a down express.
G. R. Mortimer

Right: A Tilbury tank, 4-4-2T No 41949, unusually heads a Colchester–Ipswich train at Bentley in July 1956. By this time such services were mostly diesel-powered.
Ian Allan Library

Below: 'Britannia' No 70041 *Sir John Moore* approaches Bentley, between Ipswich and Manningtree, with the 9.45am Norwich–Liverpool Street on 19 August 1960.
G. R. Mortimer

the troughs; passenger trains not booked to call would be held at the Station 'box.

Halifax Junction (67 miles 75 chains) was also the point where the branch to Griffin Wharf diverged, serving Ransomes & Rapier's agricultural works. The firm was also known for its railway cranes. The junction also marked the point where the Ipswich & Bury line had diverged from the old Eastern Union line into the first Ipswich station. The main line continued to swing round to the left as it approached Ipswich (or Stoke) Tunnel, which was itself curved and very wet. In summer trains could be drenched when passing through, and in winter some fearsome icicles could form. Today it is actually heated, thus preventing a hazard to locomotives and crew, which is much more serious for staff in the front cab of an electric locomotive or DVT (driving van trailer) than way back behind the smokebox and boiler of a steam locomotive.

Trains emerged from Ipswich Tunnel (68 miles 31 chains to 68 miles 47 chains) almost onto the platform ends. The curve of the lines meant that the station is orientated almost east–west, the lines onward to Norwich and Yarmouth swinging back in a more northerly direction by East Suffolk Junction. The down main served the inner face — Platform 3 — of the island, whilst a sharp turnout restricted to 15mph gave access to the back platform, No 4. The up main did not serve a platform, and up Norwich trains had to be turned off the main line to call at Platform 2. No 1 was a north-facing bay on the up side. Ipswich Station signalbox stood at the tunnel end of the island platform. The present station buildings, of Suffolk red and white bricks and mostly dating from 1854, were designed by Sancton Wood, and were extensively renovated by British Rail in 1986. The down side buildings and island platform were built in similar style and date from 1883.

Movements at the country end of the station were controlled by the 120 levers of Ipswich Goods Junction signalbox, which stood on the south side of the tracks, but with the down goods road passing behind it. It was a cheerful place, where the signalmen — it needed two on duty at any one time — worked well with the shunters and drivers. The signalling here had originally been two-way block, later replaced by three-position block. There had been no track circuits at Ipswich until 1952, and when they did arrive the older men didn't like them because they couldn't feel the points go over. Further to the north — 1,025 yards to be exact — stood East Suffolk Junction signalbox (69 miles 40 chains), controlling the movement of trains to and from that line and also the access to the north end of the Upper Yard. It was even busier than Goods Junction, in summer seeing a train every 1½ minutes. There were numbers of local bell codes between the Ipswich 'boxes, several in connection with the permissive working allowed in Platform 4, where groups of local trains would wait for their connection from London.

Below: Belstead Bank, south of Ipswich, provided a stern test for up trains. Here Class O2/3 No 63951, of March shed, tackles it with a goods train on 13 May 1950. *G. R. Mortimer*

Right: Class B1 No 61046 attacks Belstead Bank on 1 May 1950 with the 11.28am from Ipswich to Liverpool Street. *G. R. Mortimer*

Right: More used to fast fitted freights, Lowestoft Class K3 2-6-0 No 61926 is pressed into passenger service on the 10.55am Saturdays-only Gorleston-on-Sea–Liverpool Street, seen climbing Belstead Bank on 4 July 1959. *G. R. Mortimer*

Below: LNER Class B12/3 4-6-0 No 8566 begins its ascent of Belstead Bank with a Sunday half-day excursion from Norwich on 5 February 1939. *George Grigs*

Left: On the same day 'B12/3' No 8530 attacks Belstead Bank with another half-day excursion. How clear the linesides were in those days! *George Grigs*

Left: In the electrified era Belstead Bank poses fewer challenges, except perhaps during the leaf-fall season. On 20 August 1985 Class 86/2 No 86 222 *Fury* tackles the climb with the 12.20 Norwich–Liverpool Street. As ever, the coaches sport a variety of liveries. *Michael J. Collins*

Left: On 22 August 1987 exceptionally heavy rains resulted in severe run-off from fields, causing damage to earthworks and track on Belstead Bank. Services were not resumed until 27 August; on the following day the 13.10 Ipswich–Liverpool Street, worked by an unidentified Class 312 unit, creeps over the rebuilt embankment. *G. R. Mortimer*

Right: 'Britannia' No 70042 *Lord Roberts* heads the up 'East Anglian' over Ipswich troughs. These were located at Wherstead, just south of Halifax Junction. Note the sign (left) indicating the start of the troughs.
Author's collection

Right: Halifax troughs in GER days, with oil-burning 2-2-2 No 1007 taking rather more water than it needs.
Ian Allan Library

Right: Class K3 2-6-0 No 61880 emerges from Ipswich Tunnel with the 3.54pm Saturdays-only train for Liverpool Street on 15 August 1953. The houses above are in Luther Road.
G. R. Mortimer

Left: Headed by EE Type 4 No D202, the down 'East Anglian' runs into Platform 4 at Ipswich on 23 May 1958. *Author's collection*

Below: Class 47 No D1562 emerges from Ipswich Tunnel with the 17.30 from Liverpool Street on 3 August 1969. The board behind the locomotive was for signal-sighting and was not an advertising hoarding, as some thought. *J. H. Cooper-Smith*

Right: Fast forward to the era of privatisation, as Class 57/0 No 57 004, operated by Freightliner, heads a train for Felixstowe out of Ipswich Tunnel in 2003.
Malcolm O'Neill

Right: The main line between Ipswich and Manningtree was closed for eight weeks between 19 July and 5 September 2004, so that clearances in Ipswich tunnel could be increased to allow 9ft 6in containers to be hauled through on normal wagons. All trains terminated at Ipswich or Manningtree, with a bus link between the two. All track was removed and the trackbed lowered, after which the track and signalling were replaced. The opportunity was taken to do much other work on the affected section. By 20 August the new track was in place through the tunnel, and the signalling had been reinstated. Testing and reinstatement work lasted just over another fortnight before normal services resumed on 6 September.

Right: On 2 June 1951 Class B12/3 4-6-0 No 61555 leaves Ipswich with the 1.0pm to Liverpool Street. The layout at this end of the station is well illustrated, with a locomotive in the short siding waits to take over an incoming up service.
G. R. Mortimer

Left: Class 03 No 03 162 shunts at Platform 4 at Ipswich on 15 October 1977. The short wagon in front of the locomotive made up for the latter's short wheelbase, ensuring that it registered on track circuits. Behind the locomotive the yard is still in use as carriage sidings. *Brian Morrison*

Above: The unique Class K5 2-6-0, No 61863, was a two-cylinder rebuild from a 'K3'. Here, on 2 August 1958, it waits at the country end of Platform 3 at Ipswich at the head of the 9.56am from Liverpool Street to Felixstowe Beach. *Author's collection*

Left: Class 31 No D5679 heads a Colchester– Edinburgh train towards East Suffolk Junction, north of Ipswich, on 3 September 1969. There is a wide variety of wagons in the Upper Yard. *J. H. Cooper-Smith*

East Suffolk line to Yarmouth and Lowestoft

The East Suffolk line originally provided an outlet for Lowestoft and Yarmouth to London, avoiding the Eastern Counties' line via Cambridge, which was seen as slow and expensive by traders and passengers. It diverged from the main Norwich line at East Suffolk Junction (69 miles 45 chains), about a mile north of Ipswich station and climbed steadily to Westerfield (72 miles 25 chains), where the branch to Felixstowe diverged. It had now swung round to head east, and continued towards Bealings (76 miles 6 chains) and Woodbridge (78 miles 78 chains), emerging by the Deben estuary, which it then followed to Melton (80 miles 21 chains) on one of the few relatively level sections. To compensate, there were several level crossings and many tight curves which limited speed. Having turned to a north easterly direction the line continued its undulating course — it was said that if a driver could handle a loose-coupled goods on the East Suffolk, he could drive anywhere, so demanding was the road.

Wickham Market station (84 miles 43 chains) was located a long way from the small town that it served, and the junction of that name was considerably further on, where the Framlingham branch diverged. Continuing past Snape Junction (88 miles 12 chains), the line mostly climbed to Saxmundham (91 miles 8 chains), where it unusually passed right through the town, the station being very conveniently sited. The junction for Aldeburgh was just over a quarter mile further, with the main line continuing its progress towards Darsham (95 miles 35 chains), where the station served nearby Yoxford and

crossed the busy A12 trunk road, once the Yarmouth turnpike.

Halesworth (100 miles 53 chains) had an interesting history, having been the junction for the narrow-gauge Southwold Railway, although the Mid-Suffolk Light Railway never quite made it that far, having run out of money when it reached Cratfield. The East Suffolk climbed away from Halesworth past the original station, and undulated through Brampton (104 miles 45 chains) as far as Beccles Bank 'box, where it plunged towards the floodplain of the River Waveney and the major junction at Beccles. From here the main line strode across the marshes towards Yarmouth, rising to cross the river twice at Aldeby and St Olaves swing bridges, before reaching South Town station (121 miles 59 chains). At Beccles the line to Lowestoft diverged to the east, and the Waveney Valley line to Bungay, Harleston and Tivetshall Junction, on the Norwich main line branched to the west. The East Suffolk also crossed the Lowestoft–Norwich line at Haddiscoe, and the connection here, between Haddiscoe Junction and Fleet Junction, provided a very valuable diversionary route for Norwich trains when the main line was closed. After the East Suffolk main line north of Beccles closed in November 1959 the Norfolk & Suffolk Joint route between Yarmouth and Lowestoft was upgraded to accommodate the diverted traffic, but the longer and more expensive through journey didn't appeal to passengers, and it too closed in 1970. The loss of the direct rail link between Lowestoft and Yarmouth is still keenly felt.

Below: Class 47 No D1779 accelerates a Liverpool Street–Norwich service past East Suffolk Junction on 3 September 1969. The London Road bridge is behind the train.
J. H. Cooper-Smith

Left: East Suffolk Junction viewed in the down direction on 27 August 1975. Leaving the yard with a freight, Class 37 No 37 041 heads down the main line and passes the East Suffolk, curving away to the right. The wagons in the background are loaded with narrow-gauge bogies built by BREL for the Aqaba Railway Corporation and awaiting shipping via Felixstowe.
I. P. Cowley

Left: On 3 September 1969 Class 15 No D8242 approaches Ipswich East Suffolk Junction with an up cement train.
J. H. Cooper-Smith

Leaving Ipswich, a train for Norwich would pass Gippeswyk Park on its left, a reminder of the origins of the town's name, whilst passing under the huge and confusing signal gantry which gave problems for drivers for many years. It would accelerate through the maze of East Suffolk Junction before passing under the London Road and Hadleigh Road bridges in quick succession, and then cross the River Gipping (pronounced with a hard 'G'). The line then followed its valley until just past Stowmarket, crossing and recrossing the river several times, climbing gently all the while. Just over a mile past the junction lay the extensive Sproughton sidings, with its signalbox on the up side, almost exactly where the A14 road now sweeps overhead. There was a nine-road yard on the down side which handled large quantities of sugar beet, whilst the four up roads were used for overnight carriage storage.

Passed after a short distance was Bramford station (71 miles 76 chains), which served a large village. Here Fisons had a lime works which could handle up to 50 trucks a day, all of which might require sheeting. The signalbox was covered by a porter-signalman who did four hours in the morning and four in the evening. The 'box broke the section between Sproughton and Claydon at peak times and had to open for access to the works. The line was on a low embankment here and then crossed the Gipping once again, with a mill on the right. The wooden station had burnt down in 1911, and was replaced by the Great Eastern with a new one on the opposite (south) side of the road bridge.

Claydon station followed, with Milepost 73½ on the down platform. It had a level crossing at an oblique angle. The main station buildings on the up platform were in the ornate Elizabethan style

Right: Class D16/3 4-4-0 No 62607 north of East Suffolk Junction with an up stopping service, the 3.31pm from Haughley, on 10 October 1951. *R. E. Vincent*

Right: 'Britannia' Pacific No 70007 *Coeur-de-Lion* heads the 1.30pm Liverpool Street–Norwich between Ipswich and Bramford on 10 October 1951. *R. E. Vincent*

Right: Class 47/0 No 47 115 heads the 10.30 Liverpool Street–Norwich past the cement works at Claydon on 29 May 1976. The station, built in the same style as Needham and Stowmarket, had closed to passengers in June 1963. *I. P. Cowley*

characteristic of the Ipswich & Bury Railway, though on a much smaller scale than Bury or Stowmarket. Actually in the village of Great Blakenham, it had a small two-road goods yard with the usual facilities of a country station on the up side of the line at the London end of the layout. Though it lacked a goods shed, it did have a small cattle dock and an end-loading bay served by a short trailing spur from the up main. Claydon handled considerable traffic for the Portland Cement works on the down side, south of the crossing. This was reached by trailing connections from both the up and down lines, and sidings ran in behind the down platform, making it rather cramped. Further on trailing connections from both running lines connected with the down refuge, and this in turn gave access to a government depot by a series of sidings; petrol had been handled here during World War 2. On the opposite side of the line the British Steel Piling

Co was rail-served. New sidings installed in the 1970s at the country end of the layout served sand and gravel workings, and the area has long been well supplied with these, many now being flooded and put to recreational use.

Some 3½ miles further on the railway and river converged at Needham (77 miles 11 chains). This became known as Needham Market following its reopening on 6 December 1971, although the reconstituted parish had received the name as long ago as 1907. It had earlier closed for passengers on 2 January 1967 and for goods in April 1966. The local gas works, opened in 1846, was near the station and had been a customer. The railway approached the station again on a low bank, and unusually for East Anglia had its platforms connected by subway. The station buildings typified the style of the line, and were of quite generous proportions, in red brick with flint, though with a much smaller shelter on the

Below: A fine interior view of Needham station in GER days, with an up express approaching at speed. *Ian Allan Library*

Left: Needham was a victim of the Beeching cuts, losing its passenger service in 1967. This was soon restored, the station reopening as Needham Market on 6 December 1971. The decorations were still *in situ* on 10 December, when Class 47 No D1535 was captured hurrying through with the 09.40 Yarmouth–Liverpool Street. *G. R. Mortimer*

Above: On 13 January 1979 Class 40 No 40 002 (formerly D202, one of the five English Electric Type 4s allocated to the Great Eastern section in 1958) passes Needham Market with the 21.35 Saturdays-excepted Mossend–Parkeston air-braked freight. *John C. Baker*

Right: Class 47/4 No 47 423 at speed south of Needham Market with the 11.35 Saturdays-only service from Norwich to Liverpool Street on 19 January 1985. *John C. Baker*

draughty up platform. The signalbox, a relatively low structure at the country end of the down platform, was one that survived to the end of mechanical signalling on the line, being replaced when Colchester power 'box took over.

Still keeping company with the diminishing Gipping — which had once been navigable between Ipswich and Stowmarket (the Ipswich & Bury Railway had leased the navigation rights in 1846) — the railway neared the latter, one obvious feature on the approach being the large paint and dye works latterly owned by ICI and developed before the war by Nobel Chemical Finishes.

Stowmarket had by then become a substantial town and administrative centre for both the Urban District and Thedwastre Rural District, although its original source of trading prosperity — the river — had ceased to be navigable to barges by the 1930s. There has been much industrial development in this part of the valley, and the town boasted cycle, motor and engineering works as well as maltings, sawmills and a number of other chemical works including those of Fisons and its predecessors. There were also extensive osier beds in the vicinity. All of these were ideally placed for service by rail, and there were yards on

Left: Electrification having reached Norwich, Class 86/2 No 86 252 *The Liverpool Daily Post* hurries through Needham Market on 27 May 1987 with the 13.55 Norwich–Liverpool Street. *Michael J. Collins*

both sides of the line. There was enough work to occupy fully the pilot locomotive allocated to Stowmarket's own small locomotive depot, which in 1949 was booked on at 10.0pm Sunday and finished at 2.0pm the following Sunday. Until the mid-1950s the duty was covered by a Class J67, often No 58518, this locomotive being replaced in 1956 by a diesel shunter.

At Stowmarket (80 miles 54 chains) there were three signalboxes: Station, Yard and Silk Works, the Yard 'box being particularly busy. It was open almost continuously except for the early and late turns on Sundays, and had 70 levers controlling sidings on both sides of the line. The Station 'box on the north end of the down platform worked its gates with a wheel and electrically released the Regent Street gates.

Stowmarket had relatively short platforms, and passengers from London were requested to travel at the rear of the train; going towards London they joined the front part, and a short stroll towards the rear coaches revealed queues of motorists fuming at the crossing gates. Just over 200 yards to the north was Regent Street level crossing. Both now have lifting barriers supervised from the Station 'box, it having survived the 1980s re-signalling for this purpose. There were two Great Eastern lattice iron footbridges at the station, one in the conventional position linking the country ends of the platforms, and the other allowing pedestrians to cross the line when the gates were closed to road traffic. Most through passengers would have had little time to appreciate the delights of Stowmarket since there was no especial restriction on the line speed limit of 80mph between the country end of Ipswich station and Haughley Junction, and the sight of a 'Britannia' dashing through in full cry was awe-inspiring.

Leaving Stowmarket the main line ran through the low-lying water meadows of the upper Gipping valley, now marred by the concrete viaduct carrying the A14 overhead. This point marked the end of the association with the river which strikes off in an easterly direction, rising

near Mendlesham, of Mid-Suffolk Light Railway fame. The railway then climbed out of the Gipping valley and into High Suffolk, which presented down trains with a stiff climb of 3 miles, with Haughley in the middle. Encountered shortly after starting the ascent was a sweeping left-hand curve unusual in that the up and down tracks were very widely spaced, though they were realigned for electrification. Beyond the Gipping the countryside became more rolling, and about 2½ miles from Stowmarket the railway reached Haughley Junction, about a mile to the east of the village. This had once been a

Above: The interior of the signalbox at Needham on 12 May 1984, with most of the layout removed and only the main running lines left — almost all the levers are now white. *David Pearce*

Right: A two-car hybrid DMU formation leaves Stowmarket for Ipswich in pre-electrification days. The short platforms were greatly extended before the wires went up, the connection to the goods yard being moved some distance to the south. *David Pearce*

Right: Class 47/4 No 47 435 calls at Stowmarket station on 29 October 1983 with the 08.28 from Norwich. The new footbridge is under construction (the existing structure being visible in the background), but the platforms have not yet been extended. *John C. Baker*

Below: Class 47/3 No 47 307 keeps company with an Eastern Counties Leyland National bus in the yard at Stowmarket on 12 May 1984. The shed and tracks are long gone, replaced by the inevitable car park. *David Pearce*

Left: A view of Stowmarket station from the new footbridge on 12 May 1984, showing clearly the lengthened platforms, prior to electrification. Much of the yard remains, although the connection to the down main line has been relocated as a result of the platform extension. *David Pearce*

Left: The 13.40 Norwich–Liverpool Street runs into Stowmarket station on 12 May 1984. The original sections of both platforms are out of use, owing to refurbishment work being undertaken on the buildings and canopies. *David Pearce*

Below: Class 47/4 No 47 456 is seen near Lancaster's Crossing, near Stowmarket, with the 10.30 up Norwich express on Sunday 10 October 1982. *John C. Baker*

Right: Headed by 'Britannia' No 70003 *John Bunyan*, the down 'Norfolkman' passes Haughley Junction on 23 July 1952. Standing in the bay platform behind 'J15' 0-6-0 No 65447 is the 11.15am to Laxfield. The 'Middy' closed at the end of the week. *R. E. Vincent*

Below: One reason for the closure of the original Mid-Suffolk station at Haughley was that the site was needed for the huge silo seen here. By the time of this photograph, taken on 4 November 1983, both the 'Middy' and Haughley Junction station were long gone, and in 2008 the silo was also demolished. *John C. Baker*

market town of some importance was also notable for the ruins of an ancient fortress covering some seven acres.

Not being built at the same time as the rest of the stations on the original Ipswich & Bury line, Haughley (82 miles 72 chains) had more the appearance of the standard Great Eastern style, though constructed by the Eastern Union Railway when the line to Norwich was built. This station replaced the original, much nearer the village, which had been on the Bury line. The main building, on the up side immediately to the north of the level crossing on the road between Haughley village and Old Newton, was a solid structure of white brick with red relief. Although this had had its own signalbox it was abolished in 1933 when the layout was rationalised and the signalling taken over entirely by the Junction 'box, standing on the down side at the north end of the layout. The down platform was an island graced by a wooden building having a canopy of elliptical section, matching that on the other platform, and these gave the station a distinctive appearance.

Operationally Haughley was an interesting place, being the junction of the main lines to Norwich and Bury and also for the Mid-Suffolk Light Railway, which line's trains latterly used a bay platform on the up side of the station. Until 1939 they had had their own station, but the need to improve access between the light railway and the main line in connection with the war effort, together with construction of the large silo (which dominated the skyline until demolition in 2008), necessitated its removal. There was a small turntable on the down side, close to the level crossing, but water was available only to branch locomotives and then not at the main platform. The junction also provided one of the few speed restrictions for fast main-line trains, it being 60mph in 1947; eased to 65mph soon after. Down trains on the main line climbed through Haughley at 1 in 134, sweeping away from the junction on a right-hand curve through a long cutting. It was easier to drive (and fire) an express on the line since there was not the need to keep lifting the train away from stops on the steep gradients. 'Britannias' in charge of crack trains such as the 'Norfolkman' certainly got up to the magic 'ton' on occasion, and the fireman could then find all his fire shaken to the front of the box.

Below: Class 86/2 No 86 238 *European Community* passes Haughley Junction on 13 June 1987 with the 09.30 Saturdays-only Liverpool Street–Yarmouth express. *John C. Baker*

Haughley Junction to Cambridge and Ely

Right: Bury St Edmunds is by far the most important place along the route and has an impressive and imposing station, originally the terminus for the Ipswich & Bury Railway. In April 1960 BR/Sulzer Type 2 No D5028 arrives with a non-stop service from Ipswich, such trains being run in connection with Ipswich Town FC home matches. The station retains the through roads. *John C. Baker*

Right: On 16 April 1982 Class 40 No 40 081 runs light engine through Bury St Edmunds on its way to Parkeston from March. By this time the imposing station had lost its through roads, and all trains had to run through the platforms. *Chris Burton*

Right: An unusual view of Bury St Edmunds, recorded on 16 April 1982 from the loading dock and featuring a Class 40 working light from March to Harwich, having arrived with the 21.15 from Mossend. *Chris Burton*

Left: On a murky 23 October 1982 Class 40 No 40 085 pulls out of the loop at Bury St Edmunds with the 20.08 air-braked freight from Mossend to Parkeston.
John C. Baker

Below: Class 31/1 No 31 206 near Kentford, west of Bury, on 25 May 1978. The train is the 18.25 Ipswich–Whitemoor freight, carrying mainly agricultural machinery and fertiliser.
John C. Baker

Left: On 6 June 1987 Class 47/3 No 47 304 passes Kennett, between Bury and Chippenham Junction, with a Freightliner service from Coatbridge to Felixstowe. The yard is busy with Grainflow wagons.
Michael J. Collins

Right: Chippenham Junction, north of Newmarket, was where the lines from Cambridge and Ely to Ipswich diverged. In this photograph, taken on 27 October 1951, Class B17 4-6-0 No 61653 *Huddersfield Town* heads a train from Ely towards Bury St Edmunds and Ipswich. *Ian Allan Library*

Right: The routes from Ipswich to Cambridge and Ely were secondary main lines and carried a variety of traffic, apart from the longer-distance workings. Passing a railbus on trial on the Mildenhall branch, Class B17 4-6-0 No 61645 *The Suffolk Regiment* heads a Peterborough–Newmarket–Cambridge service at Fordham Junction in May 1958. *Derek Penney*

Right: Class 4MT No 43149 heads an M&GN Railway Preservation Society special at Fordham on 26 May 1962. *D. Rees*

Above: Soham station, between Bury and Ely, has long been famous for the heroic wartime episode in which the crew of a munitions train which had been hit by enemy fire shunted it clear of the station and thereby saved the town from being obliterated by the ensuing explosion. It was also the point reached by the LNER in its scheme to double the track between Chippenham Junction and Ely. Here, on 3 April 1976, the second man on Class 37 No 37 029 collects the key token for the single-track section onward to Ely Dock Junction. *R. A. King*

Left: Soham after complete demolition of the platforms and after the track layout had been modified in connection with re-signalling; strangely the length of single track was increased. Class 47/0 No 47 090 *Vulcan* heads the 09.48 special freight from Mountsorrell to Barham on 17 August 1982. *John C. Baker*

North from Haughley, the next station was Finningham (85 miles 31 chains), 3½ miles towards Norwich, right out in the country and with a small building of white brick on the up side. The line here passed through the almost unpopulated heart of East Anglia, and the local stations had a low passenger traffic potential. With the exception of Diss the last of them closed in November 1966, having lost their goods services some years earlier. The countryside was relatively flat, and the line straight: some very fast running could be experienced here. Up trains had to work very hard from Diss, although there was a short favourable stretch for them about a mile north of Finningham, and they did not reach the summit until nearing Haughley.

Mellis (91 miles 30 chains) was a further 4 miles from Finningham and the junction for the short Eye branch, though this had lost its passenger trains as early as February 1931. Freight services lasted until 1964, the branch closing just before Mellis lost its goods facilities. As late as March 1957 the station saw an example of the type of working that had once been commonplace, when a 'hunt special' was run from Bury St Edmunds at 9.30am. This consisted of passenger coaches, horse boxes and vans, and its 'passengers' included 13 horses and 18½ couple

of hounds. The whole village turned out to watch them set off. Three horses had also been loaded at Elmswell, whither the whole hunt returned in the afternoon, there to reboard the train and return to Bury. Mellis station buildings were on the up side, the signalbox also being on that platform, which stood in the apex of the junction. It was another survivor until the takeover by Colchester panel 'box.

The character of the line changed little as it continued towards Diss (95 miles 4 chains), though there was a considerable embankment for about a mile halfway from Mellis, before it ran into a cutting. Diss was approached by passing under the Bury road, over the infant River Waveney (which for almost its entire course marks the boundary between Norfolk and Suffolk) and then over the Scole–Thetford road. Diss was a small market town built partly on a hill, one of whose features was the Mere, a sheet of water of nearly six acres. Market day was on a Friday for corn, sheep, cattle and pigs, and there were other regular stock sales as well as two annual sheep sales — all potential traffic for the railway.

The station was about a mile from the town centre, though the latter has grown towards it, and placed where a high bank runs into a cutting. A Norwich-bound train would overlook the town

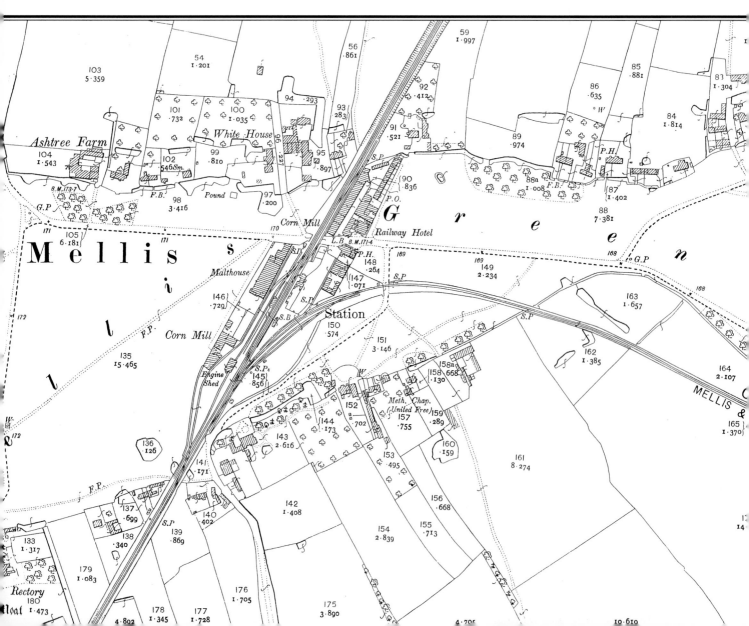

Left: Mellis station had long been closed to passengers by the time of this July 1979 photograph of Class 47/0 No 47 114 heading for Norwich with the 09.30 from Liverpool Street. Note the mirror giving the signalman a view of the level crossing. *Chris Burton*

Above: Integrated transport at Mellis? Sadly not, as this view of the level crossing was recorded on 22 June 1978, and the station had closed to passengers in November 1966. Class 47/0 No 47 156 passes with the 12.32 Norwich–Liverpool Street. *Chris Burton*

Left: The south end of Diss station on 31 July 1977, as Class 37 No 37 109 approaches with an excursion from Rugby to Yarmouth. *A. Wynn*

Above: The view north from the old footbridge at Diss on 3 September 1974, with an up Norwich express approaching. At this time the sidings on both sides of the line were in use, and the station loaded farm machinery, bitumen, fertiliser and grain.
R. A. King

on its left, with open country on the right, past the coal yards. There were granaries and maltings here, and in common with most of the stations on this part of the line grain and related products formed a substantial part of the originating freight traffic. The main buildings were small and of red brick, on the up side, with a similar but even smaller structure on the down platform; as with Stowmarket, the platforms were short. Most trains stopped at Diss — but by no means all, for alternate expresses ran fast from Ipswich — and it is a town that has benefited from electrification.

Burston station (97 miles 42 chains) had red-brick buildings on the up platforms, and again had a level crossing. It served a small village, together with the adjacent one of Shimpling, in countryside on heavy clay soil devoted to the growing of wheat, barley and sugar beet. William Smith & Son dealt in corn, coal and seed at the station. Burston's main claim to fame had been the Strike School, set up in 1914 when the two teachers at the County School were sacked as a result of a bitter dispute with their school managers. They received overwhelming support from the villagers, and as a result the Strike School was set up and operated until 1939. They had also received considerable support from local railwaymen, and the station saw a great deal of activity as supporters and campaigners — many leading lights in the Labour movement — visited the village. The school was reopened in 1950 as a social and educational centre and stands to this day on Burston Green. Unfortunately it is no longer possible to visit by rail, for the station finally closed in 1966, having lost its goods facilities two years earlier. It had enjoyed a distinctly sparse passenger service from the Ipswich–Norwich locals, although this improved marginally with the advent of diesel railcars.

Tivetshall Junction (100 miles 60 chains), a further 3 miles towards Norwich, was altogether a more important station, being the junction for the Waveney Valley line to Beccles. It served the villages of Tivetshall St Margaret and Tivetshall

St Mary, respectively about 1 and 2½ miles from the station, and together having a population of under 600, although it did boast the Railway & Commercial Hotel. It was also a traffic centre of some size for grain and malt, there being extensive maltings on the down side then owned by Watney, Combe, Reid & Co Ltd. Tivetshall was served by local trains between Ipswich and Norwich, and one or two expresses also called. The up platform was an island with its outer face served by branch trains. In Great Eastern days these had usually started from Victoria station in Norwich, though this changed to Thorpe when Victoria closed to passengers in 1916.

These trains usually stopped at the various intermediate stations on the main line, but later in British Railways days ran fast to Tivetshall; the elderly Class E4 'Intermediates' that were used on the service could show a fair turn of speed when properly handled. On one occasion a Norwich driver booked on the Waveney Valley the previous week was travelling 'on the cushions' as far as Tivetshall and was astounded to find the train ahead of time and the locomotive blowing off on arrival, since the very same locomotive had been steaming badly the previous week. The problem was caused by serious clinkering, the remedy adopted being to rake out the fire before setting out and to throw a bucket of stones over the red-hot coals; the firebox doors needed closing with extreme rapidity, but the exploding stones broke up the clinker very effectively. Norwich locomotive depot had a regular supply of stone from Lowestoft for this very purpose. Tivetshall had once had water troughs, which had been essential when using locomotives such as 'Clauds' on through trains between London and Cromer, but they were removed before World War 2. Latterly water columns were provided for up and down trains at the appropriate ends of the platforms and for branch trains at the Norwich end of the station.

The line continued on its relatively straight course, the next railway feature of note being the

Left: Diss station was extensively rebuilt when electrification was undertaken, gaining extended platforms and a new footbridge. Recorded on Sunday 29 July 1984, this view south from the new bridge shows how much the platforms have been lengthened. The train, headed by '47/4' No 47 566, is the 10.30 from Liverpool Street to Norwich. *John C. Baker*

Below: The rebuilt Diss station is well illustrated in this photograph taken from the new footbridge in July 1999 as Class 86/2 No 86 232 arrives with the 16.00 from Norwich. *Chris Burton*

Right: Tivetshall, north of Diss, was once the junction for the Waveney Valley line, and some express trains called there. However, on 20 June 1987 Class 86/2 No 86 220 *The Round Tabler* looks unlikely to do so, and even the rail connection to the grain terminal has been removed. This section was threatened with singling in the 1980s. *John C. Baker*

Right: Tivetshall station after closure, with the platforms cut back and the buildings on the up side removed. *Author's collection*

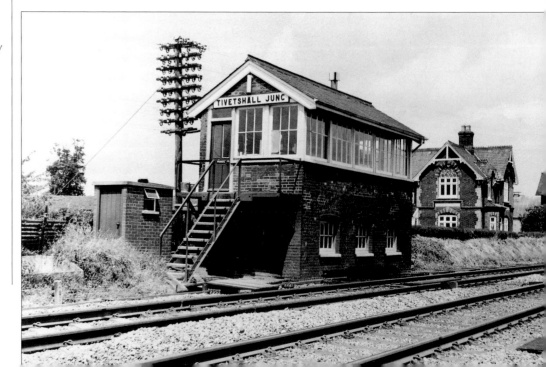

Right: Tivetshall 'box, still proclaiming its 'Junction' status long after the Waveney Valley line closed, and before the electrification of the 1980s. *Author's collection*

junction at Forncett (104 miles 33 chains). This had been the product of yet another speculative dream, of turning Wells-next-the-Sea into a major resort, and the railway access was engineered to match. As a result a high-speed junction was laid out at Forncett so that trains from Liverpool Street could sweep onto the new main line and thence to Wymondham and dash straight onto the Dereham line. Its tourist potential was never fulfilled, but there were some interesting goods workings along the main line, such as that between Beccles and Wells via the Waveney Valley and the Forncett–Wymondham line, although this had been cut back to a service between Beccles and Wymondham before World War 2. A 44ft 9in turntable was located here on the up side, though there was no water available for locomotives.

Flordon station (106 miles 73 chains) marked the first encounter with the River Tas, the course of which the line then followed almost into Norwich, albeit keeping well up the valley side for most of the way. Again there were the red brick buildings typical of this part of the line, the main ones and the goods shed being on the up side. It served a scattered village with some market gardening on the sandy soil. Swainsthorpe station (109 miles 53 chains) marked the close approach of the main A140 road to the line, though the station level crossing was over a minor road.

About a mile to the north the railway cut through the wooded grounds of Dunston Hall, and the road swung overhead on a long obliquely angled bridge, whose construction had caused considerable delay when the line was first built. One of the features of the line here was the 'Dunston dip' which ended in a short rising stretch of 1 in 200 for down trains, and where the line passed under the main road at its lowest point about a mile from Swainsthorpe station. This was certainly the fastest part of the entire line between Norwich and London. The main line then ran onto the high Lakenham (or Harford) Viaduct and swept over the lush valley of the River Yare near its confluence with the Tas, the former keeping

close company with the Ely–Norwich railway, which had been the first railway from the outside world to that fine city.

Speed was at last checked on the approach to Norwich. As they neared Trowse Upper Junction (112 miles 67 chains) down trains were required to diverge sharply to the right at 15mph, with up trains permitted to pass at 25mph. These speeds applied in 1947 and had been eased to 40mph by 1972. There was then a limit of 15mph for trains going into the goods station at Victoria. Passenger trains to London were faced with a fierce 1-in-84 climb from Trowse Lower Junction to Trowse Upper; the former was where the two main lines from the capital finally rejoined, having diverged at Bethnal Green. The reason for this curious approach by the Ipswich line lay in early railway politics, whereby the Eastern Counties Railway, proprietor of the Cambridge route, refused to allow the Eastern Union Railway's newer route access to its terminus at Thorpe, thus compelling the building of a separate station at Victoria. After the ECR took over its smaller rival the use of two stations was a considerable inconvenience, and the connecting line between the upper and lower junctions at Trowse was built, though Victoria was retained for passenger use until 1916. The sharp curves and steep gradient of the approach to Norwich have bedevilled rail travellers and operators ever since, although electric trains heading for London now make light work of the bank.

Approaching Trowse Lower Junction (113 miles 62 chains) with its signalbox in the apex of the junction, the line passed allotments on the right and the new Norfolk County Hall on the left. The mileage changed at the point of the junction, having originally been calculated for the Cambridge route which was just over 9 miles longer than the newer Ipswich line. The bridge carrying the main Lowestoft–Norwich road crossed overhead almost at once, and trains then eased through the disused Trowse station (124 miles 9 chains), closed to passengers upon the outbreak of war in 1939. Its low, short platforms

Below: Flordon, not far from Norwich, was another of the village stations on the main line. It too fell victim to the cuts of the 1960s, being shown here more or less intact but with the platforms cut back. *Author's collection*

Right: The view northwards at Flordon after closure. Track has gone from the goods shed, and the signalbox is boarded up. Station buildings on this section had a 'family' appearance.
Author's collection

Below: In 1985 Swainsthorpe station was relatively intact. This photograph shows the level crossing and signalbox before the start of electrification work.
Chris Burton

Right: Not far south of Harford Viaduct, an unidentified Class 86 climbs with the evening mail train (6.45pm from Norwich). The date is 4 May 1990.
David Pearce

enjoyed their brief final moments of glory when temporarily reopened in 1986 to cover for remodelling of the station throat at Norwich Thorpe. The main station building on the down side was rather unusual in having a very steeply pitched roof and gave the impression of having been built as a series of 'nesting' sections, each one slightly shorter than the other, forming wings on each side of the main structure. It was constructed of knapped flint and quite unlike anything else on the route from Ipswich. It had been built by the Norwich & Brandon Railway for its line into the city and even so was the second station on that site.

Although the first of the stations between Ipswich and Norwich to lose its passenger facilities, Trowse retained great importance for goods, and there were sidings on both sides of the line. These were sufficiently busy for a day locomotive to be allocated for shunting and the working of trips thence to Thorpe and Crown Point yard, and the latter had a similar engine.

Through trains were then almost on Trowse Swing Bridge over the River Wensum, a double-track electrically operated structure built in 1905 to replace a single-track version that had become a severe bottleneck. It was the twin of Carlton Colville (Oulton Broad South) swing bridge on the East Suffolk line, and was controlled by its own signalbox on the south side of the river, just over a quarter of a mile from Trowse Yard 'box, itself only 361yd from the next one, Thorpe Junction. The section of line onwards from Trowse Lower retained the old system of 'lock and block' signalling into the 1960s even though almost everywhere else had been converted to absolute block many years before, and the line as far as Chelmsford already had a great deal of automatic and semi-automatic equipment.

Below: Harford (or Lakenham) Viaduct carries the one-time Eastern Union line from Ipswich over the older Norfolk Railway route from Brandon. On 31 July 1982 Class 31/1s Nos 31 102 and 31 245 head the 14.44 Saturdays-only Yarmouth–Derby. *Dr L. A. Nixon*

Left: Norwich Trowse station was well placed for goods traffic and was very busy indeed; less so for passengers, to whom it closed in 1939. Norwich Class B1 No 61041 heads the 'East Anglian' in bright September sun in 1949. *Ian Allan Library*

Above: On 28 March 1986 Trowse station reopened to handle most of the trains that would normally have used Thorpe, closed because of remodelling of the station throat in readiness for electrification. A Cravens Class 105 DMU waits at Platform 2 before departing for Ely. *David Pearce*

Right: On 3 August 1986, during the station's brief revival, Class 08 No 08 775 arrives at Norwich Trowse with empty stock for the 14.20 to Liverpool Street. *A. Swain*

Left: Trowse Yard signalbox, controlling everything going into or out of Norwich by either main line, on 3 May 1982. *David Pearce*

Below: A BRCW Class 110 DMU forming the 14.10 from Peterborough passes Thorpe Junction on 8 April 1978. The lines to Lowestoft, Yarmouth and Cromer are in front of the signalbox, while Crown Point yard is in the background. *Les Bertram*

Above: The view eastwards at Thorpe Junction on Sunday 23 October 1977 as '47/0' No 47 213 passes with the 09.00 Yarmouth–Liverpool Street. The main line to Liverpool Street is in the foreground. *I. P. Cowley*

Trowse Bridge had two spans, one fixed and the other swinging, the moveable part having a large turntable on top of its pier. In later years it became rather temperamental, and while an Act of Parliament required it to open for shipping on demand, its subsequent closure to rail traffic was quite another matter. Trains were limited to 15mph, but in view of the other restrictions on either side, such as the 15mph over the curve to Thorpe Junction, or the same if taking the Wensum Curve round to the Cromer line, this was not too much of a problem. When the line was electrified the bridge was replaced by another very slightly upstream, and again single-track. The speed limit was raised to 40mph, although it did not prove possible to supervise it remotely from Colchester power 'box which now controls the area, and it has its own signalbox which has to be staffed around the clock. When the Sheringham line was resignalled in 2000/1 control was

transferred to the new Trowse Swing Bridge 'box, using what had been a very under-utilised resource.

Thorpe station itself (124 miles 9 chains) was approached under bridge 357, carrying Carrow Road, which gives its name to the ground of Norwich City Football Club, 'the Canaries'. Just before this bridge, with Thorpe Junction signalbox in its apex the coast lines trailed in, bringing trains from Lowestoft, Yarmouth and Cromer. Once through the bridge trains swung to the right to get into the passenger station, whilst goods trains continued straight ahead, the locomotive depot being to the left of all this. The layout was certainly complex, and a locomotive arriving at Platform 2 or 3 with a working from London would pass over three sets of scissors crossovers, the last being for locomotive-release purposes. Thorpe was always a busy and crowded station and suffered seriously from lack of capacity,

which as late as 1955 prompted the addition of a bay platform, No 6, on the north side.

Thorpe station was, of course, the original Norwich terminus for trains from London — but only via Cambridge. When the Eastern Union's line first opened trains ran into Victoria, crossing the line from Brandon by means of Lakenham or Harford Viaduct. Only after protracted wrangling and almost open warfare between the EUR and the Eastern Counties Railway was the link between the two lines constructed, allowing all services to use Thorpe. Victoria had to be retained — it was very conveniently sited for the city centre.

The line from Trowse Upper fell towards the terminus at Victoria, most of the route being in cutting. It passed under Hall Road, Southwell Road and Grove Road before finally reaching the terminus. This made use of a rotunda, formerly a circus building, which had been taken over by the Eastern Union for its new station. The building to the side of the platform and trainshed was unprepossessing, with an entrance formed by three tall arches. Opened for passenger traffic on 12 December 1849, it finally lost it on 22 May 1916, although surviving much longer for goods. It lasted well into diesel days, continuing to handle bulk traffics such as cement, and was eventually converted for use as a coal concentration depot, with modern equipment for the unloading of coal from bottom-discharge hoppers. By the time this happened, though, it had been cut short at the Grove Road bridge, with the approach from Trowse Upper having been singled in June 1953. Its demise came about with the 1980s electrification scheme and the associated track rationalisation. The erstwhile junction and crossover at Trowse Upper were abolished and replaced with plain track, and it thus became possible to release the valuable city centre site.

Above: Headed by '47/4' No 47 423, the 07.57 Yarmouth–Liverpool Street rounds the Wensum Curve on 28 March 1986, Thorpe station being closed to passengers over the Easter weekend on account of engineering work. Thorpe Junction is to the left of the locomotive, Wensum Junction to the rear of the train. *J. P. Cordle*

Right: Norwich Thorpe station and yard viewed from Carrow Road bridge in July 1977 as Class 47/0 No 47 163, adorned with Silver Jubilee Union Jacks, departs with the up 'Jubilee' for Liverpool Street. The locomotive works is in the left background, while the signalbox controlling the passenger yard can be seen beyond the fourth coach. The fuelling point is in the foreground. *David Pearce*

Right: The view towards Thorpe station from the Carrow Road bridge. Class 08 shunter No 08 868 passes the fuelling point on a trip working to Crown Point. *John Scrace*

Right: Viewed from the steps of the passenger yard signalbox, Class 31/1 No 31 313 brings in a parcels train from Yarmouth on 25 June 1975. The Carrow Road bridge is in the background, Thorpe Junction 'box being just visible through it. *Brian Morrison*

Left: The view back towards Carrow Road on 16 September 1964 as Brush Type 2 No D5543 arrives with the 12.30pm from Liverpool Street. *S. Creer*

Below: Three 'Britannias' in view from the platforms at Norwich Thorpe station on 21 July 1953. In the centre is No 70010 *Owen Glendower*, backing out after bringing in the 'Broadsman'. *T. C. H. Hill*

Right: Class 31/1 No 31 158 heads the 16.30 Liverpool Street–Yarmouth out of Norwich on 25 June 1975. At this time rolling stock was still serviced and stabled at Yarmouth Vauxhall. *Brian Morrison*

Below: An unusual combination of stock at Platforms 4 and 5 at Norwich. Converted for Royal Mail use, Class 302 EMU No 302 991 waits with Class 156 'Super Sprinter' DMU No 156 407. *Brian Morrison*

Cromer was a major traffic objective for the railways, although the system was slow in getting there. Later on, Sheringham added to the importance of the line.

Local trains started from Norwich Thorpe station, and turned off the Yarmouth line at Whitlingham Junction, 1 mile 71 chains from Thorpe. After a relatively easy exit from the terminus, the turnout at the junction was not speed-limited — apart from the ruling speed (60mph in 1947 and through to the 1980s) — but the climb up Whitlingham Bank was fierce, a mile of 1 in 80 being followed by another at 1 in 320. There was then a brief downhill respite before half a mile of 1 in 100 upward towards Salhouse (5 miles 71 chains), although there was another brief decline before reaching the station. The line then fell at varying gradients towards Wroxham (8 miles 61 chains), reached across a bridge over the River Bure, meaning that the station was actually in Hoveton. Wroxham has long been a base for Broads boating holidays (the main centres, including Wroxham Broad, being to the east of the line), but as well as being used by holidaymakers the station handled livestock traffic. At Wroxham Junction (8 miles 70 chains) the branch to Aylsham and Reepham — the 'Round the World' line — diverged to the west, whilst the main line forged onward, climbing gently

towards Worstead (13 miles 9 chains), home of the eponymous woollen cloth, although by the time the railway arrived its main outward goods traffic was in livestock.

The climb continued towards North Walsham (15 miles 75 chains, suffixed 'Main' from September 1948), the M&GN line from Yarmouth Beach converging from the east and running alongside for almost a mile, its station (Town) being adjacent. The two were sufficiently close that a connection was put in place when the M&GN closed in 1959, and companies such as British Petroleum and James Hathaway (a timber merchant), which had used facilities at the latter, continued to be served via the Great Eastern. Anglo-American Oil and R. Coller & Sons, coal merchants, used the GER station. In later years it witnessed the trans-shipment of gas condensate from the terminal at Bacton, the pipeline running under the trackbed of the Norfolk & Suffolk Joint line from Mundesley. North Walsham loaded not only the usual vegetables and livestock but also a considerable tonnage of sugar and confectionery products.

The connections at North Walsham were complex. The M&GN line curved to the west and passed under the Great Eastern to the north of the stations, but both routes had connections to the Norfolk & Suffolk Joint line to Mundesley, Overstrand and Cromer Links. Trains ran from

Below: By 1977 the East Norfolk line had long since ceased to be used regularly by through trains to and from Liverpool Street and had subsided into the rôle of a quiet backwater. Norwich- and Cromer-bound trains cross at North Walsham on 14 September, the driver of the down working exchanging tablets. *John D. Mann*

both North Walsham stations onto the N&S, but it was not until the DMU era, long after closure beyond Mundesley, that through services operated from Norwich.

Beyond North Walsham Junction (for Mundesley) the line went from double- to single-track, falling for about a mile before a level stretch of a mile and a half and thereafter resuming the climb towards Gunton (19 miles 62 chains), a small station that also handled quantities of vegetables. The alignment continued to be good, and it did not take long before trains reached Cromer High (23 miles 79 chains), although this was at least a mile from the town centre and beach, being high up on the Cromer ridge. For passengers this made it inconvenient, to say the least, although it was a substantial affair, with two platforms and a 65ft turntable. In July 1906 the line between Cromer Junction, just short of Cromer High, was opened through to Runton West Junction, on the M&GN's line between Melton Constable and Cromer Beach. This allowed Great Eastern trains to reach Sheringham, which they often did by dividing at North Walsham, the Sheringham portion being sent forward via Mundesley.

Not everything travelled to Cromer via Norwich, of course, for the Wensum Curve, opened in 1879, provided a link between Trowse Swing Bridge Junction (123 miles 43 chains) and Wensum Junction (54 chains from Thorpe station). In 1901 fast trains left Liverpool Street at 1.30pm and Cromer High at 1.00pm, running non-stop both ways between London and North Walsham via the Wensum Curve, the down taking 2 hours 42 minutes, the up two minutes less. Patronage increased sharply when the connection to Sheringham opened in 1906, and whilst the timings remained largely unchanged the loads did not. Titled the 'Norfolk Coast Express' from 1907, the trains then ran with 12 vestibuled corridor coaches, including no fewer than three restaurant cars. However, these workings were generally confined to the summer months, and most services to Cromer called at Norwich and reversed. In British Railways days there were even through workings to Liverpool Street from Melton Constable and Holt. The non-stop services between Liverpool Street and North Walsham were the longest on the Great Eastern, although there were much longer through workings, notably to York, and some of the boat trains from Harwich to Manchester.

Below: Cromer High was the GER's remarkably inconvenient station at the resort, although its distance from the beaches and hotels was doubtless a boon for cab drivers. In this splendid late-Victorian view an express from London is arriving while another stands at the adjacent platform.
Ian Allan Library

Left: Cromer Beach was the M&GN station and, as the name suggests, was much better placed in the town. It had a fine trainshed, and after Cromer High closed in 1954 it was the town's only passenger station. However, a train for Sheringham from Norwich had to reverse at Cromer if it called there rather than taking the direct line between Newstead Lane and Runton West junctions. In this view, recorded in May 1961, 'B12' No 61572 has just arrived with a local from Norwich. *John C. Baker*

Left: One of the great 'might have beens'. Mundesley was one of those places which the railway companies hoped would develop into a major resort, and the station was built on a grand scale, as this March 1956 view shows. It was not to be, although for some time portions of services such as the 'Broadsman' and 'Norfolkman' called there *en route* between Sheringham and North Walsham. *Ian Allan Library*

Left: This was the reality at Mundesley. A two-coach local headed by 'N7' No 69690 waits to leave for North Walsham around 1956, shortly before DMUs were introduced. *Ian Allan Library*

The Route via Cambridge

The layout of Liverpool Street station dictated that Cambridge-line stopping trains arrived and departed on the west side. Enfield and Chingford services used Platforms 1-4, whilst Bishop's Stortford locals used 5 and 6. Trains to and from Norwich generally used Nos 7 and 8, bearing in mind that they generally arrived via one route and departed via the other, so that crews maintained their route knowledge. In the rush hours the locomotive of an arrived service simply stayed on the stops until its train was taken back out again, thus releasing it. At less-busy times the stock would be taken out ECS (empty coaching stock) to Thornton Fields or Stratford Old Yard until required for the next peak, and the locomotive would go for turning at Liverpool Street, and for coal and water.

King's Lynn or Norwich trains by either route left via the main lines out of Liverpool Street, which were the centre pair of the six tracks, whilst local workings, and occasionally expresses, could use the suburban lines on the west side through the 'rats' hole'. Having tackled the bank up to Bethnal Green they diverged sharply to the left to head almost due north, leaving the Ipswich-line trains continuing on their generally north-easterly progress. A main-line train coming out on the suburban lines crossed back to the main lines once past Bethnal Green, much as they do today. A series of inner-suburban stations — Cambridge Heath, London Fields and Hackney Downs — punctuated their slow exit from London, the line crossing over the North London just before reaching the last-named. At Hackney Downs Junction the main line swung gently to the right, while the Enfield line veered gently left to head briefly north-west through Stoke Newington.

Clapton passenger station (3 miles 78 chains) was in a deep cutting with yellow-brick walls and buildings at street level, and heralded complex junctions allowing a variety of route choices. It was preceded by two tunnels, Queens Road

Below: BR Class 7 4-6-2 No 70000 *Britannia* stands at Platform 9 at Liverpool Street with the 12.24pm to Norwich via Cambridge on 13 June 1958.
A. E. Buckley

Left: Class L1 2-6-4T No 67727 arrives at Liverpool Street with a suburban service from Bishop's Stortford in September 1960. *John C. Baker*

Left: Class N7 0-6-2T No 69662 crosses from down main to down Cambridge line at Bethnal Green whilst working a suburban train of articulated stock in September 1960. Piles of rubble on the platform are hardly likely to impress passengers. *John C. Baker*

Below: 'Britannia' No 70039 *Sir Christopher Wren* attacks the bank as it passes the old platforms at Bishopsgate on its way out of Liverpool Street with the 12.10pm to Norwich via Cambridge in 1958. *R. E. Vincent*

(445yd) and Clapton (284yd), and followed by the spur to Clapton goods station down by the River Lea, on the east side of the main line. This crossed the river, with Clapton Junction (4 miles 38 chains) immediately after, where the main line curved to the left, leaving the Chingford branch to go straight ahead and over the line from Stratford. This trailed into the Cambridge main line at Copper Mill North Junction (4 miles 74 chains), which also accommodated the curve from the Chingford branch coming from Hall Farm Junction, lifted in 1960. All of this contrived to constrain line speed, which for most of the line's existence has been no higher than 35mph around the curves between Clapton and Copper Mill junctions. Maximum line speed — 80mph between Bethnal Green country end and Bishop's Stortford in 1972 — could not be reached until after Tottenham Hale (6 miles).

From Copper Mill Junction there was a generally better alignment. Trains almost immediately crossed the Warwick Reservoir, the most southerly of the Metropolitan Water Board's Lea Valley group, re-crossed the River Lea (often spelt 'Lee') and passed Tottenham South and North junctions, where trains could access the Tottenham & Hampstead Joint, towards Gospel Oak.

Tottenham Hale has long been an important station, and has had a good service since it opened with the line to Broxbourne on 15 September 1840. It was extensively modified when the Victoria Line opened in 1968. It had an extensive goods business and a number of private sidings, and handled a wide variety of traffic, including confectionery and preserves, paper, textiles and clothing, small machinery and livestock. The next station to the north was Northumberland Park (6 miles 73 chains). This had opened in 1841 as Marsh Lane, and appears to have closed again for a short while, reopening with a very sparse service. It became Park in 1852 and Northumberland Park in 1923. Although busy for most of its existence it had only passenger facilities. The Victoria Line depot was built on the east side of the line in 1968.

Just under a mile to the north the line went under what later became the A406 North Circular Road, with Angel Road station (7 miles 57 chains) immediately to the north. Since Tottenham Hale the alignment had been good — generally straight or with only gentle curves — and speed could finally be gained. Angel Road was important for goods, had a 6-ton crane and many private sidings, latterly including the Eastern Gas Board and Ready Mixed Concrete Ltd; there was an adjacent gas works. Ponders End (9 miles 71 chains) also hosted the Eastern Gas Board but had a smaller crane. Angel Road had once been a junction, with a branch diverging to the west to Lower Edmonton and Enfield Town. The former became 'Low Level' when the High Level station opened, on the line from Hackney Downs, and closed in 1939.

Brimsdown (10 miles 61 chains) had the usual side platforms and red brick buildings, and served the eastern side of Enfield: there were, of course, several other stations bearing the latter name. It again had many private sidings, again reflecting the industrial nature of the Lea Valley. It also marked the end of this group of Lea Valley reservoirs, the most northerly being King George's. The River Lea navigation ran along the western edge of the reservoirs, with the River Lea along the eastern side, all being to the east of the line. The level crossing at 10 miles 66 chains was immediately to the north of the station, and was followed by Enfield Lock station and level crossing at 11 miles 65 chains. By this time the glasshouses that characterise this part of the valley had started to appear to the north of the reservoirs. The station had first appeared in the timetables in 1855 as Ordnance Factory, located to the north of the level crossing of Welch's Lane, although the Ordnance Survey didn't show any such factory nearby in 1882. By this time the platforms appeared to have become staggered, with the up now south of the level crossing and a siding trailing into the down line opposite. It remained in open countryside, with Plantation Farm to the east. It was renamed Enfield Lock in 1886 and re-sited south of the crossing by 1891.

The line continued its progress through Waltham Cross (12 miles 63 chains — Waltham or Waltham Cross & Abbey in earlier years), one of the few places where the built-up area spread from one side of the Lea Valley to the other. The River Lea and the navigation were very close at this point, with the road to Epping also crossing the valley. Today the M25 sweeps all before it here. The station already had extensive goods facilities in 1882, and although largely surrounded by open country, much of the land was taken up by horticulture, notably the Royal Nurseries on the west side of the line. Waltham Lane went over the line by a bridge, and there were sidings and other facilities both north and south of this. These were used by local growers including C. J. Poupart Ltd, and the Waltham & Cheshunt Gas Co also had a siding to serve its works at the north of the station, later becoming the Eastern Gas Board.

Passing over Trinity Lane level crossing — a track leading onto Cheshunt Marsh — the line reached Cheshunt Junction at 13 miles 71 chains, where the Churchbury loop trailed in. This had had a chequered career. It branched from the Enfield Town line at Bury Street Junction, and paralleled the main Lea Valley line before rejoining it south of Cheshunt. The line had fallen victim to competition from London County Council's electric tramcars, and later, motor omnibuses. Its local stations closed after World War 1, and the line had little use until electrified by British Railways in 1960 when its stations were refurbished and reopened.

In 1882 Cheshunt station (14 miles 1 chain) had staggered platforms either side of the level crossing over Windmill Street, but no other goods facilities. Still in open country at the time, the line here is very close to the Small River Lea, the full-

Left: In the standard British Rail livery of blue and grey, Class 315 EMU No 315 801 observes a temporary speed restriction after leaving Enfield Lock with the 13.40 Hertford East–Liverpool Street service on 11 October 1986. *Roland Hummerston*

Below: Seen approaching Waltham Cross, Brush Type 2s Nos D5695 and D5699 have charge of the Royal Train transporting HM The Queen from Liverpool Street to King's Lynn on Saturday 21 December 1963. *P. Paye*

Above: Suburban services at the southern end of the Cambridge main line are currently in the hands of Class 315 EMUs such as No 315 825, in the garish Network SouthEast livery when photographed forming an up Hertford local near Broxbourne on 14 March 1987. Removal of the goods lines has left wide open spaces. *John C. Baker*

size version being slightly to the east. More reservoirs and open water characterised what is now the Lea Valley Country Park, and while the Churchbury loop stations were closed to passengers they came under Cheshunt's jurisdiction. Throughout its life goods facilities remained limited, although its passenger traffic was extensive.

Still following the edge of the valley, the line started to bear very gently to the east, passing over Slipe Lane and Wormley level crossings and reaching Broxbourne station (17 miles 17 chains). The station had once been Broxbourne Junction, for Hertford East, and later Broxbourne & Hoddesdon, the latter being much the more important. To confuse matters further the station was rebuilt 100yd to the north when the line was electrified in 1960, the new signalbox being to the north of the up platform. Prior to this it had two side platforms mostly to the north of the Station Road bridge, with extensive sidings on both sides of the line, and a gas works to the north. After electrification the new station had two island platforms, and was approached by a new road and forecourt. The platforms were linked by a brick, concrete and glass overbridge with three lift towers, and what *The Railway Magazine* described as 'a single-storey structure [which] contains an impressive modern entrance front leading to a lofty staircase hall which is glazed towards both the approach and adjoining river frontages'. The station had a private siding for the Hoddesdon Gas & Coal Co and also two for Rochford's, commercial growers. At one time there were extensive watercress beds near Broxbourne Junction.

Broxbourne Junction (18 miles 35 chains) was over a mile to the north, with the level crossing and signalbox (new for the 1960 electrification) just to the south. The line for Hertford veered away to the left, with trains subject to a 20mph restriction over the junction for many years. Continuing to swing towards the east it crossed the River Lea for the last time near Rye House

(station on the Hertford line) and continued into the valley of the River Stort, crossing the river and running between it and the River Stort Navigation. At the same time it crossed the border into Essex, and reached Roydon station at 20 miles 9 chains. Roydon Lodge and Roydon Hall were immediately to the south of the station, with Roydon Hamlet about two miles further; inevitably the settlement grew towards the railway. In 1898 the level crossing separated the staggered platforms, the down being on the west side. The road crossed the Stort Navigation immediately to the south of the station, and the railway likewise just to the east of the station, now being south of this and the river. There were also sidings on both sides of the line, and although goods facilities were limited there was a white brick goods shed at the back of the down platform, just to the west of the station building. The original wooden buildings remain on the down platform, and it is one of relatively few to retain the staggered layout. The line crossed the Stort Navigation immediately past the station, and with the transition to open countryside at last, the flat and open nature of the line became more apparent, its progress being generally easy as befits a route following a lowland river valley. Having surmounted the summit at London Fields and briefly descended at 1 in 75 through Hackney Downs, the line mostly rose very gently as far as Elsenham, with nearly four miles at 1 in 731 between Waltham Cross and Broxbourne being fairly typical.

Burnt Mill (22 miles 59 chains) was very close to the eponymous mill on the Stort Navigation, with R. E. Smith & Co Ltd's Parndon siding about ¼ mile to the west. This was worked by ground frame, the key for the hut being kept by the stationmaster at Burnt Mill. It was connected only to the down line, and there was no crossover. Up-line traffic for Parndon had to be taken to Roydon, and up-line traffic from the siding taken to Burnt Mill. When so advised the stationmaster at Burnt Mill had to send a competent man to work the

Above: 'Sandringham' 4-6-0 No 2814 *Castle Hedingham* heads an up train near Bishop's Stortford on 18 June 1931. *E. R. Wethersett collection*

ground frame, one of his jobs being to place the down distant and home signals to danger, and maintain them thus until shunting operations were complete. It was also necessary for the stationmaster at Roydon to make the arrangements to stop a down train at his station, should shunting be needed at Parndon.

Burnt Mill station served Great and Little Parndon and also Netteswell and had opened as the latter. As with many stations on the line its platforms were staggered and separated by a level crossing, with the main buildings and down platform on the east side. All this was swept away in 1960 when Harlow Town station replaced it on the same site, now having four running lines, two island platforms and brand-new buildings, bridge and lift shafts. The marshy nature of the ground caused problems for the builders and necessitated much drainage work. The level crossing was replaced by an overbridge to the west of the station. The new station was opened on 13 July by Eastern Region General Manager H. C. Johnson, and at the same time Harlow (24 miles 36 chains) was renamed Harlow Mill. It received a new signalbox with route-setting panel, which replaced the earlier 'boxes at Burnt Mill and Harlow. All of this was necessitated by the construction of Harlow New Town, which was expected to grow to some 80,000 people by 1965, from about 3,000 before. This was the first station specifically provided for a New Town. Harlow Mill continued to handle aggregates traffic on the up side of the railway.

Onwards from Harlow, the line swung back to a northerly direction, still closely following the Stort. There was a brief falling gradient approaching Sawbridgeworth (26 miles 56 chains), where the station again had a level crossing bisecting the layout. In 1897 the platforms were staggered, that on the down side being to the south of the crossing. However, the boundary between Hertfordshire and Essex also passed through the station, following the Stort to the west, but then following what was once the

A414 road towards Hatfield Heath. This meant that the line crossed back into Hertfordshire. There were extensive maltings on both sides of the line, and in the 1920s W. Lawrence & Sons and H. A. & D. Taylor both had sidings, the latter surviving until the 1950s. In 1938 they despatched over 1,000 tons between them. Today little remains of the old station, and the platforms are entirely to the north of the level crossing.

Continuing northwards past Tednambury and Spelbrook, the latter having a level crossing, the line continued to keep company with the Stort, finally reaching Bishop's Stortford (30 miles 27 chains), with an imposing signalbox to the south of the station. In earlier days there had been North and South 'boxes; the latter survived until resignalling, when the new Liverpool Street power 'box took over. Always an important town, it had been one of the objectives of the Northern & Eastern Railway. The main line snakes through the outskirts of the town on the eastern side, passing Hockerill to the north-east. On 22 February 1869 Bishop's Stortford became a junction when the line to Dunmow and Braintree opened. This had had a protracted gestation, and used a third track to the east of the main line, rising rapidly and diverging about half a mile north of the station. Branch trains could thus gain access to the outer face of the up platform without coming onto the main line. By the turn of the century a small turntable had been established on the east side for branch locomotives.

By 1898 the layout was much as it is today: the up platform an island, with the down somewhat staggered and to the north. Being on the town side the main station buildings were there. The main part was a square buff-brick block, three storeys in height, and with ashlar work at ground floor level on both the platform and road approach sides. The slate roof had a very low pitch and was enclosed by a low wall from which the downpipes emerged. From an early stage the importance of the station dictated that more buildings spread along the platform in both directions. On the up side a small

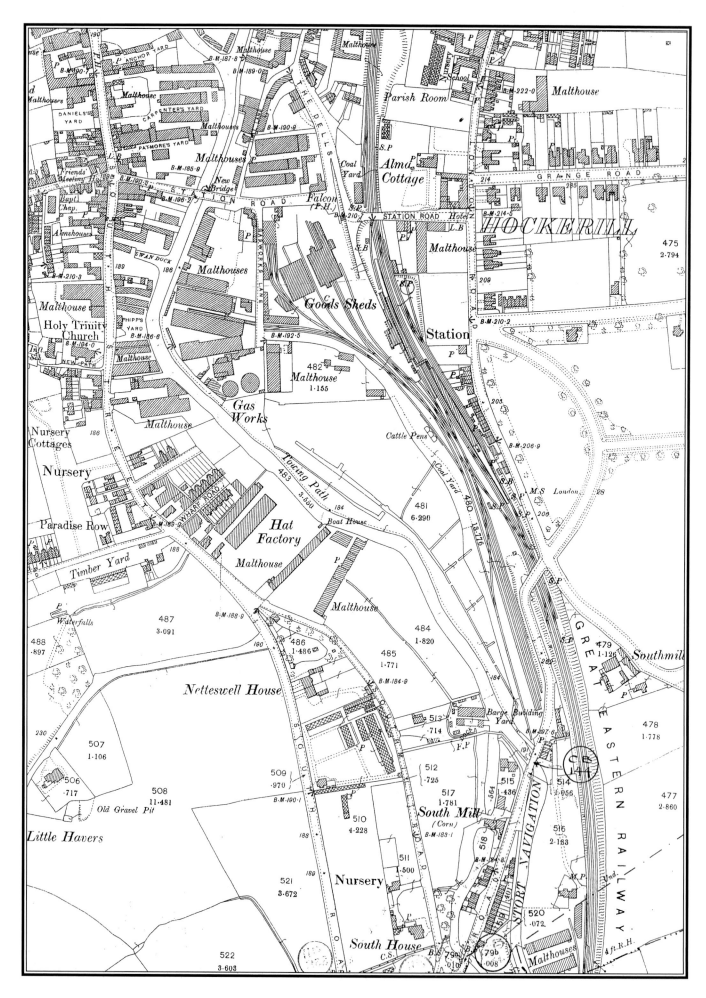

single-storey red brick booking office was located high on the side of the cutting, connected to the platforms by a footbridge. The latter was removed and replaced by the present structure at electrification in 1960, together with many other changes to the buildings.

The station had extensive goods facilities, almost entirely on the down (town) side of the main line. There were cattle pens and a coal yard to the south, another coal yard to the north and large goods sheds at the northern end. There were also large maltings to the west of the station, all rail served. Not surprisingly grain and malt traffic was heavy, well over 2,000 tons being despatched in 1938, together with substantial amounts of small and medium-sized machinery, and livestock. The station was of sufficient importance that it was the first stop out of Liverpool Street for a number of services, and in 1910 it was reached in 43 minutes by the 4.30pm London to Doncaster and York. Bishop's Stortford always had a good passenger service, although there were never many trains that made it their first call after Liverpool Street. Chelmsford and Bishop's Stortford were almost exactly the same distance from Liverpool Street, and both important regional centres. Despite the more tortuous nature of the first few miles from Liverpool Street via the Lea Valley the journey times to both were about the same in the 1880s. By 1910 they were starting to move in favour of Bishop's Stortford (about 43 as against 46 minutes), and this continued through

to the 1950s with the steam-hauled services, which were the only ones providing a non-stop service to Chelmsford before the wires were extended to Colchester and beyond. Norwich services showed a different pattern, however, and whilst times were comparable by both routes in the 1880s, they had moved decisively in favour of the Ipswich line by 1910 because of the different stopping patterns. The difference in distance — 115 miles via Ipswich and 124 via Cambridge — did not account for the faster times.

Electric trains reached Bishop's Stortford in 1960. A completely revised timetable was introduced on the lines between Liverpool Street and Chingford, Enfield Town, Hertford East and Bishop's Stortford on 21 November 1960, although some electric trains had started running to steam times on 14 November. However, the main line via the Lea Valley was not wired at this time, and all electric services ran via the renamed Southbury loop. Considerable teething troubles ensued, and the full planned service was not finally introduced until June 1963. The main line was finally electrified in 1969 under a scheme authorised in the spring of 1967. The nine miles from Copper Mill Junction to Cheshunt plugged the last gap in the suburban system and was brought into public use on 5 May 1969. It had been intended as part of the original scheme, but was omitted so that steam and heavy freight could be concentrated on the main line, leaving the Southbury loop to handle the suburban traffic.

Above: On 23 June 1957 Class K3/2 2-6-0 No 61890 arrives at Bishop's Stortford with a Liverpool Street–Cambridge train. Standing on the up road, Class B2 4-6-0 No 61615 *Culford Hall* waits to follow with a permanent-way train. *S. Creer*

Right: Class 37 No D6751 coasts into Bishop's Stortford with a Sunday-evening Cambridge–Liverpool Street service on 13 July 1969. *Chris Burton*

Right: For many years 'Stansted' meant the station at Stansted Mountfitchet, renamed when the line to the airport opened. Here an up Class H freight is headed by Class J19 0-6-0 No 64668 between Bishop's Stortford and Stansted. The four cattle trucks represent an extinct species. *R. E. Vincent*

Right: Class 47/0 No 47 010 is in charge of the 09.27 Cambridge–Liverpool Street, passes the up platform at Elsenham on 3 August 1981. The station building is set well back from the platform edge, necessitating a very wide awning. Behind the camera was once the platform for the branch to Thaxted, one of the shortest-lived in the country. Today a high footbridge soars over the overhead wires here. *Michael J. Collins*

Left: Class 47/0 No 47 158 *Henry Ford* sports Stratford's trademark silver roof as it heads the 08.35 Liverpool Street–King's Lynn through the Essex countryside between Elsenham and Newport on 26 March 1983. *Michael J. Collins*

Left: Located just south of Audley End, the station at Newport, Essex, had clearly been 'rationalised' by the time this photograph was taken in April 1967. English Electric Type 3 No D6714 passes with the 14.36 Liverpool Street–King's Lynn. *Chris Burton*

Left: Newport station had the characteristic but unassuming red-brick buildings on both platforms, with wide awnings. Here Class 40 No 40 068, of Gateshead, passes with a Freightliner for Tilbury. *Rev G. B. Wise*

Right: LNER Class D15 No 8821 on a down train near Audley End on 17 May 1930. *E. R. Wethersett collection*

Local trains remained the province of three-car DMUs, which rapidly became overcrowded. The scheme was also necessary to provide better connections with the Victoria Line, which had opened through to the West End of London on 7 March of that year. The new Mk 3 design of overhead line equipment was used on the scheme, which used the 25kV system throughout — the earlier one had used 6.25kV south of Cheshunt. Trackwork simplification also involved the removal of the pair of goods lines between Pickett's Lock, south of Brimsdown, and Tottenham South Junction, and the area was re-signalled with colour lights and AWS.

Continuing northwards from Bishop's Stortford trains were limited to 70mph as far as Ely North. The line curved again towards the north east, crossing the River Stort twice in quick succession whilst keeping company with it for another couple of miles. Eventually the river continued northwards while the railway climbed out of the valley towards Stansted (33 miles 27 chains). The station served Stansted Mountfitchet and was renamed to match in 1990; it had been Stanstead in earlier days. Passengers on both platforms were protected by red brick screens, with awnings, while the station building was also in red brick, a single-storey gable-ended structure on the down side. The line was built to the south of the town, and had two side platforms and the main facilities on the down side. There were several private sidings at the station, although it had no crane and could not handle livestock. The line approached the station for nearly a mile at 1 in 232 — the steepest adverse gradient for a down train since Ponders End — while the station itself was level. Beyond Stansted it steepened considerably, with a mile of 1 in 107 approaching the summit at Elsenham. On 29 January 1991 the new line to Stansted Airport opened, with a triangular junction and operated by brand-new Class 322 EMUs, and a half-hourly service from Liverpool Street from 19 March.

When built, Elsenham station (35 miles 49 chains) was some way north of the village, with a level crossing at a very oblique angle. The platforms were staggered either side of the crossing, with the down to the north. The station occupied a short level stretch at the summit of the line, which then fell towards Cambridge with a brief climb towards Audley End. Elsenham had sidings on both sides of the level crossing and handled the full range of goods, although it had no crane. Electric gongs were provided to assist shunting, one about 20yd on the Cambridge (north) side of the level crossing gates, and the other close to the up-side loading dock. The plunger to operate them was in a box near to where the up-side refuge sidings joined the main line, and their purpose was to allow the person in charge of shunting to signal to enginemen without having to venture onto the main line. The signalman would repeat these by flag or lamp to the enginemen if they were unlikely to hear the gongs. The signalbox was located roughly halfway along the down platform.

Elsenham's passenger-train service was that of a small country station, usually only the stoppers calling. It briefly became a junction when the Elsenham & Thaxted Light Railway opened on 1 April 1913, at which time the up platform acquired another face. It sported a wooden building which acted as a shelter for passengers, but which was set back a long way from the edge of the platform and so necessitated a very wide canopy. What at first appeared to be a triangular junction wasn't — the branch line did not join the main line at all. This was done via a spur into the goods yard on the north of the level crossing and meant that the road there also had to cross the branch. The Thaxted line lasted a mere 40 years, closing for passengers in 1952 and goods in June 1953.

In the meantime the main line dropped steadily towards Newport (39 miles 69 chains) and picked up the valley of the River Cam for its northward journey, and with gentle gradients and easy curves some fast running was possible. Again with two side platforms, this time opposite each other, the line and station were to the east of the settlement,

described by *Kelly's Directory* as 'formerly a market town and now a village'. Newport also had the brick single-storey type of building, this time in white, on the down side. The gas works was at the station on the up side, with goods facilities on the other side of the line. These were limited to general goods, although there were the usual coal merchants, including Coote & Warren. Passenger services were limited to stopping trains which called at all stations between Bishop's Stortford and Audley End or Cambridge.

Rising again towards Audley End station (41 miles 55 chains), with half a mile or so of 1 in 130 on the approach, the easy alignments continued. The line entered the station through a deep cutting and then a viaduct, with Audley End Junction following immediately, controlled by the signalbox at 41 miles 48 chains. The branch line to Saffron Walden and Bartlow was reached by a double junction, and had what amounted to its own station, with a separate platform and waiting room across the yard. The station was located in the village of Wendens Ambo, and opened as Wenden in 1845. It was given the name of the nearby stately home in 1848, since it was far from most other habitation, and served Audley End House together with Saffron Walden, which didn't get its own railway until 1865. The station had staggered platforms linked by footbridge, with the main buildings on the up side. They were

constructed of a buff brick and had two storeys and a low-pitched roof. The round-headed windows and doors were characteristic, and — as befits its service of the stately home — had a *porte cochère* on the road side. It was designed by Sancton Wood and Francis Thompson. There was a siding for Barnard Bros, coal merchants, from the 1920s, and although the station could handle all classes of traffic, the amount of originating goods was light. This was generally true of most stations on the line, and even Cambridge generated relatively small amounts for a city of its size and importance.

The line at this point left the Cam valley, which helps to explain why there was a minor summit at Audley End, and also the tunnels to the north, through the chalk ridges, where the approach cuttings are steep-sided and the chalk outcrops remain. The deviation was necessitated by having to stay out of sight of Audley End House to the east of the river, levelling out thereafter. Audley End Tunnel (456yd) started just over a mile from the station, and its south portal was designed by Sancton Wood. It is an impressive design consisting of a series of circular stone and brick rings, and the south portal of Littlebury Tunnel (407yd), about a quarter mile to the north, is also ornate. It was probably also designed by Sancton Wood, both being built at the insistence of Lord Braybrooke, then owner of Audley End House.

Above: An up freight for Temple Mills, headed by Class 8F 'WD' 2-8-0 No 90608, passes through the deep cutting north of Audley End on 30 May 1953. *R. E. Vincent*

Above: There are two tunnels at Littlebury, to the north of Audley End. This photograph, taken on 20 August 1935, shows Class B12 No 8575 at the head of a southbound stopping service.
E. R. Wethersett collection

Right: On 9 April 1983 Class 37 No 37 075 emerges from the more southerly of the Littlebury tunnels with the 14.35 Liverpool Street–King's Lynn. The portal is unadorned, in contrast to that at the other end. *Paul D. Shannon*

Left: Class J39 0-6-0 No 2726 emerges from the ornate southern portal of the southern tunnel at Littlebury with a goods train on 17 May 1930.
E. R. Wethersett collection

Left: 'Britannia' Pacific No 70009 *Alfred the Great* emerging from Littlebury (or Audley End) Tunnel with an up express on 11 August 1953. *E. R. Wethersett collection*

Left: An unusual view from over Audley End Tunnel. Class 31 No 5663 approaches Audley End with the 15.54 Whitemoor–Stratford Market Class 8 freight on 23 July 1969. *Dr R. Elsdon*

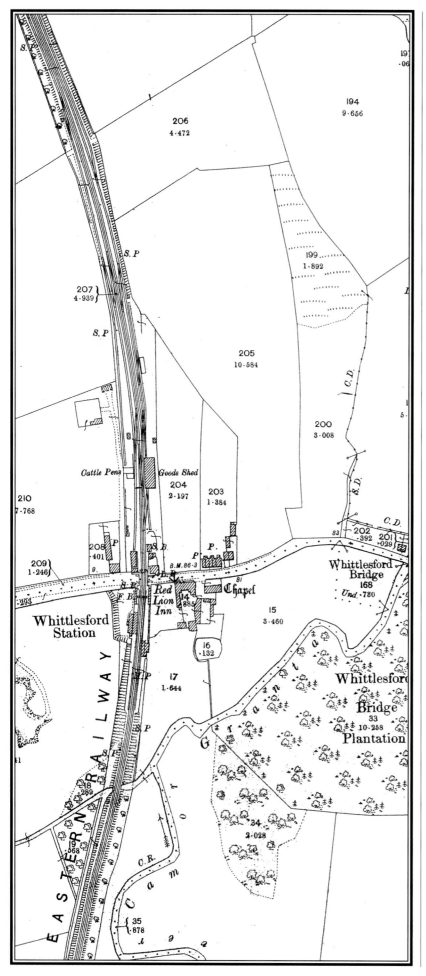

Cuttings would certainly have been adequate in engineering terms, but the railway could have been visible from the house.

Littlebury siding, on the up side of the line, served the nearby village and was used by J. Taylor & Sons Ltd, a firm of forage merchants. It was controlled by Littlebury Siding signalbox (43 miles 61 chains) but administered by Great Chesterford. That station (45 miles 56 chains) marked the boundary between Essex and Cambridgeshire, which actually passed just south of the station buildings, so that the layout was split between the two counties. The village, to the east of the line and the River Cam, is in Essex. There were the usual two side platforms, staggered and connected by a footbridge, and with the signalbox at the north end of the up. Great Chesterford was sufficiently important to warrant one of the square main buildings, on the up side, this time in a buff/white brick. The station loaded hay and straw and also vegetables, but the returns included those for Littlebury. In the 1950s the station boasted an up goods loop holding a huge 373 wagons, whilst there was also an up refuge siding and two down. Continuing northward, the line again crossed the Cam, and almost immediately passed the site of the divergence north-eastwards of the former direct line to Newmarket. This had been incorporated in 1846 and opened in 1848, but closed as early as 1851, it making no sense for trains to avoid Cambridge, despite the wishes of the colleges. From the east the village of Hinxton overlooked the river and railway, and there were three level crossings (Ickleton Road, Hinxton and Duxford) in rapid succession, the railway also crossing the Cam four times between Great Chesterford and Whittlesford stations.

Littlebury Bank, falling towards Great Chesterford, was a tough climb for up trains. Starting with 1 in 163 for a little under a mile from the latter, it steepened to 1 in 135 for half a mile, before easing to 1 in 153 through Littlebury. Special lineside telephones were provided for the use of guards of failed up goods trains, one outside the cabin at the entrance to the up refuge siding, another 1,000 yards on the Audley End side of Great Chesterford station and the third about ¾ mile nearer Littlebury. Assisting locomotives were required to cross back to the down line at Audley End and return to Great Chesterford, but could also be given a 'wrong line order' if they needed to go only as far as the outlet points at Littlebury, and so return to the up goods loop at Great Chesterford.

Whittlesford station (49 miles 1 chain) lay about half a mile from the village of that name, and a similar distance from the rather larger Duxford, also site of an important airfield. Today this is home to part of the Imperial War Museum and Concorde. The station was bisected by the main A505 road, which passed over the line by a level crossing. The platforms and the Red Lion inn were to the south of this, with the signalbox, goods shed and other facilities and loops to the north, the down loop holding 80 wagons and the up 79.

There were water columns for goods trains on both sides, between the up loops and between the down loop and main line. A warning bell was provided at the latter so that when a train was signalled on the main line the crane was not left foul of it, and men stayed clear of the running line. Originating traffic included vegetables and paper, the latter accounted for by Sawston Mill. Although the station is now suffixed 'Parkway' it was evidently not considered important enough when built for the grander style of buildings, and received only the single-storey gable-ended red brick version, albeit with a slightly higher central section at right angles to the rest.

Sawston and Dernford level crossings followed Whittlesford station, Sawston being a substantial settlement to the east of the railway. It also had a siding on the west side, accessed from the down main line, with a signalbox on the up side. This was later extended into Whittlesford Mill, which was an agricultural works owned by Maynards,

making various items of machinery, which were sent away by rail. Sawston Mill was a little way to the north.

Continuing to keep company with the Cam (also known as the Granta), the railway continued to fall gently towards Shelford (52 miles 32 chains), junction for the Stour Valley line to Haverhill, Sudbury and Colchester. The station layout was again bisected by the level crossing, with the passenger platforms to the north, and the signalbox to the south, on the up side. Shelford boasted one of the square two-storey buildings, unusually in a buff/white brick with knapped flint facing to the walls. There were sidings on both sides of the crossing, although with the main goods facilities — including the shed — to the north. The up refuge, some way to the north, held 50 wagons. The Stour Valley line trailed in on the east side, with its single line running alongside the main line for nearly ¼ mile before joining the up main and passing over the level crossing.

Below: Class B17 'Sandringham' No 2818 *Wynard Park* passes Littlebury with the 10.1am express from Cambridge on 20 August 1935. *E. R. Wethersett collection*

Left: Class J19 0-6-0 No 8267 passes Great Chesterford with an up goods on 23 June 1932. *E. R. Wethersett collection*

115

Right: Class 37 No 37 051 heads the 16.56 Liverpool Street–Newmarket–Ipswich near Great Chesterford on 30 June 1978. *Chris Burton*

Right: The south end of Whittlesford station once boasted a level crossing, now replaced by the bridge seen here. Prior to electrification the platforms were extended to accommodate 12 cars, and a very large car park was provided for commuters. Class 317 EMU No 317 308 calls with the 06.33 Liverpool Street–Cambridge on 4 October 1992. *Bob Francis*

Right: Forming the 10.18 Cambridge–Liverpool Street, Class 317 EMU No 317 305 passes Whittlesford on 27 June 1992. *Michael J. Collins*

Above: Shelford station, the first south from Cambridge, marked the divergence of the cross-country route to Colchester. Class B1 4-6-0 No 61371 is about to leave the main line with an excursion to Clacton on 25 June 1961. *Michael J. Fox*

Left: Class E4 2-4-0 No E2794 leaves Shelford with a train from Haverhill to Cambridge in early BR days. *P. Ransome-Wallis*

Left: An up freight train passes Shelford signalbox on 30 May 1953. *R. E. Vincent*

Above: At Shepreth Branch Junction the line to Royston and Hitchin diverges from the main line to Liverpool Street. On 17 May 1969 Class 31 No D5634 passes with the 10.00am Whitemoor–Broxbourne coal train. *R. Elsdon*

Right: Class 47/0 No 47 130 passes Shepreth Branch Junction with the 10.36 express from Liverpool Street to King's Lynn on 3 May 1980. *John C. Baker*

Above: In July 1969 an accident at Sandy, on the East Coast main line, caused trains from King's Cross to the north to be diverted via Cambridge. On 24 July 'Deltic' D9012 *Crepello* comes off the Royston line with the 14.00 King's Cross–Edinburgh. *G. R. Mortimer*

Left: Trumpington on 14 September 1957, with Class E4 2-4-0 No 62788 running tender-first at the head of a train of cattle wagons. *E. R. Wethersett collection*

Left: By the time Class 86/2 No 86 256 *Pebble Mill* was photographed passing Shepreth Branch Junction on 16 March 1986 with the 13.05 express from Cambridge to Liverpool Street the wires had gone up and semaphore signals had come down. *John C. Baker*

Right: Ex-Great Northern Class J6 0-6-0 No 3602 heads an up goods near Trumpington on 27 June 1932. *E. R. Wethersett collection*

Right: Robinson Class O4 2-8-0 No 6313 passes Trumpington signalbox with an up goods on 27 June 1932. *E. R. Wethersett collection*

Below: Class F4 2-4-2T No 7586 heads a train from Haverhill near Trumpington on 31 July 1934. The stock comprises an interesting mixture of four-wheelers, horseboxes and bogie coaches. *E. R. Wethersett collection*

Left: An up Freightliner service from Cambridge leaves Trumpington behind Class 47/3 No 47 372 on 4 August 1978. *Les Bertram*

Below: Class 47 No 1703 nears Cambridge with a Liverpool Street–King's Lynn train on a sunny morning in September 1973. The coal yard in the background appears to be a hive of activity. *I. J. Hodson*

Above: On 28 March 1958 Class J39 0-6-0 No 64751 passes Milepost 44, just south of Hills Road Junction, with the through goods working to the Western Region. *J. Aylard*

There was no bay platform, and trains usually continued to or from Cambridge. Shepreth Branch Junction lay a very short distance to the north, where the line from Royston and Hitchin trailed in from the west, allowing access for Great Northern trains to Cambridge. The signalbox (53 miles 4 chains) lay a short distance north. A short level stretch of about 1½ miles followed, and the line then crossed Mill Road, in earlier days by a level crossing, but later replaced by a bridge. The London & North Western's line from Bletchley and Oxford curved round from the west to run alongside about a mile and a half to the north, but always crossed Mill Road by a bridge. It finally joined the Great Eastern at Cambridge South Junction (55 miles 39 chains), just short of the Hills Road bridge; this had previously been Hills Road Junction.

Cambridge station (55 miles 52 chains) was a large and complex affair, and retains to this day its original one-sided layout, although much extended since it was first opened. The railway was deterred from passing anywhere near the city centre by the colleges, who insisted that the station had to be sited at least a mile from Great St Mary's Church in Market Street. The single main-line platform is on the down side, together with the main station buildings. There were two bays at each end, whilst up through trains had to negotiate crossovers, either at the north end or in the centre of the station, to reach the platform. Apart from the Great Eastern main line a great many rail routes radiated from Cambridge. On the south side, trains could arrive via the Stour or Colne Valley lines from Marks Tey and Colchester, from King's Cross and Hitchin via Royston, or via the LNWR (later LMS) route from Oxford and Bletchley. At the other end of the station trains left for Newmarket and Bury St Edmunds, the rural Mildenhall branch, which could also be reached via Newmarket, and the St Ives line, which also led to Ely and Huntingdon.

Trains leaving Cambridge for Norwich or King's Lynn had a relatively straightforward exit,

although in the up direction they had to cross from the up to the down line to get into a platform. With the locomotive depot on the left, a down train then passed Cambridge North signalbox (55 miles 76 chains) followed by Coldham's Lane Junction 'box (56 miles 24 chains) which controlled access to the Newmarket and Ipswich route via a very tightly curved double track. This had replaced the earlier layout which had brought them more or less into the centre of the station on a gentler alignment, but which had to go when the Great Eastern goods yards were extended on the east side of Cambridge station in 1896. Under the old arrangements bay platforms 5 and 6 were much shorter than now, and trains from them for Newmarket crossed all other lines, as could trains from what is now Platform 4. The goods lines could similarly access the Newmarket line, all of which seriously complicated working at this end of the station. Coldham's Lane Junction already existed — some distance from Coldham's Lane — and was very near the point where Stone Street approached the railway. It was the point at which the goods avoiding lines and passenger lines joined at the north end of the station. With the junction changes Coldham's Lane level crossing was replaced by a bridge taking road over rail, with the junction now immediately to the north. The signalbox continued to control the junction for Newmarket even though the latter had migrated somewhat. The short coal sidings either side of the level crossing were replaced by a small yard to the south. As a means of reducing congestion special passenger trains, such as Newmarket race trains, not booked to call at Cambridge could use the goods independent lines, at a speed not exceeding 20mph, between Cambridge South 'box and Coldham's Lane Junction.

Barnwell Junction quickly followed, where trains diverged north-eastwards for the Mildenhall branch, the station being on the branch and unable to be served by trains on the main line. There were sidings on the west side of the line serving a brick and tile works, there being several in the area

Left: An excursion to Clacton via the Colne Valley line on 22 May 1961 departs Cambridge behind Class 2MT 2-6-0 No 46465. *G. D. King*

Below: At the south end of Cambridge station Class 37 No 37 086 waits to leave with the 12.44 to Liverpool Street on 23 December 1982. The new power signalbox looms in the background. *N. W. H. Brailsford*

Left: Photographed in September 1971, the daily Whitemoor–Hitchin freight has passed Cambridge on the goods roads and is preparing to rejoin the main line at the south end of the station. Class 25 No 5248 is in charge. *I. J. Hodson*

Right: An unusual visitor to Cambridge in July 1973 as Class 55 'Deltic' No 9015 *Tulyar* prepares to back onto the stock for the 1.30pm to King's Cross. *I. J. Hodson*

Right: Class E4 'Intermediate' 2-4-0 No 7504 waits to leave Cambridge for Six Mile Bottom on 12 September 1936. *E. R. Wethersett collection*

Below: An unusual visitor, Class A1 Pacific No 60138 *Boswell*, restarts the Sunday 4.35pm King's Cross–York on 8 May 1960. Diverted because of engineering work on the East Coast main line, it had called at Cambridge to provide a bus connection to Huntingdon. *G. D. King*

Left: EWS Class 67 No 67 014 passes Cambridge on the up main line with a returning football excursion from Cardiff, using Anglia Railways Mk 2d coaching stock. A Class 170 DMU waits at Platform 1. *Chris Burton*

Below: GER 2-4-2T No 781 leaves Cambridge with a train including LNWR stock. *Ian Allan Library*

Right: Class 47 No 1525 pulls out of Cambridge down goods sidings with a train of vans for Whitemoor in September 1970.
I. J. Hodson

Right: Class E4 2-4-0 No 7503 passes Coldham's Common on 3 August 1934 with a train for Mildenhall.
E. R. Wethersett collection

taking advantage of the local clay. Chesterton Junction (57 miles 55 chains) came next, where in later years there were extensive yards used by the civil engineers. Here the St Ives branch diverged in a north-westerly direction, which also gave an alternative route to March and Peterborough via the GN&GE Joint line. The main line was almost completely level all the way from Chesterton Junction to Brandon, with very short and slight inclines around Ely and a few other locations. It started to rise about a mile before Brandon station — at 1 in 900! — with a peak about a mile short of Roudham Junction, and then undulated gently as far as Eaton Crossing, being almost completely level again into Norwich.

Crossing the River Cam by a major bridge immediately before Chesterton Junction, the line continued on its relatively straight and level course to Waterbeach (61 miles 1 chain), where the station platforms were relatively short and to the north of the level crossing over the road to Horningsea. The platforms were rebuilt and extended prior to electrification in the 1990s, when the up moved to the south of the crossing. There were limited goods facilities at the station, although a crane of 1½-ton capacity was available — larger than those at many busier stations. Electrified services to Ely and King's Lynn started on 22 August 1992, the full service starting with the introduction of the 1992/3 winter timetable on 28 September, when the main London terminus became King's Cross rather than Liverpool Street.

The countryside was flat and open, though with a few copses and ponds, and notable for the horticultural produce growing in the rich peat fenland soils. As might be expected of a line striking across East Anglian fens, there were many level crossings: Milton Fen (59 miles 10 chains) to the south of Waterbeach, Bottisham Road

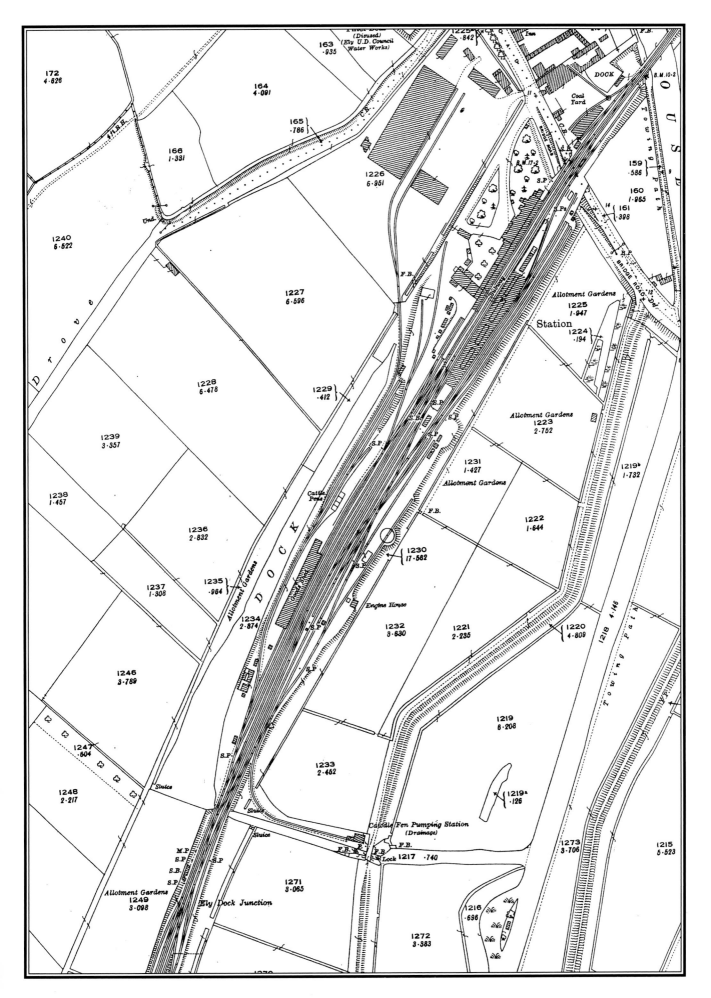

172
4·626

164
4·091

163
·935

Filter Bed
(Disused)
(Ely U.D. Council
Water Works)

1225ª
·842

Inn

DOCK

F.B.

165
·786

166
1·331

1226
6·951

Coal Yard

B.M.10·2

O
U
S
E

Towing Path

Und.

1240
6·522

F.B.

B.M.17·2

S.P.

S.P.

159
·586

160
1·965

161
·398

B.P.

Allotment Gardens
1225
1·947

Station

1224
·194

1227
6·596

Allotment Gardens
1223
2·752

1219ᵇ
1·732

1228
6·478

1229
·412

S.B.

S.P.

S.P.

S.P.

1231
1·427

1239
3·357

Allotment Gardens

F.B.

1222
1·644

1238
1·457

Cattle
Pens

1236
2·832

1230
17·582

S.P.

Allotment Gardens

D
O
C
K

1237
1·308

1235
·964

Goods Yard

Engine House

1234
2·874

S.P.

1232
3·630

1221
2·235

1220
4·809

1218 4·146

1246
3·789

S.P.

Towing Path

1247
·604

S.P.

1219
6·208

1248
2·217

Sluice

1233
2·452

1219ª
·126

Sluice

Carlisle Fen Pumping Station
(Drainage)

F.B.

1273
3·706

1215
5·523

M.P.
S.P.
S.B.
S.P.

S.P.

Sluice

F.B.
F.B.

Lock 1217 ·740

Allotment Gardens
1249
3·098

Ely Dock Junction

1271
3·065

1216
·696

1272
3·383

D
r
o
v
e

127

Right: The Whitemoor–Hitchin freight, hauled by Class 25 No 5237, passes Barnwell Junction on a sunny March day in 1971. The only sidings were on the down side of the main line, while the station's only passenger platforms were on the branch, the remains of which are seen in the foreground. *I. J. Hodson*

Above: The main line crossed the River Cam by an impressive girder bridge to the south of Chesterton Junction. Here 'K1' 2-6-0 No 62052, on a parcels train from Liverpool Street, is held while the 1.0pm Leicester–Cambridge, headed by a Class 2F Mogul, clears the junction in February 1951. *Ian Allan Library*

Right: 'Britannia' Pacific No 70011 *Hotspur* passes Chesterton Junction in May 1960 with the 8.20am Sundays-only Liverpool Street–Norwich. *G. D. King*

Left: In charge of a southbound express, Class 47 No 1524 encounters a Cambridge–Norwich local worked by a Gloucester RCW DMU as it passes Chesterton Junction in July 1971. *I. J. Hodson*

Below: Green-liveried Class 37 No 6782 approaches Chesterton Junction in May 1971 with a down mixed goods consisting largely of permanent-way wagons. *I. J. Hodson*

Above: Waterbeach signalbox and level crossing on 13 May 1982, with '47/0' No 47 014 passing at the head of the 08.35 Liverpool Street–King's Lynn. *B. J. Windle*

(61 miles 47 chains), Bannolds (62 miles 72 chains) and Dimmocks Cote (66 miles 25 chains) to the north, where the road from Stretham to Fordham and Soham went over the line. Bannolds also boasted a break-of-section signalbox with a crossover. Stretham Fen 'box (65 miles 53 chains) had refuges either side of the running lines. Before long Ely West River level crossing (68 miles 29 chains) and Sutton Branch Junction (69 miles 42 chains) heralded the approach to Ely itself, the line from Bury St Edmunds and Ipswich trailing in on the east side at Ely Dock Junction (69 miles 79 chains). This line was scheduled for doubling in the 1930s, and this had already been done between Chippenham Junction and Soham when war broke out. The Ouse bridge had been replaced by a double-track structure, although the second track was never laid. It was itself replaced in 2007 after the deck collapsed, depositing much of a freight train in the river below. Ely Dock Junction (69 miles 73 chains) controlled access to and from this line, and also to sidings on the east side of the passenger station. The 55ft turntable was also located here, and Ely South 'box (70 miles 22 chains) was just off the end of the island platform. There was another extensive yard on the west side of the line. Originating goods traffic was considerable, the largest tonnage being in sugar (over 10,000 tons in 1938), but the highest value

in oil cake. Vegetables were also a major traffic, together with scrap metal, seeds and livestock.

The original Ely station was another single-sided affair where the present down platform is located. The buildings were probably designed by Francis Wood, and appeared similar to what is there today, although the frontage was rebuilt by the LNER around 1929/30. By the time the first edition of the 25in Ordnance Survey map was published in 1885 a new platform and buildings had been constructed for up trains, with two faces as now, although apparently also with a footbridge connecting up and down sides. The goods shed on the down side was at a right-angle to the line and was shown as having rail access via a wagon turntable. This was removed when the down platform was extended towards the south, and the shed was incorporated into the other buildings. A new and much larger goods shed, served by a through rail siding, was built to the south. Ely Dock was a small facility on the river, from which the junction gained its name. The single rail siding dropped down via a tight 90° curve to a small staithe on a cut from the River Ouse, access for water-borne traffic being via a lock. The small turntable and locomotive facilities were also located nearby, on the up side of the line.

Ely station has thus had three platform faces for most of its existence, was laid out as a side

platform where the main buildings are located on the west, with an island on the east. These main buildings were of white brick, with ashlar work on the approach side. They had two two-storey blocks flanking the main entrance and booking hall, with the remainder being single-storey. On the platform side the brick was not faced, although extensions to the south, including the approach to the subway, were in red. To the north end of the building were various extensions housing such as porters' rooms, toilets and so on. Extensive awnings covered much of the platform, utilising standard cast-iron columns and spandrels. When the down platform road was taken out as part of the 1990s electrification scheme the platform itself was widened to reach the down main, leaving a wide gap between the edge and the awning. Ely station is a bleak place for waiting passengers at the best of times, and this certainly didn't help their creature comforts.

By the time of the survey for the 1925 OS map the island platform was connected to the other by a subway, unusual in this part of East Anglia, and which replaced the earlier footbridge. This was authorised in 1897. The low embankment on which the station is built also allowed an underpass for light traffic to avoid the level crossing at the north end, controlled by Ely North signalbox (70 miles 38 chains), and this

arrangement was also in place by the time of the first OS survey in 1885. The island had an assortment of buildings which appeared, after rebuilding around 1960, to be largely an afterthought. It was again remodelled in the 1990s, and did at least have the benefit of extensive awnings which also covered the subway approaches. Goods lines and sidings lay to the east of this platform. The main lines, No 3 platform road and the goods road all passed over the level crossing, there to cause some monumental hold-ups to road traffic. The line crossed the River Ouse a very short distance north of the station, with water meadows on the east side, and quays, moorings and Ely on the west. The cathedral towered over the town and was a major landmark visible for many miles across the fens, making it easy to visualise why it has always been known as the 'Isle of Ely', especially after heavy rain brings the river over its banks.

Continuing through a succession of carr and water, the line passed over Kiln Lane level crossing (71 miles 35 chains) and reached Ely North Junction at 71 miles 72 chains. The route straight ahead led to King's Lynn and Hunstanton, whilst divergence to the east took trains to Thetford and Norwich. There was a sugar factory on the east side of the line at Ely North, now better known as the Potters depot.

Above: On Sunday 8 August 1976 Class 31/1 No 31 198 and Class 37 No 37 102 pass Ely South with ballast train. In the sidings can be seen withdrawn EMU stock awaiting transfer to Meyer-Newman's scrapyard at Snailwell. *David Pearce*

Right: Seen from the station's island platform Nos 31 198 and 37 102 pass through Ely on the down main with their ballast train on Sunday 8 August 1976. *David Pearce*

Below: Ely South, and '47/4' No 47 577 *Benjamin Gimbert GC* waits with the 15.36 Norwich–Liverpool Street on 5 September 1983. *J. C. Hillmer*

Left: An interesting view of the down platform, an up train and a glimpse of Ely South 'box in November 1981, as Class 47/0 No 47 004 restarts a King's Lynn–Liverpool Street service. When the down platform road was taken out the platform was extended to reach the through road, next to the train. Sadly the awning wasn't extended. *Chris Burton*

Below: Ely North signalbox controlled the busy level crossing and junctions at the north end of the station. Class 47/4 No 47 544 passes with a football excursion from Norwich to Northumberland Park on 28 January 1984. *John C. Baker*

Ely to Peterborough East

Ely North Junction was also the point at which many trains from Cambridge to March, Whitemoor, Peterborough and beyond curved around to the north west, striking off across the Fens. Others used the GN&GE Joint line to St Ives. One of the unusual features of the junction was the South Curve or avoiding line, also known as the West curve, constructed in 1890, and which had been initially intended to allow goods trains between Norwich and Peterborough to run through without reversal at Ely. It soon became useful for passenger traffic, and especially excursions. The line was more or less level for most of its length, rising to cross rivers and drainage channels, notably the New Bedford River or Hundred Foot Drain and the Counter Drain and River Delph, or Old Bedford River, between Black Bank and Manea. There were many level crossings.

The junction for the avoiding line was facing for southbound trains and then curved through 180° before rejoining the March route at Ely West Junction. The total length of the curve was 78 chains — a shade under a mile — whereas the distance between the two junctions via the main line was a mere 54 chains. The speed limit on the curve was always low: 15mph in 1947, raised to 25mph in the 1980s. It was double-track until singled in the 1990s in connection with the electrification between Cambridge and King's Lynn. Chettisham station was immediately to the west of the level crossing (73 miles 55 chains) and

had a number of sidings on the down side. Black Bank (75 miles 23 chains), served the village of Downham (not to be confused with the one on the Lynn line) and also had a level crossing at the station. The station did a good business in vegetables and potatoes.

Rising to cross the Old Bedford River by an impressive girder bridge the line was carried on an embankment between this and the bridge over the River Delph, the area between the two being allowed to flood in the winter months to provide somewhere for the surplus water. It then fell towards Manea (80 miles 13 chains), most of the village being a mile or more to the south of the station and its level crossing. The station did a good trade in vegetables and potatoes from the fertile fenland farms, and in 1938 this amounted to over 15,000 tons, worth over £5,500 to the LNER. Stonea (82 miles) was likewise busy with this traffic; it also shipped livestock and at one time had been a possible destination for the Wisbech & Upwell Tramway. At March South Junction (85 miles 35 chains) the line finally curved northwards, having been straight all the way from Chettisham, and the St Ives line trailed in on the west side. The speed limit was severe to and from St Ives (only 15mph in 1947), and the main line then swung towards the west to pass through the extensive sidings, past the goods sheds, March East Junction (85 miles 65 chains) before entering the station. Trains for Whitemoor and the joint line diverged to the right, and had

Below: Class 37 No 37 308 approaches Ely North Junction with a train of coal empties from Hythe and Claydon to Toton on 14 May 1988. The relative heights of the signal arms shows the importance of the different routes at the junction: the board is off for the March line, with Lynn in the centre and Norwich on the left of the picture.
Michael J. Collins

Left: Monday 8 August 1983 finds Class 40 No 40 080 venturing onto the avoiding line at Ely West Junction with a summer-dated Manchester–Yarmouth holiday service. *Chris Burton*

Left: On 20 December 1986 a two-car Class 114 DMU forming the 08.49 Lincoln Central–Cambridge crosses the bridge over Twenty Foot Drain, between March and Ely. At the time this section of line was subject to severe speed restrictions because of heavy engineering work. *Michael J. Collins*

Below: Class 31/1 No 31 325 near Manea, between Ely and March, on 9 June 1975 with a train of coal empties from Ipswich to March. *Stanley Creer*

Right: Class 40 No 40 001 ambles through Stonea, between Ely and March, with an additional freight between Whitemoor and Norwich on 4 January 1983. *John Rudd*

Below: Class K3 2-6-0 No 61976 bypasses March station with an up freight from Whitemoor in September 1960. *John C. Baker*

Right: On 6 August 1960 ex-LMS Class 5MT 'Black Five' 4-6-0 No 45111 leaves March with a Saturdays-only Birmingham–Clacton service, which it is believed to have worked as far as Colchester. The train was routed via Bury St Edmunds. *G. D. King*

136

Left: Class 31 No No D5581 leaves March with the 10.00 York–Yarmouth on 24 February 1970.
David Wharton

Left: Class 37 No 37 087 passes the Joint Line platforms at March with a Whitemoor–Eastleigh working on 14 April 1984.
Chris Burton

Above: On 19 June 1984 Class 08 No 08 526 passes through the Joint-line platforms at March on a trip working from March down yard, where the Grainflow wagons had been loaded by lorry. *John Rudd*

Right: Class 31/1 No 31 164 arrives at March on 10 December 1977 with the 10.15 from Birmingham to Norwich. Note that the canopies have been cut back and that the decorative boarding has been replaced by very plain work. Early preparation for electrification? *Alan Brooke Baylis*

Right: An unusual visitor to March on 1 September 1984 was this three-car Swindon 'Cross-Country' DMU on a Norwich–Birmingham working. *Chris Burton*

their own platforms on the north side of the station, whilst Peterborough services used the pair to the south. There were also dock platforms at the west end, which could be reached from the Joint line. There was a further junction (March North) at the west end of the passenger station, where a further double-line connection was made to the Joint line and Whitemoor Junction. There was also a west-facing bay alongside the main down platform.

The station (85 miles 76 chains) had been completely rebuilt in 1885 following the opening throughout of the GN&GE Joint line. This had a long gestation, the March–Spalding section having been opened by the Great Northern in 1867. The route was completed by the opening of the Spalding–Lincoln line in August 1882, and at that time the Great Northern & Great Eastern Joint Committee was formed. This took over a number of GNR and GER lines, and gave the Great Eastern its long-sought direct access to the Yorkshire coalfields. They diverted their traffic to the new line, and this put a great strain on March station. The GER started its Liverpool Street–Doncaster service, and soon added a Harwich train, further straining the junction. It therefore resolved to rebuild completely, including new locomotive sheds, the station itself moving towards Ely.

The main line to Peterborough continued past March West Junction (86 miles 17 chains), where the curve to Whitemoor Junction diverged to the north. Having cleared Norwood Road level crossing (86 miles 30 chains) the line was again straight as far as Whittlesea (94 miles 55 chains). In the meantime the Benwick branch diverged at Three Horse Shoes (91 miles). This had opened as far as Burnt House in September 1897, and was intended to tap the agricultural traffic of the Fens, which it did with some success. Eastrea briefly boasted its own station at the eponymous level

crossing (93 miles 28 chains), although it seems to have closed by 1866. Whittlesey, a much more substantial settlement, had a station whose name has always differed in spelling, about half a mile to the south. This is brick-making country, and the station boasted extensive sidings to serve the industry, especially the London Brick Co, which had a works near the station. Whittlesea also had oversight of sidings at Three Horse Shoes and King's Dyke. The station handled large tonnages of vegetables and potatoes — over 20,000 tons in 1938 — as well as livestock, but this was dwarfed by the brick traffic, which in that year amounted to 265,018 tons, worth £106,296 to the LNER. The line curved slightly northwards after Whittlesea, and on the final stretch towards Peterborough the brick pits and the characteristic smell of firing bricks pervaded the air. There were more brick works at Kings Dyke (96 miles 73 chains) and beyond.

The line approached closer to the River Nene, crossing Moreton's Leam as it did so, and reached Peterborough East. There were extensive sidings on the down (south) side at Stanground, reached from both ends via Standground (Great Eastern spelling) and South Bank signalboxes, and again between Standground and Middle Bank 'boxes. Peterborough East itself had a very large yard on the down side, with goods sheds, locomotive depot and more facilities on the north side. It was served by the Great Eastern itself, the London & North Western's lines from Northampton and Market Harborough, and the Midland via Stamford. One curiosity was that the East and North stations were in different counties, the former being in Huntingdonshire, the latter in Northamptonshire. As might be expected, goods facilities were very extensive, and both the GER and LNWR maintained full services, the GNR having its own parcels office. All had their own passenger facilities.

Below: Passing March East Junction, Class 45/0 No 45 040 takes the Whitemoor line with a freight from Norwich on 15 July 1984. *John Rudd*

Right: Ivatt Class 2MT 2-6-0 No 46465 comes off the Wisbech line at Whitemoor Junction with a General Manager's special in September 1960.
John C. Baker

Below: Class 37 No 6753 heads an up rail train for the Cambridge line out of Whitemoor Yard in October 1971, at which time the yard was still intact. *I. J. Hodson*

Left: Class 31 No 5578 heads a Harwich–Peterborough service away from March on 9 February 1972 as another of the class waits to come off the line from Whitemoor. *J. H. Cooper-Smith*

Left: The imposing frontage of Peterborough East station seen in 1950, with a fine selection of cars on the forecourt. *Ian Allan Library*

Below: Class J6 0-6-0 No 64251 leaves Peterborough East for Peterborough North with a breakdown train in September 1960. *John C. Baker*

Ely to King's Lynn

The line to Norwich continued straight ahead at Ely North Junction, following a generally north-easterly direction. The route to March curved through 90° to strike off straight across the fens, whilst the King's Lynn line went between the two, heading just east of north. There are no significant gradients at all on the route, and for most of the way it follows the Great Ouse, occasionally rising to pass over it. Much of the line is also straight, although level crossings are relatively numerous, and speed limits have never been particularly high, in 1947 being generally the 70mph ruling limit between Liverpool Street and King's Lynn, and 60mph through Littleport. On the route between Liverpool Street and Norwich via Ipswich at the same time the ruling speed limit was 80mph.

Once over Queen Adelaide level crossing (72 miles 17 chains) the Great Ouse came close alongside on the east side, although the river wall prevented sight of it from the train. Sandhills level crossing (75 miles 35 chains) heralded the approach to Littleport station, although the town is nearer this crossing than that at the station. The platforms were opposite and to the north of the level crossing, where there was also an underpass provided for light vehicles, immediately to the north. The road, between Ely and Lynn, later became the A10, but is now superseded by the bypass to the north. There were extensive goods yards at the station, to the south of the level crossing, and necessitating their own signalbox in

addition to the station 'box. The station could handle all classes of goods traffic, but had a relatively small crane. Tonnages were very large, especially of potatoes, and in 1938 11,234 tons were shipped, with a value to the LNER of over £10,000. There were also large tonnages of other vegetables, seeds and livestock. Most passenger trains between Ely and King's Lynn called, although the service was sparse, and a few were routed via Wisbech.

Continuing north the line crossed a succession of minor level crossings including Black Horse Drove and Southery, both of which once had signalboxes, before reaching Hilgay level crossing and station (Hilgay Fen until October 1896) at 81 miles 39 chains. Black Horse Drove had a public siding which could handle general goods traffic, and Sir Frederick Hiam — a farmer living at Ten Mile Bank — also had a siding between Hilgay and Littleport. All of these came under Hilgay for administrative purposes. The nearest significant habitation was Ten Mile Bank, nearly a mile north-east of Hilgay station, by Hilgay Bridge over the Ouse. Hilgay village was a further 2 miles away, and Southery was as near to the station as the crow flies, if not as the cart travels. In fact, the nearest station by far to the village was Ryston, on the Stoke Ferry branch. The Railway Tavern was right by the station. The goods facilities at Hilgay itself were not extensive, and it could handle general goods, parcels, general livestock and horse and prize cattle vans. It also handled large tonnages of

Below: The 10.24 from Ely to King's Lynn via March, formed by a two-car Cravens DMU, swings round at Ely North Junction on 1 October 1964. *G. R. Mortimer*

Left: The view south from the level crossing towards the station at Ely North on 1 May 1977, as Class 37 No 37 264 runs in with the 18.22 King's Lynn–Liverpool Street. Down trains now have to use the platform loop. *David Pearce*

Left: A pair of Cravens Class 105 DMUs forming the 17.40 Saturdays-excepted fast service from King's Lynn to Cambridge leave Littleport on 25 August 1985. *John C. Baker*

Left: The 'Eastern Counties Limited' railtour visited, among others, the Stoke Ferry branch. Here it is seen diverging from the main line at Denver, with Class J69 0-6-0T No 68566 in charge. *C. J. Sarah*

143

Above: Class 47/0
No 47 180 *County of Suffolk*
rushes past Denver Junction
with the 10.36 Liverpool
Street–King's Lynn on
29 March 1980. The remains
of the station can just be
made out beyond the signals
and signalbox, while the
branch to Wissington
diverges in the foreground.
David Pearce

Right: The view southwards
at Downham Market on
1 May 1982, with the level
crossing, signalbox and
up starter prominent. The
buildings in the background
started life as the Eagle flour
mills. *David Pearce*

potatoes and other vegetables — respectively 6,025 and 9,297 in 1938. The former were worth much more to the railway. Passenger services were always sparse, with four or five trains a day each way: only the Ely–Lynn stoppers called.

Onward from Hilgay the line crossed the River Ouse just over a mile to the north, followed almost immediately by the Wissey. Denver Junction followed, at 84 miles 32 chains, where the Stoke Ferry branch trailed in from the east. This line had opened in August 1882, but lost its passenger service as early as September 1930, probably because the local population was so sparse. Goods services continued until 1965, although the private Wissington Light Railway, serving the local farms and ultimately the beet sugar factory just south of Abbey station, ensured that part of it survived for much longer. Denver station (84 miles 38 chains) had a history tied to that of the branch, and closed

for passengers with it in 1930, although not for goods until July 1964. It had been Denver Road Gate until 1847, and closed for main-line trains in 1870, reopening for branch trains only in 1885. Denver village was about a mile from the station, but Downham Market, with a much better train service, was almost as near.

The main line now converged closely with both the Great Ouse and its Relief Channel, both to the west. Downham station (86 miles 4 chains) — 'Market' was added in 1981 — was immediately to the north of the level crossing over the main road from Downham to Outwell, and had two side platforms, with the main station building on the up side. This was a single-storey structure with steeply pitched roofs, with two Dutch-gabled structures at right angles to the line, linked by another section with a road-side entrance set back somewhat. The walls were mainly made of brown carstone, giving

Left: The view northwards from the level crossing at Downham station in GER days (probably Edwardian). There is an interesting contrast between the awnings on each platform. *Lens of Sutton Association*

it a distinctive appearance, with quoins and architraves of buff brick. The building was extensively restored in 1990 when the corrugated asbestos on the roof was replaced with tiles, and the awnings and their supports restored to their former appearance. The other prominent structure on the up platform was the large brick water tower, topped by the tank itself, with a crane for filling locomotives between it and the level crossing.

On the down side a much smaller Great Eastern waiting room, mostly brick with some wooden panels, was provided. There were maltings near the station, and large flour mills in the town. Many concerns had sidings at the station, and in 1929 these included J. L. Bennet & Sons (corn, cake, seed and coal merchant), F. & A. Bird (miller and corn merchant), Boyce & Sons, B. F. Haylett, Scarnell, Wood & Co (also a firm of corn, cake, seed and coal merchants), Wilsons Healey (corn and coal merchant) and the Downham Market Gas & Coke Co. The traffic was worth a good deal to the railway, and in 1938 included nearly 28,000 tons of vegetables, 11,000 tons of sugar products, 7,000 tons of grain and flour, 7,500 tons of potatoes and 5,000 tons of oilcake, worth a grand total of £27,258 to the LNER. The passenger service was never very frequent, but Downham did get calls from almost all trains, in July 1922 including the 8.30am restaurant car service from Liverpool Street to Hunstanton, its only intermediate call between Ely and King's Lynn.

Continuing northward, the line remained close to the Great Ouse Relief Channel. Stow Bardolph station (88 miles 33 chains) was immediately to the north of the level crossing over the road between Stow Bardolph village to the east, and Stowbridge to the west. It had been plain Stow until July 1923, when it was renamed to avoid confusion with Stow, near Galashiels on the Waverley route of the North British Railway. It had side platforms opposite each other, and only limited goods facilities with no crane. Its main goods traffic was vegetables and potatoes.

The next station to the north was Magdalen Road, or Watlington (91 miles 13 chains), depending on the era. It opened as Watlington, from the village about a quarter mile to the east. It was renamed as Magdalen Road — after Wiggenhall St Mary Magdalen, about half a mile to the west — in 1875, closing to passengers in 1968. It reopened, unstaffed, in 1975, and reverted to 'Watlington' in 1989. To confuse the issue, the level crossing had remained as 'Watlington', while the junction was 'Magdalen Road'. It had the usual side platforms, opposite each other, to the south of the level crossing. This was also the junction (90 miles 74 chains) for the single line from March and Wisbech, which trailed in on the west side, and which provided another route between Cambridge and King's Lynn. Goods traffic outwards was mostly vegetables and potatoes. Goods facilities were generally on the down side and included private sidings, used in 1929 by (among others) English Oilfields and Read & Wildbur, the Lynn Manufacturing Co Ltd, Somerfield & Thomas and Technical Oils Ltd. English Oilfields and Technical Oils, shale-oil manufacturers, were based at Setchey, a hamlet some two miles to the north east, where there were what were described as 'extensive oil works'.

English Oilfields also had a siding at St Germans (92 miles 68 chains), between Magdalen Road and King's Lynn Junction, which had had a passenger station when the line first opened. There was a siding on each side of the line here, each reached by a trailing connection, plus a crossover between up and down lines. Public goods facilities were available, the whole being to the north of the level crossing over the minor road between Wiggenhall St Germans and Setchey. The signalbox was on the down side.

Towards King's Lynn the main line remained straight and level, apart from rising to cross the River Nar, north of which Clarke's Drove siding, linking with English Oilfields at Setchey, trailed in on the east side, having run for a short way alongside the main line. The junction was about

Right: On 19 October 1991 the level crossing and signalbox at Stow Bardolph see an unusual visitor in the form of LNER 'A3' Pacific No 4472 *Flying Scotsman*, heading a 'Fenman' special. This was part of a Network SouthEast steam weekend which saw a number of workings by *Flying Scotsman*, SR 'West Country' Pacific No 34027 *Taw Valley* and No 70000 *Britannia*. *David Pearce*

Above: Class 31/1 No 31 325 near Magdalen Road on 11 June 1975 with a trainload of sand from Middleton Towers. *Stanley Creer*

Right: 'Claud' No 62580, formerly No 8829, pulls out of King's Lynn with the up 'Fenman' on 21 May 1957. *K. L. Cook*

Left: Magdalen Road station reopened to passengers on 5 May 1975. Here Class 31/1 No 31 160 is taking empty stock from a reopening special on to Downham to run round. *G. R. Mortimer*

Left: King's Lynn on a sunny 29 October 1956, as Class B17 4-6-0 No 61635 *Milton* departs on an up working. *L. G. Marshall*

three quarters of a mile north of St German's siding. This was a product of exploration by English Oilfields Ltd in the period immediately after World War 1, which sought to exploit oil shale in the area. The branch served two works, one of which had its own internal tramway, and a number of sidings near what is now the A10 just north of Setchey, and was around two miles in total length, with a passing loop halfway along.

King's Lynn Harbour Junction (95 miles 25 chains) was the connection to the Midland & Great Northern Joint line. The double-track connection trailed into the Great Eastern line, making the connection from South Lynn and the M&GN's harbour lines, while the junction for the GE harbour branch was facing and also on the down side. The M&GN main line passed over the GE a short distance to the south. Extons Road level crossing, at 96 miles 27 chains, had its own signalbox, although this had been downgraded to a ground frame by 1947. This was also the site of extensive sidings on the up side of the line, which employed a system of gongs so that the man in charge of shunting operations did not have to go onto the main line to signal to the enginemen.

Extons Road was quickly followed by King's Lynn Junction (96 miles 54 chains), where both the lines to Swaffham and Hunstanton trailed in on the up side in quick succession; the 'box was on the down side of the tracks. Having curved gently towards the west since Extons Road, passenger trains continued to do so to reach the station, with King's Lynn Passenger Yard signalbox on the down side of the line a short distance from the end of the platforms. Goods trains continued into the depot, which was on the north side of the passenger station, or on to the docks branches of the King's Lynn Dock & Railway Co. There was both a goods shed, constructed with two terminal rail platforms, and a warehouse with three roads, and goods offices to the west of this, fronting onto Blackfriars Road. The docks branch went round the north of the town, and was worked by the main-line railway. King's Lynn was a busy port for smaller shipping,

and also had connections with many of the waterways of the Fens. The docks branch was considered to be a goods station for much of its length, and had a maximum permitted speed of 5mph. Enginemen had to be prepared to stop promptly if necessary, and any propelling movements required a shunter to precede them. Any level crossings en route, such as Pilot Street, had to be protected by the shunter.

King's Lynn station (96 miles 75 chains) was a terminus, although with relatively modest buildings for such an important location. A single-storey white-brick structure orientated across the ends of the terminal platforms provided the frontage onto Blackfriars Road. There were two main platforms, on the north and south sides of the station, with two centre roads, and both having bays on their outer faces. This was a replacement for the original East Anglian Railway station, the site of which became the goods yard to the north, and was built in about 1871 as a joint concern by the Great Eastern, Great Northern and Midland railways, reflecting its function as terminus for the GER and M&GN lines. When built the main entrance had a fine portico supported by cast iron columns and brackets. Alterations were undertaken by the LNER in 1937, additional space being made available on the concourse and in the booking hall, and a new booking office provided. A new refreshment room was built. The electric lighting on the station was upgraded, and the signs replaced with illuminated box indicators. A new train indicator was provided. All of this was facilitated by the recent agreement between the LNER and the LMS whereby the former took over all the responsibilities for the former Midland & Great Northern Joint system, so that King's Lynn effectively ceased to be jointly managed.

King's Lynn locomotive depot was squeezed in between the approach lines to the passenger station and the goods depot. By 1950 there was a four-road locomotive shed, accessible from either end. The turntable had always been small, and in 1927 was recommended for replacement by a 50ft example from Berwick, which seems to have been

Below: Ivatt Mogul No 43089 waits at King's Lynn on 24 August 1960, at the head of the 4.15pm to March via Wisbech. The train started at Hunstanton and had arrived with No 62613, the last surviving 'Claud Hamilton', at its head.
Leslie Sandler

extended by at least 2ft by 1932. However, Lynn remained the preserve of smaller locomotives such as the 'B12s' or 'B17s', and closed around 1959.

Any service with King's Lynn as an intermediate station, such as the 'Fenman' from Liverpool Street to Hunstanton, had to reverse there, although this was often used as the opportunity to strengthen trains. For example, on Hunstanton services the restaurant car portion usually worked only as far as Lynn, and not right through. The Passenger Yard signalbox closed at night, which necessitated some complex arrangements for trains still needing to use the station. The down mail train had to be accompanied from the Junction 'box to Platform 3 by the Yard Inspector, who then had to go to the 'box to return the signals to their normal positions. After station work was completed the train then had to be accompanied back up the down main as far as the Junction 'box, where the locomotive ran round and set the train back into Platform 3, after which it went to the locomotive depot. The enginemen were authorised by the Yard Inspector to pass the necessary signals at danger. It was permissible to work trains of up to 50 wagons between the Town yard and the Docks branch without a brake van, in either direction. It was also possible to propel up to 45 wagons, in clear weather only, and this rule also applied on the Harbour branch.

There were very many private sidings and depots at King's Lynn, almost all on either the Docks or Harbour branches. Others were reached via the M&GN station at South Lynn. Some were associated with shipping companies, such as the East Coast Steamship Co at the harbour, or the Lynn & Hamburg Steamship Co at the Docks. There were many coal merchants, including the King's Lynn Cooperative Society and Vynne & Everett, oil companies including Anglo-American and Shell-Mex, and agricultural concerns such as Fisons and the West Norfolk Farmers' Manure & Chemical Co-operative Co. Morgans Brewery was there, and King's Lynn Corporation had sidings on both branches. The range of traffic handled was immense, grain and flour being top of the list, followed closely by 'inflammable liquids' (oil, petrol and so on), timber, manure, livestock, vegetables, confectionery, and to the LNER in 1938 collectively worth over £45,000 — a huge sum.

Left: A general view of King's Lynn station during the British Rail era. *Ian Allan Library*

Left: King's Lynn station on 23 May 1984. Class 31/4 No 31 423 has arrived with the 10.35 from Liverpool Street and is about to run round to head the 13.05 return working. *David Pearce*

Right: The King's Lynn docks branch generated a great deal of traffic for the railway. Here a Class 08 pulls a long train of steel coil into King's Lynn station yard on 6 August 1985.
John C. Barrett

Right: Alexandra Dock at King's Lynn produced much traffic for rail. Here the MV *Candourity* discharges bulk urea into rail wagons on 19 February 1986.
John C. Barrett

Right: Pure LNER at Wolferton, on the Hunstanton branch, although the date is May 1949. Class D15 'Claud' No 2507 of King's Lynn shed slows to give up the tablet, having just come off the single-track section.
Ian Allan Library

The Hunstanton branch came about through the efforts of the Lynn & Hunstanton Railway Co, which had been incorporated in 1861, and opened its line on 3 October 1862. It was intended to develop and promote the new resort at the terminus, as well as the surrounding area, and also served Wolferton, the station for Sandringham. Freight revenue was good, and development took place rapidly.

The line left King's Lynn heading in a south westerly direction before diverging at King's Lynn Junction and curving sharply towards the north. It had a favourable alignment that allowed a ruling speed of 70mph in 1947, although other restrictions applied for much of the route. It was double-tracked as far as Wolferton, and easily graded. It kept to the coastal plain of the Wash, the only significant earthworks being at Sandringham Warren, just north of Wolferton station.

The first station from King's Lynn was North Wootton, with two side platforms and rather limited goods facilities. Wolferton, as befitted a station numbering royalty among its passengers, was always well maintained and with Royal waiting rooms. The up platform was open to the roadway, allowing carriages and cars to be brought close to the trains. The signalbox, on the down side by the level crossing, was unusual in being incorporated into adjacent houses.

The line onwards was single, controlled by electric train tablet. Dersingham and Snettisham were both passing places with two platforms. Both had full goods facilities; the latter had a one-ton crane and by 1929 had acquired a private siding for Vynne & Everett Ltd, coal merchants with headquarters at Swaffham. Heacham boasted a substantial station north of the level crossing over one of the access roads to the beach, and had two platforms on the Hunstanton line plus a bay at the north end for Wells trains; W. H. Smith had a bookstall there. The passing loop was extended to accommodate two 13-coach trains in 1937. The main buildings, goods yard and shed and turntable were on the up or east side, and the West Norfolk Junction line had direct access to these facilities. There was a private siding for A. Lewis, and Anglo-American Oil had a depot. From the station the Wells line curved away sharply towards the east with a speed limit of 20mph, the junction being immediately to the north of the station, with the signalbox on the west side of the main line.

The terminus at Hunstanton was well placed for the beaches and town: New Hunstanton had grown up around the railway. One of the features of the journey from Heacham was the long row of beach bungalows, almost entirely consisting of old railway carriages, which were within sight of the line almost all the way. Hunstanton station had two double-sided platforms, with the buildings and offices across the ends and on the east side. Facilities were extended in 1937, so that Platform 3 was increased from 520 to 770ft long, and Platform 4 from 515 to 740ft. The circulating area was enlarged, new awnings being provided over the concourse and east side, and new offices for the stationmaster, ticket collectors and porters. Additional sidings for another 43 carriages were provided. Complete goods facilities were available, including a 1-ton crane, and the goods shed on the east side of the passenger station. A footbridge across the throat of the station provided an excellent vantage point. There was a small locomotive depot on the west or seaward side of the line, which was substantially rearranged in 1937 to cater for the increasing excursion traffic; the resort had long been a popular destination from the Midlands and North.

Services on the line were relatively infrequent in earlier years, with around seven or eight trains each way daily, mostly calling at all stations between Lynn and Hunstanton. One or two reversed at Hunstanton and went through to Wells, and there was usually at least one through train from Liverpool Street, such as the 5.12pm restaurant car service shown in the April 1910 timetable. By July 1922 this had increased to 13 each way, with extras on certain days of the week, and with through restaurant car services to Hunstanton from both St Pancras and Liverpool Street, and Pullman cars from the latter. By the summer of 1938 the number of trains had risen further, especially on Saturdays, many calling only at Heacham between King's Lynn and Hunstanton. There were through services from Nottingham and Leicester, and King's Cross had replaced St Pancras as a London terminal. The Liverpool Street trains remained, of course.

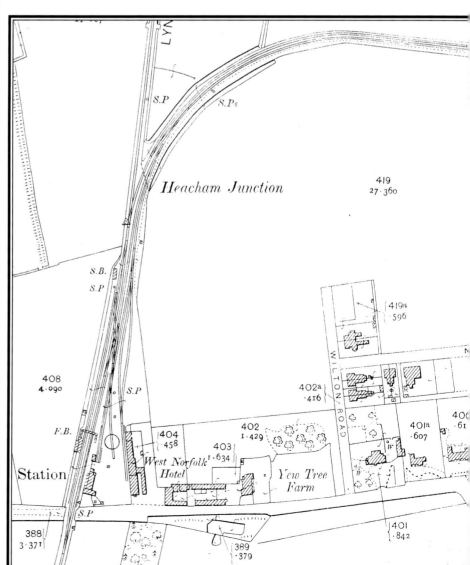

North of Ely the Norwich line diverged from the Lynn route about 7 chains north of the signalbox, and passed first over Queen Adelaide level crossing (72 miles 32 chains), where there had once been a signalbox. The crossing was one of triplets, as there were two others of the same name over the Lynn and March lines, which derived from a local public house on the road from Prickwillow and Shippea Hill to Ely. However, it managed to cross the avoiding line by a bridge and so the level crossing never became quadruplets. Further crossings at Padnal (73 miles 17 chains) and Mile End (74 miles 76 chains) followed in quick succession, the line rising to cross the River Lark between the two. There was a public siding at Padnal, and another at Duck Drove, between Padnal and Shippea Hill. Goods trains calling there had to collect the key for the ground frame from Padnal signalbox, and the guard was responsible for lowering the signals and locking

the frame on completion of the work. The key then had to be returned to Shippea Hill 'box, being sent back to Padnal by the first available train. Both sidings were accounted at Shippea Hill.

Onward from Mile End the line continued almost dead straight through Shippea Hill (77 miles 25 chains). This had been opened in 1845 as Mildenhall Drove, becoming Mildenhall Road later the same year, Burnt Fen in 1885, and finally Shippea Hill in 1905. Just a few feet higher than the surrounding fens, Shippea Hill had a level crossing immediately to the east of the platforms, and also a public house and a school, drawing its pupils from the many farms scattered around. The station was sited where the line crossed the road from Littleport to Mildenhall, and while there were several farms in the area — including Shippea Hill itself — there was little else. Not surprisingly, traffic was almost entirely agricultural and reflected the fenland through

Below: Having travelled via the Ely avoiding line, Class 31/4 No 31 423 passes Queen Adelaide level crossing with the 08.04 Birmingham–Norwich on 19 March 1983. *John C. Baker*

Right: Class 47/3 No 47 357 calls at Shippea Hill with the 14.44 Saturdays-only Yarmouth–Derby service on 29 May 1982. The call by this otherwise non-stop train, along with the Police presence and that of the ticket-collector, was occasioned by an open day at RAF Mildenhall. *John C. Baker*

which the line passed — over 20,000 tons of potatoes was shipped in 1938. The signalbox was on the down side, with the station buildings on the up. Chivers & Sons had a siding at the station in the 1920s, all the goods facilities being on the up side. The sidings on the Norwich side of the level crossing were installed later than the others, and whilst they do not appear on the 1885 Ordnance Survey sheets, they are clearly shown on the 1927 edition. By then a tramway had been built, connected to these sidings, initially running parallel to the main line but then diverging to the south to serve first the Shippea Hill Chicory & Herb Drying factory, and then going on to a number of other farms.

Crossing into Suffolk, trains passed through more wooded carr before reaching Lakenheath (82 miles 44 chains). Unlike Shippea Hill the station here did serve a sizeable community (1,713 in 1923), although it was over 2½ miles distant.

There was also the village of Hockwold, just over a mile away across the border into Norfolk. The station itself had a simple building of white brick, with the signalbox on the Norwich side of the crossing, on the down side. The goods facilities, including a shed with a through siding, were again on the up side, and the station could handle most traffic except furniture, and could not load motor cars or carriages. Lakenheath station was officially the base for Home Grown Chicory Ltd, chicory growers and dryers, which traded under the name 'Chicory, Phone, Lakenheath'.

About 2½ miles beyond the station the line, still level but now keeping close company with the Little Ouse River, finally rose over it and crossed into Norfolk. The approach to Brandon station (86 miles 32 chains) continued across the flat open countryside, with the signalbox and level crossing 6 chains short of the station itself. The Great Eastern Hotel, a fine flint building, was located on

Left: Brandon signalbox overlooks a pair of Class 25s — Nos 25 129 and 25 124 — double-heading the 08.32 Saturdays-only Derby–Yarmouth service on 29 July 1978. *John C. Baker*

Left: Brandon station was the first in Suffolk to be served by trains from London. It features some very fine buildings, constructed mostly of knapped flint, while the platforms are staggered and are linked by footbridge. Class 40 No 40 084 passes with the 09.19 Saturdays-only from Manchester Piccadilly to Yarmouth on 26 August 1978. Today the Friends of Brandon Station are making great efforts to return it to its former glory. *John C. Baker*

153

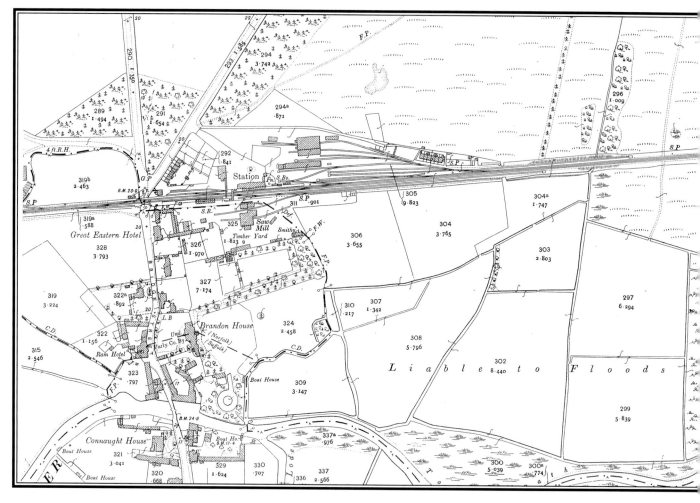

the south side of the crossing. At this point, despite the county boundary looping northward away from the Little Ouse to accommodate parts of Brandon, the line had not crossed back into Suffolk, so the station was actually in Weeting in Norfolk. The main station buildings were on the down side and of knapped flint, and were similar to those of other significant stations along the line, such as Attleborough and Wymondham. The platforms were staggered, the up being nearer the level crossing, and were linked by a footbridge. There were also offices and waiting rooms on the up side in similar style. There were sidings on both sides of the line, with goods sheds and a sizeable yard on the down side, but at least in the 1930s the station was not particularly busy for originating goods traffic, with the main item being potatoes. The town was also noted for its hare and rabbit skins, used for felt- and hat-making, and also size and glue. The red brick goods shed served a sawmill on the up side, and water was available for locomotives. A further set of sidings served another saw mill on the west side of the level crossing, as shown in the 1905 OS map. Forestry traffic developed greatly in the post-World War 2 period following the planting of Thetford Forest, which had been intended to reduce Britain's reliance on imported timber.

Beyond Brandon the line started to gently gain height and continued to follow the Little Ouse. At one time it had been intended to take a relatively direct route eastwards between about Two Mile Bottom (91 miles 16 chains) and Roudham Junction, Thetford being served by a branch. Sense prevailed before work had started, although the rather abrupt loop southwards — continuing to follow the river whilst rising out of the valley — was the result. The station (93 miles 50 chains) was to the north of the town, with two platforms opposite each other connected by a footbridge. The signalbox was on the down side at the Ely end of the station. The main station building, including the booking office, was on the down side, and was constructed of red brick in 1889, as proclaimed on the outside, over the main entrance. Older structures, which remained in use, were of the knapped flint construction of other stations along the line. Both platforms had very substantial canopies supported by cast iron stanchions, on the down side with a red brick building and screen along the back of the platform.

The main goods facilities were on the up side. There were also sidings on the up side at Two Mile Bottom for Fison & Sons and the Yorkshire Pitwood Association Ltd, which were administered by Thetford, while at the station itself sidings served two large malthouses, one for Cronshey & Sons in the 1920s, and later — in the 1950s — J. Crisp & Sons. At the Brandon end of the station were more facilities serving local factories, and here also was the goods shed.

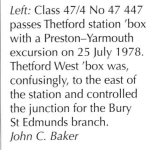

Above: Norwich 'Britannia' No 70011 *Hotspur* between Brandon and Thetford, *en route* to Norwich on 25 May 1951. The 'Britannias' were designed as mixed-traffic locomotives, and this photograph amply demonstrates that capacity. *P. M. Alexander*

Left: Class 47/4 No 47 447 passes Thetford station 'box with a Preston–Yarmouth excursion on 25 July 1978. Thetford West 'box was, confusingly, to the east of the station and controlled the junction for the Bury St Edmunds branch. *John C. Baker*

Left: The goods yard at Thetford on 22 March 1975, this being the view west towards Ely. *David Pearce*

Right: Class D16/3 4-4-0 No 62569 near Thetford with a Cambridge–Norwich van train in the early 1950s. Formerly open heathland — the Brecks — this area has now largely been planted with conifers to help supply timber. *P. M. Alexander*

Below: An unusual interloper on the Breckland line. Seen near Two Mile Bottom on 4 April 1978, HST No 254 010 heads back to King's Cross on the return leg (17.05 from Norwich) of a special run in connection with the opening of the Sainsbury Centre at the University of East Anglia. *John C. Baker*

Right: The remote Roudham Junction marked the divergence of the Thetford–Swaffham line, and trains called only for the purpose of making connections. In this view the main line to Norwich goes straight ahead, while the branch curves to the left behind the signalbox. *H. C. Casserley / M&GN Circle*

General originating traffic was mixed, including manure, malt and grain.

To the east of Thetford station was the confusingly named Thetford West Junction. This arose when the line from Bury St Edmunds was constructed, opening in March 1876 after a prolonged gestation. When planned, this line's station in the town was to be Thetford Bridge, and it would then have continued more-or-less northward to cross over the Norwich line at Roudham, without making a physical connection. Wiser counsels prevailed — doubtless linked to a lack of money — and a triangular junction was built with the main line, joining it at Thetford West and East junctions, both to the east of the station. The curve between Thetford Bridge and Thetford East was little used and soon abandoned, leaving only Thetford West.

The line headed out of Thetford in a north-easterly direction, continuing to rise as far as Croxton level crossing (96 miles 45 chains), near the summit of this section. It then fell gently until about Milepost 100, passing Roudham Junction (97 miles 59 chains) on the way. This was where the branch to Watton and Swaffham diverged to the north, and although it had been a public station in its earlier years it progressively lost its facilities, culminating in its final closure to passengers on 1 May 1932. It never handled goods traffic.

The line continued roughly eastwards to Harling Road (101 miles 38 chains), where it crossed the road between East Harling and Watton. The former was about 1½ miles from Harling Road station, where the up platform hosted a modest L-shaped red brick building which housed the booking office and other facilities, there being little on the other side. The signalbox, also of red brick with wooden superstructure, was on the Norwich side of the level crossing, on the up side of the tracks. The station handled grain traffic and some livestock, with a small yard and goods shed on the down side. The line continued to rise towards Eccles Road (104 miles 39 chains), having passed over Heath level crossing (104 miles 9 chains) — officially two crossings, Heath No 58 and Heath No 59, the heath being Eccles. Today Snetterton motor-racing circuit is very near, on what was Snetterton Heath. Eccles Road is nowadays the site of modern sidings which occasionally handle grain, but the station once saw a small amount of livestock traffic. It was remote from almost everywhere, the only settlement of any note being Kenninghall, some four miles to the south. To the east of the station was a level crossing over the road from the Lophams and Kenninghall, and this was followed by Hargham No 1 (105 miles 30 chains) and Poplar Farm (107 miles 21 chains) crossings.

After falling for about 2½ miles the line then rose again to Attleborough (108 miles 19 chains), where the passenger station consisted of two staggered platforms on each side of the level crossing, controlled by the adjacent signalbox at

Below: BR/Sulzer Type 2 No D5071 near Roudham Junction in July 1960 with a train from Yarmouth Vauxhall to York. The coaching stock is quite mixted, as is the surrounding countryside, with open fields one side of the line and woodland on the other. *John C. Baker*

157

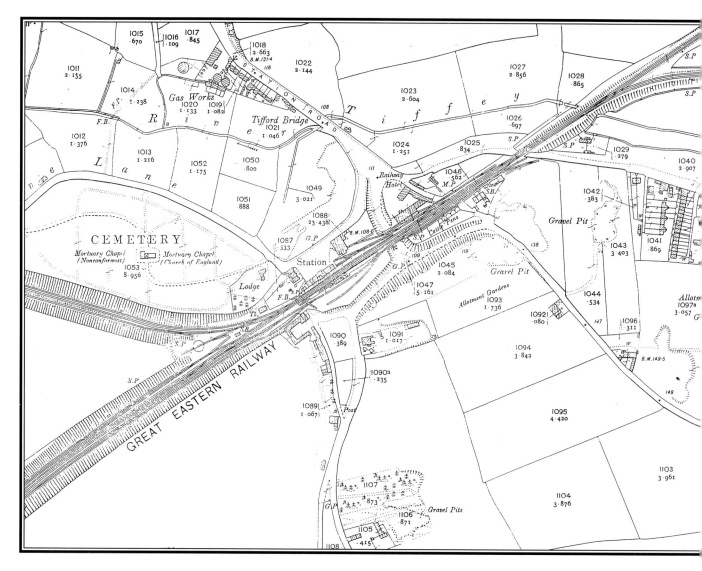

the Thetford end of the down platform. The main station buildings were also on this side, of red brick with a number of gabled windows on the road side, with a relatively imposing platform façade featuring a short canopy. The station was dominated on the up side by W. Gaymer & Sons' cider factory, which had its own siding, together with Thomas Moy, the coal merchant, and Tyrrell & Byford Ltd, a corn, coal, cake and seed merchant. In general terms, the station handled vegetables and livestock as outward traffic. The goods shed, a substantial red-brick building, was on the Norwich side of the crossing opposite the down platform, and there were also several sidings on the down side.

Continuing to rise the line swept onwards, reaching a minor summit soon after Milepost 110½, and passing over Spronces level crossing at 112 miles 30 chains and Besthorpe soon after. Spooner Row (111 miles 27 chains) was another of the wayside stations serving a very small settlement, although this was close to the station. It also had its own level crossing and signalbox, the platforms being staggered either side of the crossing.

Suton level crossing (112 miles 30 chains) was almost exactly a mile away, and was followed by

Wymondham. On the southern edge of the market town, the station had two opposite platforms with the knapped flint principal buildings on the down side, but with matching offices and other facilities on the up platform. There were sidings on both sides of the running lines by the South Junction signalbox (113 miles 65 chains). There was also a small turntable, 45ft 9in in diameter, which could be reached from both the sidings on the down side and the Wells line, and water was available for locomotives on both platforms. Wymondham was a double junction, with the line from Wells and Dereham trailing in at South Junction (113 miles 70 chains), and that for Ashwellthorpe and Forncett, on the Ipswich main line, facing at Wymondham North Junction (114 miles 7 chains). There were goods facilities on both sides of the line, and a loop ran behind the up platform. There were a number of private sidings, including in the 1920s, those of S. G. Page & Sons Ltd and John Standley & Sons Ltd, the latter being corn, seed-cake and manure merchants. By the 1950s the sidings were used by Ayton Asphalt, the Home Counties Tarmacadam Co Ltd and the Briton Brush Co Ltd. Throughout the period A. King & Sons had a siding, this firm being a furniture manufacturer but later known for scrapping redundant railway rolling stock on the remains of the line to Forncett. General traffic was mostly grain and livestock.

Continuing onwards the line rose towards Ketteringham signalbox (115 miles 77 chains), which was towards the end of a level stretch of about a mile, and which marked the highest point on the line from Cambridge. The village was around 1½ miles from Hethersett station (117 miles 73 chains), which was thus inconvenient for both villages. There the staggered platforms were either side of the level crossing, and there was a siding on the up side, latterly used as an oil terminal. The line fell from Ketteringham, through Hethersett and on to Eaton Crossing signalbox (120 miles 30 chains), passing over Intwood and Keswick level crossings on the way. The line reached the River Yare just before Eaton Crossing, passing over it three times in quick succession before reaching Harford (Lakenham) Viaduct, where it passed under the Eastern Union main line from Ipswich. Swinging gently round to the north-east a succession of river crossings followed before Trowse Lower signalbox was passed at 122 miles 74 chains, the physical junction being a further six chains on. The main road from Beccles went over the line on a bridge almost immediately, with the platforms of Trowse station on the far side. Closed immediately before World War 2, Trowse had its main buildings on the down platform, of knapped flint, and looking as if they were a 'nested' series of three. The up platform had two faces and formed an island. The station had its final flourish in the 1980s when Thorpe was closed for track remodelling prior to electrification, and Trowse twice reopened while the work was carried out.

The two routes thus came together for the first time since leaving Liverpool Street, and for very many years it was normal practice for express trains from Norwich to work out via one and back via the other. Note that the mileages for Norwich are via Cambridge, since this route is the older. Trowse Lower Junction was 113 miles 68 chains via Ipswich, but exactly 123 miles via Cambridge, and this slight difference in distance, combined with the generally higher line speeds via Ipswich and the necessarily slow running between Bethnal Green and Clapton mean that the Eastern Union line has finally prevailed over the older Eastern Counties.

Below: Class 31/1 No 31 262 passes Eccles Road, between Thetford and Attleborough, with the 13.15 Birmingham–Yarmouth on 3 July 1982. *John C. Baker*

Above: Class B1 4-6-0 No 61311 leaves Eccles Road — the station can just be seen behind the train — with a Norwich–Liverpool Street service. All stations to Ely, it then joined with with an up train from King's Lynn. *John C. Baker*

Right: Wymondham station on 12 August 1983, as Class 37 No 37 253 passes through with a Saturdays-only Yarmouth–Chesterfield train. In recent years the station has won many awards for the high standard of its restoration and for its 'Brief Encounter' restaurant. *Chris Burton*

Left: A stopping train from Norwich to Attleborough, headed by a grimy Class J15 No 5470, passes Keswick crossing, near Norwich, in 1948. *Reginald E. Batten*

Left: Class K3 2-6-0 No 61867 has been pressed into passenger service on the 11.33am Saturdays-only Yarmouth Vauxhall–Sheffield Victoria in July 1955. it is passing beneath Harford Viaduct, which carries the one-time Eastern Union line from Ipswich to Norwich. *R. E. Vincent*

Left: On 23 July 1955 Class B12/3 No 61565 pilots Class B17/6 No 61633 *Kimbolton Castle* on a cross-country express from Yarmouth and Lowestoft, the train having just passed Trowse Lower Junction. *R. E. Vincent*

Principal Locations

Liverpool Street

Below: The older west side of Liverpool Street station was home to Great Eastern suburban services via Hackney Downs. Here is an orderly scene in the morning peak hour in 1920, with every platform occupied by a 'Jazz' train, and every passenger wearing a hat.
Ian Allan Library

Here there were orchards, gardens, ditches and marshes. Monks from Bethlehem settled here, and the Bethlehem Hospital stood on the site until 1676. Where? the site of Liverpool Street station, although the rural delights describe it as long ago as 1247. The station itself was built by contractors Lucas Bros for the Great Eastern, under the design of the then GER Civil Engineer Edward Wilson, to replace the former Eastern Counties terminus at Shoreditch, whivh later became Bishopgate Goods depot. The new line from Bethnal Green to Bishopsgate Low Level — some of the platforms can still be seen — opened in 1872, with the final section on to the new terminus in 1874, but only for suburban trains. The long-distance traveller had to wait until 1875 before Liverpool Street was fully open for all traffic. The eastern suburban side was finally added in April 1894, bringing the total area to 16 acres.

The initial route from London to East Anglia was from Shoreditch via Stratford, either continuing towards Romford or Tottenham. However, in June 1872 the line via Hackney Downs, Clapton and Copper Mill Junction opened, shortening distances on the Cambridge line by 2 miles 22 chains. This and several other Great Eastern lines in the area had been authorised by a series of Acts in 1864, 1865, 1867 and 1868, and were designed to increase the company's traffic from the rapidly growing suburbs. Part of the same scheme, the first section of Liverpool Street station opened for suburban traffic on 2 February 1874, which transferred from Shoreditch. Eighteen months later, on 1 November 1875 main-line traffic also started to use the new station, and Shoreditch closed to passengers, becoming part of Bishopsgate goods station. When opened the new terminus had nine platforms, with another added later, but demand rapidly outgrew them, and a further eight were added in April 1894. Additional approach lines and other developments were also undertaken,

Left: Released by the removal of the train with which it arrived, one of James Holden's GER Singles, No 14, prepares to reverse to the turntable at Liverpool Street. *Ian Allan Library*

making it the largest London terminus for many years, until overtaken by Waterloo. The steep bank from Bethnal Green was necessitated by the demands of the City to keep the railway out of sight, which has proved an operational inconvenience ever since, and has also required arriving passengers to ascend back to street level.

At the time of opening the lines through Platforms 1 and 2 continued in tunnel to make a junction with the Metropolitan Railway just east of its Bishopsgate station (later Liverpool Street), although this was a temporary arrangement pending the Met's extension to Aldgate. The tunnels remained, disused, until about 1920, although the junction had long been taken out. Platforms 9 and 10 were longer than the others, extended back towards the Great Eastern Hotel, and were used by main-line trains. The 1894 enlargement provided additional capacity on the east side of the station, when the opportunity was also taken to add a further two tracks on the western side, making six in all.

Alterations were made to station working in 1920, with new connections at Bethnal Green. Fast and slow trains could use any line, although platform arrangements segregated the different types of traffic as far as possible. The tracks on the station approach were designated, from the east side, as 'through', 'fast' and 'local' lines; Bethnal Green had no platforms on the through lines. Platforms 7 and 8 at the terminus were double-sided. Liverpool Street itself occupied an area of some 16 acres, and was controlled by the West 'box, with 240 levers and located under the Primrose Street bridge, and East 'box, adjacent to the turntable, with 136.

After all this the passenger approaching the station from Bishopsgate descended considerable flights of stairs to reach the concourse; the approaching cab drove a long way down the steep and tortuous cab road from Liverpool Street itself to deposit its fare by the entrance to the booking office. For very many years this approach was guarded by sets of iron gates supported on sturdy

stone pillars, whilst in the centre, between the cab roads, was Edward Cash's newspaper pitch. It had been founded by his father, among whose first customers were Lord Claud Hamilton, one of the Great Eastern's most distinguished chairmen, and Sir Henry Thornton, its last General Manager. In those early days there was a choice of six London evening papers, the *Pall Mall Gazette*, *St James's Gazette*, *Globe*, *Star*, *News* and *Standard*, of which only the last survives today. Broad Street station towered over the suburban platforms on the western side of the station, while to the north Pindar Street and Worship Street crossed the Great Eastern line by imposing bridges but passed under the adjacent North London line.

The station's position in the square mile was invaluable in the development of traffic. The main entrance was in Liverpool Street itself, which was completely dominated on its north side by its buildings, especially the Great Eastern Hotel. The façade here was of white stone up to first-floor level and of red brick above, with ornate mullions, arches and the like executed in a red stone. A plaque on the front noted that this was 'The site of the First Bethlehem Hospital 1247–1676', this being framed by the legend 'The Corporation of the City of London'. The station buildings themselves, of yellow brick, abutted the west side of the hotel and were graced by some ornamental stonework. A stone plaque on the wall read:

> THIS MEMORIAL TO THE MEN OF NORFOLK, SUFFOLK, ESSEX AND CAMBRIDGESHIRE WHO FELL IN THE GREAT WAR 1914–1919 IS ERECTED BY THE LONDON SOCIETY OF EAST ANGLIANS

It also bore also three shields, composite coats of arms of the counties, including the City of London. Around the corner was the entrance to 50 Liverpool Street, latterly housing the Treasurer's

Department of the British Railways Board. One of the gate pillars stood sentinel outside the door until early 1988, when redevelopment finally overtook it.

Pedestrians from Liverpool Street jostled with taxis down the steep approach road to reach the ticket office, extensively remodelled in the 1960s, but retaining the Great Eastern war memorial (now relocated at street level) along its north wall. The old company's coat of arms was still fully painted; railwaymen had played a full part in both world wars at home and abroad. On the left side of the main memorial was a commemorative plaque to Capt Charles Fryatt, who died on 27 July 1916. He had rammed a German submarine but had been captured and shot. The Great Eastern brought his funeral cortège to London via the main line, hauled by a 'Claud' bearing a wreath with the letter 'F' on its smokebox door, and railwaymen at Stratford turned out in force to stand and show their respect as the train passed. On the right of this plaque was another, to Field Marshal Sir Henry Wilson, Bart, 'whose death occurred on Thursday 22 June 1922 within two hours of his unveiling the adjoining memorial'.

The booking office connected the outside with the concourse adjoining Platform 9. The station was divided into an east and west side, the platforms of the former being generally somewhat longer. In earlier British Railways days the barrier ends of Platforms 1-8 formed a uniform line about four coach lengths shorter than in the new station, with the familiar standard black iron railings. Platforms 9 and 10 were much longer, and tended to be used for the more important expresses such as the boat trains. There was a kink in the face of Platform 10, due to its origins: both lines (and the associated release roads) had once continued on to wagon turntables and coal hoists. Alongside Platform 10 was the roadway, which gave access for Post Office vehicles, newspaper vans and the like and which effectively split the station.

East and west sides were covered by partly glazed trainsheds which had suffered badly during the war. That on the east side was particularly impressive, though this only became really apparent after the demise of steam, when it became possible to see it! A great deal of damage was done in World War 2. In 1940, when the Luftwaffe began the bombing of London, all 260,000sq ft of glass was removed and put into storage; this constituted just over half the total roof area of 500,000sq ft, or nearly 12 acres. On 11 January 1941 two high-explosive bombs fell on Hamilton House, which fronted Bishopsgate, and on neighbouring shops, and the wall of the station fell onto an empty train standing in Platform 18. Debris also blocked the entrances to Platforms 14-18. On 10 May of the same year the station was hit by a number of incendiary bombs, with high explosives falling nearby. Six platforms were put out of use, and one block of headquarters offices was completely gutted.

With all the damage to the station there was a great deal to do after hostilities ended, and renewal of the roof started in 1946. However, the original stored glass had also been damaged by enemy action, and replacement material was in very short supply, although about 130,000sq ft was renewed over a period of two years. The work was made more difficult by the need to replace the eaves, and the whole roof had suffered badly from weathering whilst uncovered. Temporary sheeting was used over much of it, and open spaces were left over Platforms 9-12. These were covered in 1950, though of the 60,000sq ft needing attention only 10,000 could be glazed, because of the shortages. At the same time new long-stroke buffers were installed on Platforms 13-18, and the glazing over this section was renewed to protect the new apparatus. Another 15,000sq ft had been re-glazed by 1954, a further 22,000 being done in 1957 and 17,000 in 1958, leaving about 20,000sq ft needed to restore the roof to its prewar condition. The

Right: Spot the spotters! A suburban service leaves Liverpool Street c1960 as an unidentified 'Britannia' backs onto its train at Platform 10.
Author's collection

buildings were also refurbished and repainted throughout in 1957.

The west-side trainshed consisted of two main bays, that on the west covering Platforms 3-7, and the other Nos 8, 9 and 10. Platforms 1 and 2 were covered by a series of smaller transverse bays, and there was a corresponding arrangement on the east side of the shed. The roof was supported by massive columns, a double row marking the junction of the two main bays. The brickwork of the side walls and of the office and station buildings was mostly of yellows, but with some reds used for arches and relief work, and the new work of the 1980s rebuilding (partly financed by the Railway Heritage Trust) faithfully follows this pattern. The buildings themselves occupied the space that would otherwise have been taken by the trainshed had it continued back towards Liverpool Street (as it now does) in the same manner as the east side. In the subsequent redevelopment of the station in the late 1980s the main office buildings were demolished and the west trainshed extended over the site in a style matching the earlier parts. This allowed the platforms to be lengthened, for the first time creating a uniform barrier line right across the station.

Platforms 9 and 10 extended back towards the front of the Great Eastern Hotel, whose imposing red-brick façade with stone mullions, arches and ornate decorative work dominated the concourse. This area of the station was separated from the east side by a brick wall which continued to form

the retaining wall for the access road from Liverpool Street and was elsewhere pierced by numbers of arches. One of those nearest to the hotel gave access to the subway, but there were various other ways through for passengers. Another was by means of a long and meandering footbridge which gave access to all platforms, though this was latterly somewhat restricted. In early 1959 a new walkway was completed between Platforms 9 and 10 at the buffer-stop end, which meant that passengers no longer had to use the congested area under the hotel, or even the footbridge. It was constructed of brick cross-walls which supported concrete planks topped with *in situ* concrete, which method was economical and allowed access to telephone cables in Platform 9.

The east-side trainshed was in itself a splendid edifice, covering Platforms 11-18, but with the remodelling of Liverpool Street in the late 1980s this roof and associated structures were demolished to make way for the new buildings over the platforms; it had gone by mid-July 1987. The low level of the tracks was accentuated by the stairs up the side of the retaining wall on the Bishopsgate side, and the flights of stairs down from the pleasantly wood-panelled suburban booking offices. The barrier line was further forward than on the west side, though in a similar style, with slatted departure boards between each pair of gates to the platforms.

The rail approaches to Liverpool Street station had been extensively remodelled in preparation

Above: 'Britannia' No 70003 *John Bunyan* leaves Liverpool Street with the down 'Norfolkman' on 15 August 1951. *R. E. Vincent*

Right: A typical off-peak scene at Liverpool Street's Platform 1 in July 1960, as 'N7' 0-6-2T No 69670 prepares to leave with a suburban train formed of a single quint-art set.
John C. Baker

for the electrification in 1949. Before the war the three pairs of tracks out to Bethnal Green had been designated respectively 'suburban', 'local' and 'through', reading from west to east. The suburban lines effectively had no connection with Platforms 11-18, which were accessible from the local and through lines by double junctions; on the other hand, all approach tracks gave access to the west-side platforms, Nos 1-10. Part of the problem was the location of the retaining wall on the east side, which followed a curve from the end of Platform 18 round to the Norton Folgate bridge and which made the approach to the east side very narrow. One of the steps taken to relieve this was to set the wall back and straighten it out, allowing the provision of several extra tracks whilst retaining full access to the turntable near the end of Platform 11.

With the alterations, the running lines were renamed 'suburban', 'through' and 'local', the entire station throat having been remodelled. The intention was to confine the suburban traffic to the extreme east and west sides of the station, the main-line trains being accommodated at Platforms 5-14. To this end the suburban and through lines still had access to the west side, but the new local lines curved very sharply in line with the new retaining wall and now gave access only to Platforms 13-18. The new power signalbox was built onto this wall by the Worship Street bridge. The layout was designed with electric services in mind: out went the old scissors crossovers for locomotive release, and in came reversible running so that the new trains could arrive at and depart from any of the electrified platform lines. At this time the west side of the station remained substantially unchanged apart from the alterations to the throat, which were completed shortly before the electric services were inaugurated in September 1949. When the full service came into operation Platforms 11-18 had been provided with overhead equipment, though it was anticipated that only Nos 15-18

would be used by the new trains, operating at a frequency of 21 per hour in the peaks.

To help handle the extra traffic and allow an increase in train lengths several platforms were altered. No 11 was extended under the Pindar Street bridge, occupying the site of the East signalbox and almost reaching the turntable. Platforms 12 and 13 were also extended almost to this bridge and retained the dock for the pilot. Demolition of the East signalbox allowed Platforms 14 and 15 to be considerably elongated, but a change in the track alignment caused 16 and 17 to be rather narrowed at the country end and 18 to be shortened slightly. This layout remained to the end of steam, when the opportunity was taken to eliminate the turntable and many of the pilot docks, the need having largely gone with electrification of all the suburban services. This remodelling and simplification was not finally completed until 1962, by which time 98 sets of switches, 186 crossings, one set of switch diamonds and four new scissors crossovers had been relaid in long-life high-manganese steel. This layout persisted until the major reconstruction over Easter 1989.

Operationally, Liverpool Street's problems stemmed almost entirely from the intensity of the service operated, its famous 'Jazz' trains providing the busiest steam service in the world. Engine crews had their turnrounds down to a fine art: they would run in with the fireman already hanging on the tank side, ready to 'put the bag in' from the water column on the platform's inner end; he would then jump down and unhook. Meanwhile the turnround locomotive had come onto the other end of the train and within five minutes would depart with the outward working. The first locomotive had to follow immediately to get into the dock and thus free the platform and be ready to take up its outward working: if the fireman had reversed the order of taking water and uncoupling there would only have been time to take half a tank, with disastrous results.

Left: A feature of Liverpool Street was its two pilots. The smaller of the pair, 'J69' 0-6-0T No 68619, is pictured looking immaculate — as ever — on 1 August 1961. *Author's collection*

Left: 'B12' 4-6-0 No 61622 *Alnwick Castle* leaves Liverpool Street with an express service on 11 May 1957 as both large and small pilots — Nos 69614 and 68619 — look on.
R. C. Riley

Left: Monday 13 May 1985 witnessed the official start of electric haulage between Liverpool Street and Ipswich, although Class 86/2 No 86 222 *Fury* was already in use the previous Friday, being seen arriving at the London terminus with the 10.17 from Norwich. The state of the track leaves something to be desired.
Michael McGowan

Right: An unusual view of Platforms 1 and 2 at Liverpool Street on an untypically quiet Saturday afternoon in 1983. The Class 305 EMU bears on its cab front a 'Jazz Train' logo recalling the GER's steam service. *Chris Burton*

Right: Liverpool Street in 1985, with reconstruction work in progress. The three forms of electric traction are a Class 86/2 locomotive in the then-new InterCity livery, a Class 312 EMU and a Class 305 EMU. It is some time since any of them has been seen at the terminus. *Chris Burton*

The Stratford crews working such services had to carry out jobs such as tube cleaning at the country ends of the runs, such as Chadwell Heath or Shenfield, and had also to ensure that they carried the day's full supply of destination boards when they started in the morning. Even in the late 1940s the elderly 'Buckjumpers' were still working these services, albeit soon to be displaced by the new Shenfield electric sets.

For many years it was the practice to work chimney-first out of Liverpool Street, but this was no longer considered essential in the 1950s, by which time Class N7 0-6-2 tanks had replaced the earlier 0-6-0s, and even the powerful 'L1' 2-6-4Ts were occasionally to be seen. Indeed, the destination boards had also become a rare sight. These trains were usually formed of articulated stock for the maximum efficiency of usage of space, two 'quint-art' sets being used in the peaks, while some off-peak workings were formed of a single set; the length and loadings of the 'Jazz' trains diminished after the war. At the time of its introduction the new electric stock caused great embarrassment: the first trains had run out to Hackney crush-loaded, whereupon it was found that the doors could not be opened; the greater length of the new coaches had allowed them to become bowed under the weight, distorting the door frames, and they had to be prised open with pinch bars and the like! Curiously, it probably took just as long to turn around one of the new electric sets at the terminus, as the driver had to change cabs by walking the length of the platform.

The Norwich and other long-distance trains had a more leisurely turnround, if anything at Liverpool Street could be so described. The train would run in to its appointed platform — some, such as the 3.40pm to Ipswich and Norwich only, loaded to 15 bogies and had to use 9 or 10, the only platforms long enough — and the locomotive be unhooked. There would then be a wait of around 45 minutes before the stock departed on its down working. The locomotive could then reverse out to the locomotive depot, where it would be turned and oiled up and take up its place ready to back down onto its return working.

Liverpool Street boasted two pilots, the large and the small, also known as west- and east-side pilots respectively, and often to be found together between Platforms 9 and 10. The large pilot had once been a 'Claud', which covered for main-line failures and which was replaced from Stratford if called out, though in later years it was normally an 'N7'. The small pilot was a tank engine, and in the late 1950s Stratford restored Class J69 0-6-0 No 68619 to the blue livery of the Great Eastern for this duty. It covered tank engine failures and general shunting; the driver and fireman were allowed half a day's pay per week for cleaning it, and it was kept in spotless condition. This concession did not apply to the large pilot, the reason being something of a mystery, although crews did their best to keep it smartly turned out. Another duty that — perhaps surprisingly — they did not perform was that of banking out of Liverpool Street. The incline did not start until some distance beyond the platforms; because of the steep gradient the down lines had a number of trap points, and if a main-line train stopped, perhaps when heavily loaded and with adverse signals, it could not set back to restart. In such cases one of the Spitalfields pilots would be summoned, and back down wrong-road onto the train, which then had to stop at Bethnal Green for it to be detached. The Liverpool Street pilots were not called upon to push.

When Liverpool Street station celebrated its centenary in 1974 traffic was falling because of events such as the opening of the Victoria Line, which had siphoned off passengers from Walthamstow, Tottenham Hale and Seven Sisters. The extraordinarily high potential value of its prime City site was thought to mean that it would not survive much longer in its existing form and would be replaced by an underground station beneath a high-rise office/hotel complex. Initial proposals later that year envisaged reconstruction of Liverpool Street and Broad Street, with a new hotel to replace the Great Eastern, and a shopping centre. The plans published the following year envisaged closure of Broad Street and diversion of its services to Liverpool Street via a new connection at Graham Road, Hackney, four extra platforms at Liverpool Street (taking the total to 22) and two extra tracks to Bethnal Green. A single concourse with a glass-domed roof would offer greatly improved passenger facilities. Only the Abercorn Rooms section of the Great Eastern Hotel would be retained from the old station.

Controversy predictably followed. After a lengthy public enquiry in 1976/7 it was decided that the hotel and Abercorn Rooms would both be retained, together with the western trainshed. In 1981 the British Railways Board submitted a detailed planning application for the scheme, having delayed doing so because of concerns over tax liabilities. Work started in mid-1985 and was expected to be complete by the end of 1991. Broad Street closed on 27 June 1986, and some services were diverted into Liverpool Street, although the proposal for extra platforms and running lines had quietly been dropped. The new Liverpool Street was opened by HM The Queen on 5 December 1991, having cost £2,400 million, mostly financed by the Broadgate development on the site of Broad Street station. Sixteen of its 18 platforms were now able to accommodate 12-car trains, and the whole station was controlled from a new power signalbox at Worship Street. Although the loss of the proposed extra tracks to Bethnal Green continues to constrain operations in and out of the terminus, these will be strongly influenced by the Crossrail scheme, one section of which is proposed to take over local services as far as Shenfield, going into tunnel just west of Stratford and having new underground stations at Whitechapel and Liverpool Street. There will be much of interest here for many years to come.

Stratford

Below: In many ways Stratford was the hub of the Great Eastern system, being the site of the railway's main works and locomotive depot as well as the point at which the two routes to Norwich had diverged. Class J20 No 64697 comes off the line from Chobham Farm Junction and Temple Mills with a transfer freight in May 1961. *John C. Baker*

After rebuilding to cope with electrification Stratford station boasted three island platforms. No 10 served down main-line trains and was in the 'V' of the junction with the Cambridge line, whilst No 9 served those going towards London. Although one face of an island, the other side was not used nor even numbered, being bypassed by down through trains not calling. No 8 was the north face of another island, fairly long and serving down local trains — Gidea Parks, Shenfields and Southends — whilst tube trains on the Central Line, bound for Epping, served the much shorter south face, No 6. There was a London-facing bay at the west end of this platform, No 7. The arrangement of the third island was much the same, with the north face, No 5, served by up stopping trains and the south face, No 3, served by the tube, which arrived late in 1946. The bay at the London end was built by the LNER in 1947 for the abortive service to Fenchurch Street, envisaged as part of the electrification scheme, but never used. The line

via Bow Junction had been electrified for this purpose, but the only service trains that used it were some diverted from their normal route from Southend Central when the LT&S was flooded. The bay was redundant until 1987, when it was used for the fully automated trains of the Docklands Light Railway, in turn being replaced in 2007 by two new platforms, the first opening on 18 June.

The station also operated at quite a different level, the line to North Woolwich, Beckton and Thames Wharf passing underneath. Stratford station's architecture was an interesting mixture of styles, with much of it dating from earlier days and built of red brick. The severe outline of the signalbox contrasted with this, though the grime of years has brought a much closer match in external finish. By the end of the 1980s many of the buildings on the main line and Cambridge platforms were derelict, and Nos 9 and 10 were only used for the occasional emergency services which started at Stratford when Liverpool Street

was out of action, or the engineers had possession. However, at the end of 1989 Network SouthEast refurbished Platforms 11 and 12 in connection with electrification work which allowed it to run a service from Liverpool Street onto the Cambridge line via Stratford, considerably improving the appearance of the station. At the same time it restored Stratford's effective function as a junction between Cambridge- and Norwich-line services.

Stratford also bore the postwar style of buff-and-blue tiling and 'art nouveau' décor characteristic of the LNER's modernisation schemes, though completed in 1948 by British Railways. On the suburban platforms the new buildings had characteristic semi-circular ends, with bronze horizontal rails for protection, the style extending down into the subway and to the exterior; the blue and white Gill Sans enamel signs persisted, having been adopted as standard by British Railways. Inside the booking office — as at other stations at this time — there was something of a revolution in appearance and working conditions. Out went the racks of tickets, manual date stamps and the single incandescent light bulbs. In came the newly standard automatic 'Bellmatic' ticket machines, light oak furnishings and fluorescent tubes. The tiny ticket windows were replaced by a long panoramic glass frontage with several positions, well-lit on both sides, and flanked by poster spaces built-in to the design of the tiling. This pattern was repeated down the line at many of the inner-suburban stations such as Maryland and certainly appeared in other London-suburban modernisation schemes. Out on the platforms the canopies were more conventional, being to an inverted 'V' configuration and supported on steel columns and brackets.

Another change that took place at the same time was in the station announcements, which became partly automated. With the introduction of the new electric service a large number of trains stopping at Stratford had a very limited number of destinations and calling patterns, and it was felt that ordinary vocal announcements would 'produce a suggestion of monotony or boredom'. The system installed was worked from a control desk in the signalbox, and actuated by the trains themselves via the track circuits. Approaching the station, the taped 'girl with the golden voice' would be activated to announce that 'the train now approaching Platform ..... will call at ......', changing when the train entered the platform to 'the train standing at Platform .....' and so on. In the signalbox, groups of up to four announcements could be preselected from a total of 24, so that when the first train of the sequence entered the approach circuit, a red light showed on the control panel telling the operator to press the button and so start the broadcasting sequence. It was possible to override the system and make emergency announcements, or to press another button and have no announcement if a freight or non-stop passenger train were approaching.

Interesting and busy though the passenger station has always been, this has never been its primary importance. Stratford has figured as a place of locomotive maintenance for East Anglia's railways for almost as long as the lines themselves have existed. The first section of the Eastern Counties had opened on 18 June 1839 between Mile End and Romford, to be followed on 1 July 1840 by the sections from Shoreditch to Mile End, and Romford to Brentwood: Colchester was reached in 1843. The slightly newer Northern & Eastern Railway opened its first section between Stratford and Broxbourne on 15 September 1840, and it was this company that first established locomotive facilities here. By 1843 it had built a 16-road roundhouse, situated in the apex of the junction formed by the Shenfield and Broxbourne lines, near the present station and Stratford Central Junction. This building was known as the 'Polygon' and was later incorporated into the works.

As the demands for motive power grew the Stratford complex expanded, running sheds appearing to the south of the Cambridge line, more or less on the site of the later locomotive depot, and eventually the carriage works was also sited here. The works proper remained on the cramped site in the apex of the two lines, with its limited access, this becoming considerably worse as the years went by and the size of locomotives inexorably increased. It had been based around the magnificent office block, which had an archway through the middle giving access between the main line and the erecting shop. Eventually, as locomotives of the size of the 'Claud Hamiltons' and the later '1500s' appeared, it almost seemed the case that items such as chimneys and cabs had to be fitted or removed whilst the locomotive stood on the main line outside the works. The real cause of the problem was that everything using the track through the archway into the works had to use a turntable to gain access, and it was just too small.

Eventually, just before World War 1, the situation became so pressing that the Locomotive Superintendent, James Holden, persuaded the Great Eastern's board that the works be expanded by the construction of a new Engine Repair Shop (ERS) for the heavy maintenance and repair of the locomotive fleet. Space could not be found on the works site, so the new building was placed to the north of the running sheds, near to the Channelsea Junction–Loughton Branch Junction line. It measured 450ft by 150ft, was 40ft high, consisted of three equal-size bays, the outer ones containing full-length roads traversed by two 40-ton overhead cranes, and was intended to be used for locomotive dismantling and erection. The centre bay was to be used for motion and other component repairs, with only a single 10-ton overhead crane, the main machining processes remaining in the old works.

This shop was essentially complete at the outbreak of World War 1 but had not been occupied for its intended purpose. It was commandeered by the Ministry of Munitions, and is rumoured to have been completed and adapted by German prisoners of war. The Great Eastern finally took control in 1919, and it was altered back to fulfil its original purpose. However, before new locomotive construction could be transferred there the Grouping took effect, and LNER policy discontinued building at Stratford, where the last locomotives to be built were erected in the old works in 1924. The ERS continued to be used for maintenance of the motive power inherited from the Great Eastern, and for incoming classes such as Gresley's 'Sandringhams'. The ERS was used again for munitions work in World War 2, and later the Thompson 'Bongos' and Class L1 2-6-4 tanks which were employed on the East Anglian lines took their turn in these fine shops. Meanwhile activity continued on the original works site to the north of the Cambridge lines. Among the huge variety of locomotives handled at Stratford were the diminutive tram engines such as worked the Wisbech & Upwell Tramway and Ipswich Docks, which would be sent back to their depot on a Sunday morning to keep them clear of other traffic. Their cowcatchers and the like travelled in a brake van and were refitted at the home shed. For economic reasons it was the practice to return locomotives from the works in groups coupled together, and on at least one occasion a 'Sandringham', tram and another express locomotive were coupled, in that order. It was necessary to warn the crew on the 'Sandringham' to take it easy!

After nationalisation the works remained under the control of the Regional Chief Mechanical & Electrical Engineer, but it was inevitable that its status would come under wider scrutiny. After the inception of British Railways the Eastern Region stretched only as far as Doncaster and Sheffield, the North Eastern Region covering the portions of the former LNER system in the more northerly parts of England. They were finally amalgamated on 1 January 1967, Gerard Fiennes taking over as General Manager of the new enlarged Eastern. The parts of the old company north of the border were incorporated into the Scottish Region from the very start, of course.

The Great Eastern section had been one of the first to get the new diesel locomotives, just as it had been in the forefront when the new BR Standard steam classes appeared, and it was decided to convert the Engine Repair Shop for them, steam eventually being restricted to the old works. Larger locomotives such as 'Britannias' which needed overhaul were sent away to Doncaster or Darlington. Conversion work started in July 1957, and the first diesels arrived in the ERS in about 1958, many of the pits in the north bay being filled in at about this time so that power-unit repairs could be undertaken there. However, this new use did not last long, since Stratford was identified as one of those places whose capacity was surplus to requirements, and the works closed in September 1963. However, this was not the demise of the ERS, even though the rest of the complex was demolished fairly quickly.

Below: Retired locomotives were often transferred to the Departmental list and continued working at places such as Stratford. No 44 is seen so employed in April 1961. *John C. Baker*

Stratford shed, not to be confused with the works, was for many years the largest in the country, supplying motive power for the most intensive steam-operated suburban service in the world. In January 1955 there were approximately 500 locomotives allocated. Some were shedded at the smaller outstations which included Hertford East, Bishop's Stortford, Enfield and Walthamstow Wood Street, all of which contributed to the west-side suburban service, as well as at various locations along the Ipswich main line. These ranged from Devonshire Street, with its 'coffee-pot' 0-4-0 necessitated by the right-angled entrance to the yard, to more rural places such as Braintree and Maldon. About 50 locomotives were outbased at Colchester, and another 30 at Parkeston, both of which were in the Stratford District.

There were two main running sheds, both orientated roughly north-east–south-west, as with most of the rest of the depot. The 'New Shed' of 1871, with no ventilation and six roads, did not have locomotives lit up in it, for obvious reasons, and was used entirely for 'stopped work' — in other words, where a locomotive had had to be taken out of traffic. No 6 road had all the unusual jobs, whilst Nos 2 and 3 were used as boiler roads, for tubing and the like, and No 1 was used for 350hp diesel shunters. The New Shed had a welding bay, which was also the site for the boilermakers' shanty and rest-room. As in the works, boilermakers regarded themselves as being rather above the fitters, and there was a good deal of rivalry between the two.

The main building at Stratford was the 'Jubilee Shed', to the west of the New Shed, opened in 1887 and extended about 10 years later, with 12 very long roads. It was divided into two halves, the tank and tender sides, accommodating the freight and passenger tenders and the suburban and shunting tanks, the latter being on the side

Stratford Shed

Left: Departmental Class Y4 0-4-0 No 33 on duty at Stratford in April 1961, with an electric unit lurking in the shed behind. *John C. Baker*

Left: A line of locomotives at Stratford on 2 May 1959, including 'D16' No 62588, 'J39' No 64715, 'N7s' Nos 69659 and 69634, 'J17' No 65574 and 'B12' No 61575.
Author's collection

nearer the passenger station. The Jubilee was mainly a running shed, only two roads being used for daily repairs: No 2 for tank engines, and No 9 for tenders.

Overall there were about 2,500 staff at Stratford shed, this total comprising a huge number of drivers and firemen, about 460-500 artisans and many conciliation-grade men, such as boilerwashers. Mess facilities were unbelievably crude for drivers and virtually non-existent for other staff until a new block was opened in 1955 for conciliation grades. Other staff had their own official and unofficial messrooms such as old air-raid shelters, and it could be very difficult to find people when they were wanted. Working conditions were appalling, oil and dirt often soaking through the men's overalls and shirts, with a fitter having to wash up in a bucket in the open road by his tool cupboard, hot water being obtained from the nearest locomotive.

In many respects working conditions in both the Works and Shed at Stratford had not advanced since the turn of the century. This led to a great deal of discontent, which came to a head with a number of strikes in the 1940s, when there was a shortage of both men and motive power. When Richard Hardy was appointed to Stratford, first as Assistant District Motive Power Superintendent and later in charge, he had the considerable task of rebuilding the bridges between the management and the men. Much was done in the period of transition to diesels, and many of the restrictive practices of the steam era were buried.

Temple Mills cannot escape without mention, although it was not really a part of Stratford. Located on the old line between Stratford and Copper Mill Junction, the area had once been a Roman camp site, and traces of this survived into the 19th century, when the railway finally obliterated them. The huge marshalling yards were built on both sides of the line between Loughton Branch Junction and Lea Bridge (on the original route to Cambridge), to the north of the Stratford complex. They had been developed more-or-less piecemeal over the years and by the early 1950s consisted of nine flat and one hump yards, the former having a rather limited capacity of about 1,000 wagons per day. Although a large number of freight trains was scheduled to serve Temple Mills, six of its yards received almost no traffic directly from this source: they were fed by transfer trips from other yards. Because of the poor layout each wagon had to be shunted at least twice, which was expensive in terms of time and manpower. It also caused considerable delays to goods in transit.

In 1954 the British Transport Commission authorised the complete reconstruction of the complex, which would then take over from a number of other yards in the London area as well as the old Temple Mills; only Goodmayes down yard was scheduled to remain untouched. The new layout was to consist of one main 'hump' distribution and two 'reservoir' yards. There were to be 12 reception lines, six of which could be entered from either direction, and 10 departure

Below: Class D16/3 No 62536 looks a sorry sight at Stratford on 2 May 1959. *Author's collection*

Left: Class L1 2-6-4T No 67729 receives attention outside Stratford MPD offices on 2 May 1959. *Author's collection*

Left: A sign of changing times at Stratford: shiny new English Electric shunter No D3071 poses outside the locomotive depot in the mid-1950s. *Author's collection*

lines, all of which could be used by either east- or westbound trains. There were to be 50 sorting sidings, and locomotive release roads, cripple roads, cattle pens and brake van storage lines were to be provided, together with a miniature hump serving the southernmost 12 sorting sidings at the departure end of the main yard. This was to be designated the 'Manor Yard' and used for secondary sorting of express freight to Cambridge, Whitemoor and Norwich. The passenger lines were to be routed round the south side of the yard. A number of features were designed to speed shunting generally. Careful attention was given to the gradients, and electric primary and secondary wagon retarders were planned. Colour-light signalling and electric point operation were to be provided, all being operated from a new control tower. The new Temple Mills was scheduled to take four years to build, whilst normal work went on in the old yards, and when it opened it represented the latest in railway technology. It was rapidly overtaken by the Beeching report and the withdrawal from wagonload traffic, the latter being replaced by the 'liner train' concept, the precursor of today's block and container trains.

In recent years all of this has been swept away. The new International station has been built in a giant trench running across the middle of the site, and Thornton Fields sidings, which once provided stabling for stock needed for peak services next to the River Lea, have been replaced by more at Orient Way, to the north and east. Temple Mills, briefly a depot for EWS (English, Welsh & Scottish Railway), is now home to Eurostar, replacing the latter's first facility at North Pole, in West London. The whole Stratford area is being remodelled for the Olympic Games in 2012, with high-speed domestic services, further extensions to the Docklands lines and Crossrail all in the pipeline, while much of it will be occupied by the new Westfield shopping centre, destined to be one of the largest in Britain. Whatever happens, Stratford will play a pivotal rôle, both nationally and internationally.

Colchester

Colchester had been some distance short of the halfway point on the Eastern Counties Railway's plans for its line from London to Norwich but in the event marked the limit of its construction. Norwich was eventually reached via Cambridge, and Ipswich was left in great alarm, so the Eastern Union built the line onwards, eventually becoming the route used today. The ECR station (later Colchester North) lay at an inconvenient distance from the town and might have been bypassed by the EUR line, although after the connection was made relations were so bad for a time in 1852/3 that the latter's trains were blocked from even entering the station, and passengers to and from the north had to continue their journeys to London by steamer!

Although the later St Botolphs station (now Colchester Town) was more convenient for passenger access to the town centre, North station attracted growth towards itself and was in turn enlarged and improved to cope with the increasing demands on it. Officially North was divided into passenger and goods stations, the whole handling the full range of parcels and miscellaneous traffic, furniture vans, cars and wheeled machinery, livestock and horse boxes, and carriages and motor cars to go by passenger train, a 1½-ton crane being available. However, most of the goods traffic was handled at Hythe, on the Clacton line, where in 1929 there were 18 private sidings, reduced to 11 by 1956 and by then including those for Crosse & Blackwell Ltd, Colchester Coop,

Marriage & Sons (millers) and Thomas Moy, coal merchants. The station handled only goods and passengers and had a 6-ton crane, this having replaced the 15-tons example in use in 1929. St Botolphs, on a spur off the Clacton line, handled passengers but not livestock and had a 6-ton crane, as well as a siding for Paxman, Davey & Co Ltd. The range of goods forwarded included grain and flour, scrap iron, bricks and tiles, machinery, hay and straw, and hides, as well as livestock and vegetables from North. Tonnages were reasonable but not enormous, the total in 1938 being 8,077, worth just over £9,000 to the railway.

The main station is known to this day as Colchester North and was described as such by the Railway Clearing House in 1956, but the 'North' suffix did not appear in the RCH's 1929 handbook or in railway timetables, including Bradshaw; the LNER's goods-traffic returns did use the name, but traffic from Hythe was allocated to St Botolphs. The main line at this point ran almost due west to east and swung back towards the town from its smooth progress from Chelmsford, a consequence of the conflicts when the line was under construction. Even so, the station was still a fair way from the town centre, and reaching the latter entailed a long pull up North Street. The LNER had embarked on modernisation at the end of the 1930s but was prevented by the war from completing it. The station was finally rebuilt in conjunction with the electrification of the main line, the new layout being approved on

Below: Colchester marked the limit of the Eastern Counties Railway's original scheme to reach Ipswich and Norwich, and the layout of the North station bedevilled operations until electrification. Great Eastern Class T19 No 773 departs with a train for Ipswich. *Ian Allan Library*

31 December 1959. The Clacton and Walton lines had been the pilot scheme for the 25kV system, and this was inaugurated in 1959, although at Colchester the wires extended only into the Clacton bay platform and did not allow the new trains to enter the main part of the station. Part of the scheme also involved installation of the new standard Automatic Warning System on the electrified lines, and this was actually done in 1957.

In its LNER and earlier British Railways form the station was approached from the London direction on a sweeping curve, which then reversed quite sharply to bring it into the platforms. This curve bedevilled the line until the rebuilding in the early 1960s, and immediately after World War 2 the limit was 40mph for through trains and just 20mph for those taking the crossover onto the Clacton branch. The old Colchester North had two side platforms which served all through trains on the main line and for Clacton. There was a bay on the up side for local services to Clacton, and another at the London end, together with end-loading docks. The goods depot had been at the London end of the station. Under the rebuilding the former main lines became the goods lines, with a connection at the Ipswich end into the new down Clacton road. Much of this change was dictated by the need to build the new motive power depot onto the adjacent site, between the old and the new main lines.

The old station had major buildings on both up and down platforms. That on the up side was an elegant red-brick structure, with stone sills and arches, some of the latter being square and others semi-circular. It comprised a central two-storey portion, containing the main entrance, and an ornamental balustrade on the road approach side, which in turn sported what appeared to be ornamental stone 'temples' at each end. This part of the building had a fully hipped roof topped by a small bell-tower. On either side of this central block extended a single-storey portion parallel to the platforms, each having at its outer end another square two-storey block, featuring four large stone spheres on its balustrades. A glazed canopy extended along a large portion of the road side of this building, whilst the platform side was so graced along its whole length.

The buildings on the down side were the principal ones, somewhat larger and of two storeys, but similar in style. Both sides were provided with generous awnings, and laid out to match the curve of the platforms. The two were connected by subway, and road access was easier on the down side of the station. The reorganisation of the station for the main-line electrification from Chelmsford involved drastic changes to the track and station layouts, which had been foreshadowed in a report forming part of the Modernisation Plan in 1956. Where there had been a conventional flat junction between the main and Clacton lines, there was to be a

Below: Before the start of the electrification Class K3 2-6-0 No 61963 approaches Colchester on the up Norwich line. The two tracks in the foreground are the Clacton lines
Author's collection

Above: A fine postcard view of Colchester North station, showing the main up platform and the relatively sharp curvature of the tracks.
Lens of Sutton Association

Right: Colchester North station on 15 November 1905, with a down local service calling.
Lens of Sutton Association

Right: A general view of the north end of Colchester North, with a down train signalled for the Norwich line, and also showing the Clacton bay platform.
Lens of Sutton Association

Above: A typical scene at the south end of Colchester station as a 12-car train for Clacton, made up of three Class 309 units, passes the depot, with Class 37 No 37 260 on shed.
J. C. Hillmer

completely new down Clacton line some 1,200 yards long on the north side, which would then burrow under the main lines at the east end of the layout; the cost of this alone was £150,000. The original junction was singled and simplified. The new down Clacton line obliterated much of the existing locomotive depot, which was re-sited at the west end, with the down platform converted to an island of rather restricted width. Reconstruction involved the complete obliteration of the fine down-side buildings, and their replacement by a less-than-inspiring single-storey edifice which continues to look decidedly temporary more than 50 years later.

On the up side the main face extending towards London became the new Platform 3, for the principal departures to Liverpool Street, whilst at the other end it was reduced in width, though extended in length, and an extra up loop installed adjacent to the main, having its own platform face now designated No 4. This necessitated moving the previous Clacton bay over, and the southern face of this much-extended platform became No 5. A new fish dock was provided at the end of this road, but the run-round facility was not renewed. The combined length of the up-side platforms became 1,920ft, with No 3 having a face 810ft long, and No 4 825ft, the discrepancy with the total being explained by the fact that the connection between the two could not be used for passengers, since there was a trap point protecting the up main where the loop ran into it.

Considerable use was made of aerial surveying for the rebuilding. The new station boasted the longest platform in Britain, although many discount this claim since it does not have one continuous face. Road access to the station was altered so that buses now came up to the station entrance from the roundabout that had been built by the newly widened bridge carrying the lines over Station Road. There had been a large BR laundry in the junction between Bergholt Road and the station approach on the down side, and its water tower had dominated the skyline.

The original locomotive depot was on the down (north) side, at the Ipswich end of the layout, and boasted a considerable allocation of both tank and tender engines, though it was described by staff from other depots as a 'one-horse affair'! In GER days it had come under the control of the Ipswich District, but was transferred to Stratford when Ipswich lost its district status. It was notable for its extremely cramped layout: a three-road shed stood immediately adjacent to the main lines, with the various buildings clustered around it. These included some ex-GER carriage bodies and a wooden hut housing the Shed Master's office. The carriage body housing the cleaners' mess had burnt down in dubious circumstances in August 1952, and had been replaced by one of similar vintage; another replaced the Running Foreman's office and signing-on lobby, and an ex-North British Railways coach body served as a new locker room. Another feature of the Colchester scene was the 'Residence', its appearance revealing that it had indeed been adapted from a pre-existing house, that of the keeper of the erstwhile level crossing No 38, which was not finally stopped up until the rebuilding. It had carried only a footpath for many years, and a diversion was built to avoid the crossing; the house had been taken over many years before by the locomotive department for stores facilities. The whole lot was replaced with a modern purpose-built block at the end of 1956, incorporating offices for the shedmaster and his staff, a signing-on lobby, messroom/kitchen and locker room. The buildings were wooden and designed for speedy assembly — and dismantling for use elsewhere. In the event it was just five years before the depot closed.

John Bellwood, who retired as Chief Mechanical Engineer to the National Railway Museum in April 1988 and who sadly died later that year, was shedmaster at Colchester from August 1952 to 1956, when there were about 50 steam locomotives allocated. Colchester, in common with far too many other ex-Great Eastern

sheds, was an appalling place for working conditions. There was a serious problem with disposal, there being only a single pit, and this was done in the yard (or almost anywhere), with the result that there were heaps of ash all over the place. One way of raking it out was to use a dart, bent at right-angles, which could be poked through the spokes of the wheels in order to work the ash out into the four-foot. Even so, for a Stratford District depot at that time the standard of maintenance was very high.

In John Bellwood's time Colchester had a varied allocation of locomotives, although there were no 'Clauds'. Colchester 'B2s', including Nos 1607, 1614, 1616, 1632 and 1644, worked to London, Ipswich, Cambridge, Parkeston and Clacton. One of his achievements had been to exchange the old inside-cylindered 'B12s' ('1500s') for 'B17s' with outside cylinders, which eased the problems of preparation without pits. Colchester had very good artisans but few relief staff, which was in contrast to Ipswich, by now a part of the Norwich District. There each depot was more or less independent and expected to cover its own sickness or other

Below: Colchester locomotive shed was a cramped affair with poor facilities located on the down side of the main line. Having rested on shed between turns, Cambridge-allocated Class J39 0-6-0 No 64751 leaves to take up its return working on 26 August 1957. *Author's collection*

absence, whilst sheds in the Stratford District depended on the parent to send fitters out to provide cover, so that staffing was tighter at Colchester than at Ipswich. Coaling was by a lightweight tub-elevator system, installed by the LNER in the 1930s, and there was a 65ft turntable at the station end of the site. The track layout of the depot, quite apart from its dangerous proximity to the running lines, imposed many restrictions. There was only one through road in the shed, No 1 (nearest the running lines), which provided the only connection between the two ends of the depot, so if this were blocked locomotives had to go out onto the down main to get from one end to the other. The congestion was such that at peak times locomotives had to be stabled in the goods yard or in the carriage sidings opposite the depot.

The main station area at Colchester was controlled by two signalboxes. The junction with the Clacton line at the country end of the station was controlled by Colchester Junction 'box, on the up side, the branch tracks then descending sharply and curving away to the south. Colchester station 'box stood at the London end of the up platform, and both were replaced in the modernisation scheme by a new 'box (also called Colchester Station but almost opposite its erstwhile namesake on the down side) worked by three regular men. In due course it was itself replaced by the new panel 'box, and many men felt a great deal of stress in changing to the new system. Previously they could 'take it out' on the levers, which is simply not possible with a push-button system. Some of the old mechanical frames had been very heavy, and it was necessary to 'feel the frame' and gain the knack of working it. The precise placing of the compensation — those cranks in long rodding or wire runs — mattered greatly in allowing it to work in extremes of hot or cold weather. Many older staff felt that signalmen no longer had knowledge of the personalities with whom they had to deal (and *vice versa*), so that they became disembodied voices on the end of a telephone. The present Colchester panel 'box controls much of the main line, sharing this with Liverpool Street, and during 2008 work was continuing to install bi-directional signalling within its area.

Below: Class E4 2-4-0 No 62785 stands outside Colchester shed in 1959, after the wires went up for the Clacton electrification but before the layout was remodelled. *Author's collection*

Right: A fine view of LNER Class B2 No 1603 *Framlingham* about to leave Colchester with the 12.39pm Clacton express on Saturday 21 June 1947. *Ian Allan Library*

Below: After the main line was electrified and the connections to the Clacton line reorganised Colchester locomotive depot was relocated some way to the London end of the layout. A Brush Class 31and two Class 08s, Nos 08 226 and 08 715 outside on 19 April 1975. The main up platform, No 3, is in the foreground with the up and down main lines and the connection to Platform 1 between it and the shed roads. *Norman E. Preedy*

Left: Colchester Junction 'box looks over 'Britannia' Pacific No 70040 *Clive of India*, arriving at the head of the down 'Essex Coast Express'. Meanwhile a two-car lightweight Metro-Cammell DMU sets back into the station, probably to form a Brightlingsea working. The photograph dates from 1959; what would today's Health & Safety Executive have to say about the work going on up the ladder?
Author's collection

Below: Engineering work involving track re-laying in progress at the London end of Colchester station on 7 March 1982. Modern machinery has made life easier for those working under the wires.
Michael J. Collins

Ipswich

Ipswich was a town almost completely surrounded by the Great Eastern Railway. It had first approached from the south-east from Colchester, changed direction a little and skirted around the southern side before turning north again to Stowmarket and Bury, following which the East Suffolk covered the north-eastern quarter, with encirclement almost completed by the Felixstowe line. The branches to the docks and quays on either side of the Orwell made the embrace even closer.

The first Ipswich station had been on the site of the later locomotive depot, on the London side of Stoke Hill. It was by-passed when the line onwards to Bury St Edmunds was built, which diverged at Halifax Junction. This also necessitated the construction of the tunnel, and a new station was proposed — meantime trains had to reverse in or out of the old station. To complicate matters the Eastern Counties Railway had taken over operation of the Eastern Union, which had built the line from Colchester to Ipswich (and had itself taken over the Ipswich & Bury), and relationships between the EUR and ECR were fraught with difficulties, both legal and practical. It was not until 1860, some months after the East Suffolk Railway opened its line between Yarmouth and Ipswich, that the new station was ready on its present site, essentially consisting of that part which now serves the up (north) side. Like Colchester its orientation is roughly east–west, and the line curves quite sharply at each end. The LNER also maintained a parcels and ticket booking office at 27 St Matthews Street, which facility was shared by — of all companies — the Great Western.

The station building was a very fine structure in white brick (unlike most on the line), red being used for quoins, plinths, lintels and so on. The arches were almost all circular. The central section was of two storeys, with a hipped slate roof and with prominent chimney stacks at each end and on both platform and road sides; the latter also had a small bell-tower. On the road approach side a large awning spanned the front of this block. The down main line served the north face of the island, No 3, which had been added in 1883, whilst a sharp turnout, restricted to 15mph, gave access to the back platform, No 4. The up main did not serve a platform: up Norwich trains calling at the through platform, No 2, had to be turned off the main line. No 1 was a Norwich-facing bay on the up side. Ipswich station signalbox stood at the tunnel end of the island platform, and was provided as part of the 1883 station rebuilding. Two sharply curved short dock roads trailed into the up line close to the tunnel and were used for locomotive changing, the relieving locomotive waiting there for the up train to run in. The incoming locomotive, probably from Norwich or Yarmouth South Town depots, would come off and set back onto the middle road, whereupon the relief would emerge from the spur and couple up. After the train had gone the Norwich crew would take their locomotive through the tunnel and into the depot, although much of the need to change locomotives was

Below: An early view, from Ipswich Goods Junction 'box, of the west end of Ipswich station. Note that Platform 1 is extensively covered by a trainshed, and compare this with later photographs showing the awnings here.
Russell Whipps collection

Left: Ipswich station on 12 August 1947. Austerity 2-8-0 No 79198 is halted on the up main line, while just visible on the right is LNER 'B12/3' No 1577, performing station duties.
G. R. Mortimer

Left: On 21 June 1957 Class L1 2-6-4T No 67739 waits in the Felixstowe bay at Ipswich station. The overall roof has been dismantled to make way for a new structure. *Author's collection*

Below: Class B1 4-6-0 No 61160 heads the 10.5am Fisons special to Windsor on 31 May 1958.
Author's collection

Above: Colchester 'B1' 4-6-0
No 61311 backs along the
up main line through
Ipswich station on 5 March
1960. Notice how the
platform awnings differ from
those of earlier years.
John C. Baker

obviated when the 'Britannias' were introduced and through locomotive working between Liverpool Street and Norwich became the norm. Splitting of trains into Norwich and Yarmouth portions also involved locomotive changes, and this practice also diminished.

On the west side of the station were the carriage sidings, reached by trailing connections at the north end. Movements there were controlled by Ipswich Goods Junction signalbox, which stood on the down side of the tracks but with the down goods road passing behind it. Further to the north — 1,025 yards to be exact — stood East Suffolk Junction signalbox, controlling trains to and from that line, and access into the upper goods yard from the north. Congestion here could be considerable, as a northbound goods train had to cross the up and down East Suffolk and the up main line to get onto the down main, the pair of East Suffolk running lines extending right into the station, rather than being single, as today. Between here and Ipswich Goods Junction were six running lines, the main, East Suffolk and goods roads, the down East Suffolk leading straight into Platform 2. Ipswich had been considered for rebuilding in 1956, when lengthening of the platforms, improvements to running facilities and revision of the signalling was proposed at a cost of some £500,000, in order to meet traffic requirements. Apart from the work in connection with the change to diesel traction, nothing was done until

the advent of electrification in the 1980s.

Near Goods Junction 'box was one of the great railway features of Ipswich, the magnificent Great Eastern signal gantry which bore a total of 22 arms and which was erected in 1912, when two goods roads were added between Goods and East Suffolk junctions. It spanned all six running lines, and apart from three down distants, all its arms were for up trains. The up Norwich home and up Yarmouth home were the highest at 45ft above rail level, and the gantry sported several GER 'draw-ahead' arms to the very end. This came on the weekend of 27/28 July 1957, when it was replaced by just three four-aspect multi-lens colour-light signals with theatre-type route indicators. The one controlling the goods lines was at ground level for reasons of restricted clearance.

On the north side of the main line between the two 'boxes was the Upper goods yard, which handled considerable quantities of freight, and which is currently largely used for containers in transit to Felixstowe. It also gave access to the Dock branch, which wound down across Ranelagh Road, under Princes Street, through the lower yard and goods station, and then continued across Bridge Street to St Peter's Quay, where it divided. One branch went around the north side of the Wet Dock, serving a multitude of private sidings and wharves, including Albion Wharf, Common Quay, Neptune Quay and Orwell Quay and housing firms such as the Meux brewery and Ransomes,

Left: Class B1 No 61054 shunts in Ipswich carriage sidings on 18 July 1958. *Author's collection*

Left: Ipswich carriage sidings in 1959, with 'B12' No 61535 collecting coaching stock. *Author's collection*

Sims & Jefferies. Much of the quay area on this side was not constructed until after World War 1, although authorised before. By 1937 Cliff Quay extended to 1,800ft and could accommodate ships of 28ft draught; electric cranes were installed.

The other branch went round the south side and, again, served a wide variety of concerns. The two branches were united at their eastern end, where a swing bridge took the southern part over the entrance lock to the dock. From here a line extended along to Cliff Quay. The dock working necessitated the use of tram engines, and consequently Ipswich had an allocation of Class J70 0-6-0s, which survived until at least 1954. Following 'dieselisation' some of the new shunters were specially fitted with the appropriate skirts. There were two tram duties, one from 6.0am on Monday to 6.0am Sunday, the other from 6.0am to 10.0pm each weekday. A Class J67

was also allocated to shunt at Cliff Quay, and could take over from the No 1 tram after 6.0pm. Incoming trade, largely from Scandinavia, the Netherlands, Belgium, France and the USA, included all kinds of grain, timber, raw materials for fertilisers, slate and stone, whilst much of the export trade comprised products manufactured from these — agricultural and railway plant, fertilisers, flour and so on. It was all good for the railway.

The Griffin Wharf branch diverged from the main line at Halifax Junction, south of the station and locomotive depot, and served sidings and quays on the south and west sides of the New Cut, the south part of the Dock branch serving the north and east sides. Terminology is a little difficult because the Wet Dock is more-or-less right angled, whilst the New Cut (of the River Orwell) cuts off the corner. Ransomes & Rapier

Right: In the carriage sidings was a fuelling point, where Class 37 No 37 113 was photographed on 24 April 1976. *I. P. Cowley*

had its works here, complete with its own shunting locomotive, and the branch also served maltsters and others. The first Ipswich station had stood on the site later occupied by the locomotive depot, and its latter-day successor the electrification depot. This was not extended when the Ipswich & Bury Railway was being promoted — it had always been considered temporary, and so the new line by-passed it. The depot had an entrance in Croft Road, opposite which two pubs commemorated the origins of the railway, being respectively the 'Great Eastern' and the 'E.U.R.', where the initials of the Eastern Union remain in the stonework. Around the corner in Wherstead Road, close by the bridge taking the Griffin Wharf branch over the road was the new locomen's block — signing-on point, messing and so on, with the depot in the area bounded by the main line and these streets.

In April 1950 when Richard Hardy started as shedmaster Ipswich had an allocation of approximately 90 locomotives and about 450 staff of all types, which included clerical, footplate, artisan, supervisory and conciliation grades. The last included storekeepers, boilerwashers, softening-plant attendants, labourers and so on, whilst the artisan staff included fitters and boilermakers in a ratio of about four to one. The shedmaster had a very good office, once used by the District Locomotive Superintendent in the days when Ipswich had that status. He was responsible for the general running of the depot, the maintenance and running of locomotives, administration, law and order and general supervision, as well as making general

improvements where possible. The supervisory staff under him included the mechanical foreman, boiler chargeman and running foreman, the latter responsible for the booking of locomotives and for preparation and disposal and the like. The shedmaster in turn was also responsible for the timekeeping of both men and trains and for the five outstations: Aldeburgh, Framlingham, Laxfield, Stowmarket and Felixstowe, all of which were small. Aldeburgh and Framlingham each had two drivers, two firemen and one cleaner. Stowmarket had three drivers and firemen and a coalman. Felixstowe had two drivers and firemen, and a man was sent out from Ipswich daily to do general labouring and tidying. Laxfield had two drivers and firemen, and a steam raiser.

The administration at Ipswich had to be tight. The stores were well run by a very good clerk, who kept the place clean and tidy. A major difference between now and the early 1950s is that there was then no budget, and the shedmaster was not financially accountable, except that if excessive overtime were being worked, he would be asked to explain. The number of operating staff required at the depot was calculated on the basis of a fixed number being needed for the amount of work involved in covering the number of running jobs done, such as the number of Ipswich–London turns. Artisan and conciliation staff levels were calculated on locomotive allocation and the requirements of the depot. In summer there were extra trains, and some of the younger men got driving turns.

There were three shed turners — drivers who did all the shunting around the shed: setting for the

Left: Ipswich Upper Yard on 11 February 1977, with Class 31/1 No 31 315 preparing to leave with a working for Derby Road, on the Felixstowe branch. Ipswich Goods Junction signalbox can just be seen on the extreme left.
I. P. Cowley

fitters and placing the locomotives correctly for going off shed the following day. Working conditions in the old depot at Ipswich were dreadful. There was no coaling plant, and coalmen stood on a truck and heaved coal directly into the tender. When the coal pile was getting low, the bucket loader would dig into the ground, and a mixture of coal with ash and chalk would be gouged out, which was hardly conducive to good steaming! The coalmen were in a strong bargaining position as much depended on them: they worked in shocking conditions and were pretty forceful at times.

The artisan staff were very good indeed, and both the Norwich and Ipswich men were high-quality craftsmen. There were three chargehand examining fitters who did the daily examinations of all the locomotives. It was no good their demanding a pit for this work —

there weren't any that were suitable! The old Eastern Union shed had very shallow pits, which weren't much use at all, and there was one disposal pit for the entire shed, which was usually full of hot ash. There were pits in the shed itself, but this was often full of locomotives. Examinations had to be carried out in the open, crawling in underneath or going over the top of the motion.

There had been several plans over the years to rebuild Ipswich depot, and the LNER had approved a scheme just before the outbreak of World War 2. A new wheeldrop and 70ft turntable were obtained from Ransomes & Rapier, which firm's works was served by the Griffin Wharf branch, but although the wheeldrop was installed the turntable had to wait until the war period. After that hostilities prevented the execution of the remainder of the scheme, though it was

Right: Class 08 No 08 708 shunts container flats in Ipswich Upper Yard on 16 April 1984. Brake vans and shunting locomotives are no longer to be found at this location, but the yard itself is busier than ever with container traffic and is to be extended. *Michael J. Collins*

Right: The view from over the east portal of Ipswich Tunnel towards the locomotive depot, recorded on 28 May 1966. The 14.30 Liverpool Street–Norwich is about to enter the tunnel, BR/Sulzer Type 2 No D5036 piloting a failed Brush Type 4, No D1781. At Ipswich English Electric Type 4 No D202 took over for the onward journey to Norwich. *G. R. Mortimer*

substantially to the LNER plans that the new depot was built. Reconstruction started in 1953, and during the work conditions were worse than ever, and standards slipped, though they were fully restored when the new depot started operating — and remained high until closure. By the end of the year a new wet ashpit, with a steam grab crane for ash removal, had been installed, together with the new 200-ton coaling plant, which was of modern reinforced concrete and stood over the inlet road. The wheel drop had been re-sited, equipment in the machine shop repositioned, and the new administrative and amenities block built, the last including first-aid and lecture rooms for ambulance and mutual-improvement classes.

Completed in 1954, the new depot featured a main shed with six roads, four in the running shed proper, and another two designated as the locomotive-repair bay. It was built of reinforced concrete and contained the proper inspection pits, lighting and so on — all the facilities that had been missing from the old depot. Part of the original building alongside was retained and refurbished, this becoming the machine shop. The new administrative and mess block was separated from the shed by the inlet and outlet roads, and itself had access from Wherstead Road, near the bridge where the Griffin Wharf branch passed over. In 1957 there were still 257 footplate staff, together with 151 workshop and shed staff, with 72 locomotives (including nine diesel shunters) allocated to Ipswich. The shedmaster was W. J. H. Pennell.

On 2 November 1959 Ipswich depot, which had been designed with the new form of traction in mind, became the first in the country to convert completely to diesels for both passenger and freight work, all the drivers (who numbered more than 200) having already been retrained. Among its allocation of 27 main-line locomotives, said to be replacing 60 steam engines, were Brush and North British Type 2s; there were also some 20-30 shunting locomotives. The sheds were modified for the diesels, and a locomotive washing plant was installed as late as 1963. Notwithstanding its modernity, the depot closed in 1968, the site thereafter remaining disused for many years; it has now disappeared under housing. Remaining work, such as refuelling, was transferred to part of the carriage sidings on the Norwich side of the tunnel, where a new administrative and mess block (still used today by Freightliner) was erected.

Above: On 5 March 1960 Class 03 No D2043 was on pilot duties at the country end of Ipswich station, being seen in charge of an elderly parcels van. *John C. Baker*

Norwich

Below: Norwich Thorpe
station is an imposing place,
as befits its status in such a
fine city. It is mainly of red
brick, with much stonework
as ornamentation, and has a
fine *porte cochère*. The
hipped roof on the right of
the domed section was
matched in the original
building to the left, but this
was destroyed during World
War 2 and has been rebuilt
in more recent times by
Railtrack. The forecourt has
undergone many phases of
remodelling, this being the
layout in the 1960s.
Ian Allan Library

The present-day passenger station opened in 1886
and replaced the original, which was then turned
over to goods usage. The main building, a lofty
structure in red brick with white Bath stone
dressing, featured a fine dome, and had a covered
colonnaded approach for carriages. The main
concourse was covered by a very high roof
supported on massive pillars and steelwork, with
much ornamentation on some of the supporting
brackets. Canopies extended along the platforms
providing considerable shelter; Platform 1 was
screened from the adjacent goods depot by a brick
wall. Refurbishment work took place in 1953
when a new ticket, seat reservation and enquiry
office was provided at a cost of £8,000. By this
time the station was issuing 500,000 tickets
annually (including 5,000 seasons), and 20,000
seat reservations. The Great Eastern main line still
rode high in the 'fastest trains' league with the
'Broadsman' covering the 46.3 miles from
Ipswich in 44 minutes, an average of 63.1mph.
Further reconstruction of the station waiting
rooms occurred in 1957. There were carriage
sidings next to Platform 6, and at the end nearer
the buffers, whilst the train control office was set
into the bank. Next to Platform 1 was a bay known
as the 'Royal dock', not for its use by Kings and
Queens but because the Royal Mail was loaded
there.

The area between the tracks going into the
passenger and goods stations was occupied by

Thorpe Station signalbox (which appeared on the
plans as 'Passenger Yard Signal Box') and the 70ft
turntable, installed in 1936 to replace a smaller
one. This was vacuum-operated, and all that was
needed was for the locomotive to be run onto it,
connect up the pipes and simply 'blow it round'.
Close by was the single-storey brick staff
accommodation block, which housed oil and tool
stores, a report room where drivers filled in details
of locomotive defects and the like, the fitters'
mess, cleaners' mess and the drivers' and
firemen's mess. Across the tracks into the goods
depot was the Goods Yard signalbox. The depot
had extensive facilities as befitted a city of
Norwich's importance. The shed boasted three
covered platforms, served by tracks joined in the
conventional manner, but also having another
running across its mouth at right angles, and
connected by a series of wagon turntables.
A separate structure covered a further two tracks,
and allowed direct loading or unloading between
rail and road vehicles. Rowntrees and Lyons had
depots; Shell-Mex and Charringtons had rail-
served oil terminals, and Boulton & Paul's private
siding handled large quantities of raw materials
and finished products from its joinery works; there
were the usual coal merchants, including Messrs
A. Dawnay and H. Parker.

The Norwich area had been a heavy user of
containers for freight for many years, much traffic
being associated with the Birds Eye factories at

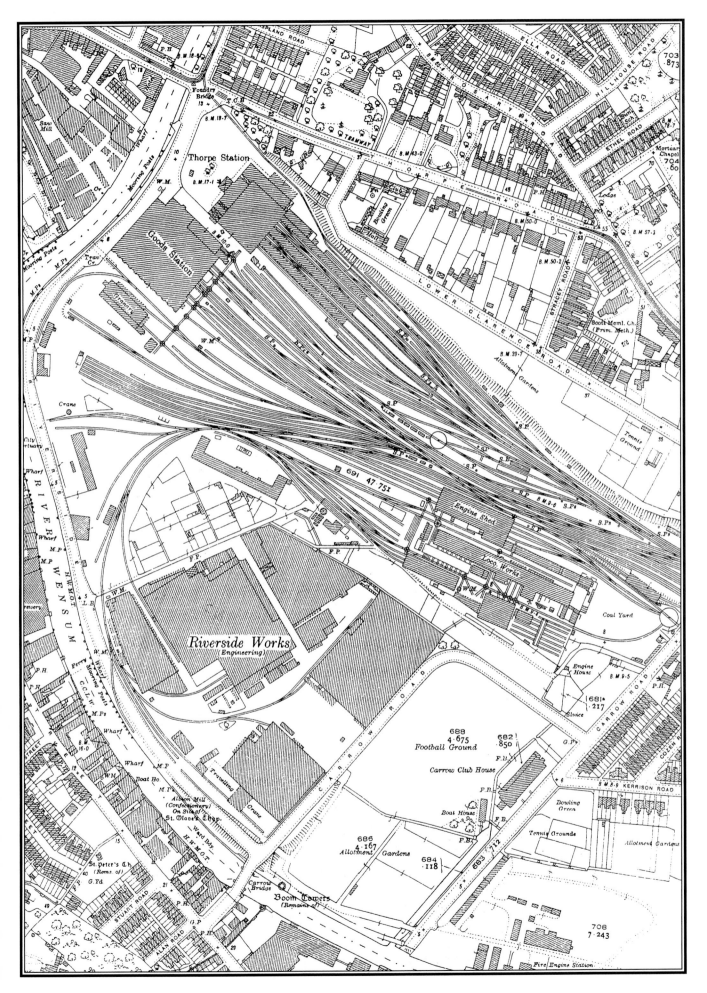

Above: An Edwardian view of Platforms 1 and 2 at Norwich, with another train standing at Platform 3 (right). *Lens of Sutton Association*

Right: Norwich Thorpe plays host to a pair of DMUs on 15 April 1982. At Platform 4 a Metro-Cammell Class 101 will form the 16.28 to Yarmouth, while a Cravens Class 105 waits to depart Platform 5 as the 16.14 to Ely. *Michael J. Collins*

Right: The concourse of Norwich Thorpe on 19 January 1991: 'Sprinters' and luggage lockers abound. The concourse has since been extensively remodelled, and the roof renovated. *David Pearce*

Left: In August 1953 'Britannia' No 70008 *Black Prince* waits to go on shed at Norwich, having brought in an express from Liverpool Street. Partially visible on the left is No 70009 *Alfred the Great*, ready to depart on an up working. *John Robertson*

Left: Monday 19 September 1983 finds Class 47/4 No 47 574 leaving for London while Class 03 No 03 180 potters about the yard. The passenger-yard 'box is in the background, while the old locomotive sheds are on the right. *Peter Doel*

Below: Class 47/0 No 47 010 passes the passenger-yard 'box with the 14.36 to Liverpool Street on a sunny 25 June 1975. The rolling stock is mostly early BR Mk 2, although there is a Mk 1 brake at the front. *Brian Morrison*

Right: The interior of
Norwich Thorpe Passenger
Yard 'box, recorded in
November 1979. *David
Pearce*

Lowestoft and Yarmouth. Originating goods also included boots, shoes, electrical appliances and Colmans' many products including mustard, Robinsons cordials and Wincarnis wines. Much seasonal traffic passed through Norwich and created its own demands on the locomotive depot. Whilst the summer saw very heavy passenger traffic to and from the coastal resorts, extra trains had to be run in the spring to carry fruit and vegetables, and there were heavy express fish workings during the autumn herring season. The western end of the layout was bounded by Riverside Road, separating it from the River Wensum, and at the other end was the somewhat tortuous Carrow Road. This crossed the railway by bridge 357, and nearby was the 55ft hand-operated turntable, a survivor from an earlier era. It could not handle the new 'Britannias', although the 'B12s' could be turned, provided that the

balance was exactly right. Engines frequently got stuck, and the crew would then have to summon three or four of their mates to give an extra push. This table connected with the coaling plant, whose huge concrete tower dominated the skyline of Norwich depot, and had been built in 1936. Prior to this there had been an affair of staging: coal trucks would be run up the bank behind it and their contents shovelled out, and then into tubs on rails, which would be run up to the locomotive and tipped. At least four men had been permanently employed on this coaling stage.

Locomotive coal in two classes arrived by the trainload from Whitemoor: ordinary for goods locomotives and best for passenger work. Wagons were stored on sidings by the coaling plant, and when required, one would be hauled up the side of the tower and its contents tipped bodily into the hopper. This also had the effect of tipping the oil

Left: Norwich had a large and important locomotive depot with a sizeable allocation of motive power. Class J15 0-6-0 No 65469 is turned in March 1960. *John C. Baker*

Left: By Saturday 14 January 1961 'B12' No 61572 was the last of its class but managed to remain active thanks to a shortage of motive power and the efforts of Norwich shedmaster Bill Harvey. In this view it is being shunted over a pit. *Colin P. Walker*

Below: Norwich MPD on 9 March 1980, with an assortment of locomotives in view. *David Pearce*

Right: Class N7 0-6-2T
No 69706 potters around
Thorpe station on 8 July
1952. *F. J. Saunders*

out of the axleboxes, so they had to be carefully checked and topped up after a visit to the plant. The hopper held about 250-300 tons of coal, which was enough to last through a day and the following morning. Coaling a locomotive involved positioning it under the plant, and the driver getting up via steps into the small control room. There was a moveable chute which could be positioned appropriately for the particular locomotive; the driver then operated the electrical controls which activated a slide, which released the coal into the chute. It took about four minutes to coal a locomotive using the plant, which was demolished in 1963.

The locomotive depot at Norwich had started with the arrival of the Yarmouth & Norwich Railway, which had opened for traffic in 1844. It constructed a long, low brick building with square central section and water tower over, and a four-road locomotive shed, and this remained until the depot finally closed with the transfer to Crown Point in the 1980s. The District Mechanical Engineer's office and ambulance room joined on at the south-east corner of this original structure. Another track coming from the depot turntable separated this from the shops: fitting, smithy and machine, and in Yarmouth & Norwich days this had also included the erecting shop. It had eight transverse pits, each with its corresponding doors; the overhead crane survived to the closure of the depot. For many years Norwich handled main works overhauls with the exception of new fireboxes, but this capability was downgraded in the 1930s. Later, when it became necessary to do heavier work on the 'Britannias' than was officially deemed possible, tools seemed to appear from various holes where they had lain hidden. Norwich and its men rose to the latest challenge.

The water-softening plant with its great upright cylinder was at the eastern end of this complex. Water was supplied to the site via a dyke from the river, which led into the reservoir from where it was pumped into the softener, a tall structure which removed the lime. Adjacent to this naturally enough were the sludge pits, formed with earth banks. After a few weeks in there the residues would set, and being mostly lime much of it was sold to farmers for spreading on their fields. A particular problem would arise when Boulton & Paul was galvanising and let the effluent run into the dyke, which caused the water to develop a thick foamy head, looking rather like Guinness. The locomotives would then prime very badly, having to be run with no more than a quarter glass of water. Even under normal circumstances and with treatment, they had to be washed out at least once a week because of the state of the water supply.

The various messes were at one end of the shops complex, each grade having its separate facilities. Beyond the softening plant and separated by another turntable road was the three-road locomotive repair shop, and the road motor engineer's depot, with the new canteen building in the angle formed by one of the doglegs in Carrow Road. It replaced all the former messes, and was for all grades. The running foreman's office was also there, and remained even after the opening of the new Crown Point depot. The timber yard and store adjoined this area, and in later years the new three-road diesel maintenance shed was built there. In 1945, when the 'B1s' (Nos 1042-52, with 1040/1 spare) had been allocated to Norwich, some had been single-manned only. This meant that they went to London and back with the regular crew, and then either sat around doing nothing or went with another set of men to Whitemoor and back (or similar), which rather defeated the object of having regular crews. This was changed to double-manning *c*1949.

From early in 1947 the renowned D. W. (Bill) Harvey took over as Shedmaster at Norwich, leaving only when steam finally departed in 1962. He had had long experience of a variety of depots, both on the LNER and in Nigeria, and moved to Norwich from the post of mechanical foreman at Cambridge. His long stay allowed a continuity of policy, which was lacking at some of the places regarded as training depots, such as Ipswich or Melton Constable, where men would remain in charge only a short time before moving on. He was very well liked and respected by the men under him, and he was especially skilled in matters relating to valves and their setting. He had much to do with the new 'Planned Servicing System' instituted in 1948 by L. P. Parker, Motive Power Superintendent first of the Eastern Section of the LNER's Southern Area, and later of the Western Section as well, this occurring after nationalisation. It permitted much greater precision in the provision of fitting and maintenance staff at depots by accurate monitoring of costs. It aimed to throw the emphasis onto preventive rather than curative work, and locomotives were regularly examined on their 'shed day'. This scheme was later superseded by the 'X examination' system, derived from LMS practice, but which was similar in general principle.

In 1958 there were about 400 enginemen at Norwich, and about 100 mechanical and workshop staff, including labourers. The traffic manager was responsible for all of these, and for the carriage & wagon and outdoor staff including the wheeltapper (examiner), who might be called out to carry out repairs to vehicles in transit, for example to a hot box. He was also responsible for the Plant & Machinery section, which covered items such as the turntable, coaler and water softener, and the running repairs section of the Road Motor department. The total staff numbered 796.

Norwich had a number of pilot engines. The Crown Point pilot was a three-shift duty (6.00am, 2.00pm and 10.00pm), and so worked round the clock. It was available for transfer trips to Thorpe or Trowse yards, but was mainly concerned with shunting its own yard. Long-distance freight trains would arrive from Whitemoor with items such as bricks, coal and general merchandise, which would be re-formed into local goods trains for Lowestoft, Yarmouth and Cromer, and also for the 'round the world' line from Wroxham to Dereham. There were two pilots at Thorpe, one operating continuously for yard shunting, and the other on two shifts for Boulton & Paul's siding and shunting the coal ground. The Trowse pilot dealt with traffic for Wymondham and Wells, Beccles via the Waveney Valley, and with cattle. This latter was important on Saturdays when up to three trains could be run to London following the sales. A Norwich crew would work 35 trucks with a six-coupled locomotive to Stratford, lodge, and return with the empties. These would then be cleaned and disinfected, and stored at Trowse ready for the next Saturday, though they might be used during the week for the carriage of other livestock such as pigs from Acle, where Harry Pointer was the main dealer, and the sale on a Thursday. Alternatively, a local station might ring up for a few trucks for a consignment.

Many trains conveyed horseboxes, which were passenger-rated, and stations such as Foulsham, Aylsham or Dereham would attach them to local trains. This often happened on Saturdays, and on arrival in Norwich they would be detached by the passenger pilot. This was also kept busy forming and re-forming trains, since numbers of them conveyed through coaches to places such as Yarmouth or Cromer. The Victoria pilot was booked to leave the locomotive depot light-engine at 4.30am on weekdays and run to Trowse, where it would pick up the wagons for Victoria. If there were more than about 30 of these it might require banking as far as Trowse Upper Junction by the Trowse pilot; the train would then be backed into Victoria. The pilot was then booked as being available for shunting from 6.15am 'until done'. The station dealt with coal — about a trainload a day — and general merchandise. Working between Trowse Yard or Thorpe and Victoria required reversal at Trowse Upper junction. As coal arrived via the Thetford line, trains would have a locomotive attached in the rear and be drawn back past Trowse Lower to Upper, where the train engine would take it over the crossover and down the branch. It was quite possible to see a 'Britannia' being dragged back up from Trowse on such a working.

Victoria retained much of the appearance of a passenger station right to the end. Passengers had approached through a relatively small building with an imposing entrance, with three tall arches and nameboard over them. The station had been built on the site of the Ranelagh Gardens, later the Victoria Gardens, and the main building had started life as the 'Pantheon', part of the gardens, and used for circuses and the like. It was converted to house the booking and luggage offices, and retained the lofty rotunda. The platforms were in a 'V' formation, each with a trainshed, though the effect was later spoiled by the cycle shed and odd bits of woodwork. The trainsheds over the platforms were wooden and covered with corrugated sheeting, and were later used for the loading and unloading of wagons. A brick water tower topped by an iron tank fed a column off the platform end, and to one side stood the goods shed, and then the coal roads.

Norwich today retains a great deal of its former importance, having had the new Crown Point depot built for locomotive, diesel-multiple-unit and carriage maintenance. The main-line service has been speeded up with electrification. Some of Norwich's radiating branches have gone, notably the Wells line, and the M&GN's City station is long closed. The main buildings have been extensively cleaned, rebuilt and refurbished, and the old locomotive sheds and workshops have gone, and buses have returned to the station forecourt to link Thorpe station with the shopping and business areas.

Right: The new diesel depot at Norwich was purpose-built and offered a clean, well-lit working environment, in stark contrast to the steam shed. Class 31/1 No 31 291 awaits attention over a pit in October 1982.
Ian Allan Library

Right: Multiple-units were also maintained at the new depot. Here a Cravens Class 105 receives attention in October 1982.
Ian Allan Library

Above: It was distinctly wintry at Norwich on 14 January 1987. Signal NO586 demonstrates why the red lamp is always the lowest; meanwhile a three-car Tyseley Class 117 DMU is unusual visitor.
David Pearce

Left: Norwich Thorpe on 30 May 1987: Class 86/2 No 86 245 *Dudley Castle* waits at the head of the 17.55 to Liverpool Street as Class 47/4 No 47 564 *Colossus* runs back out of Platform 4.
Michael McGowan

Cambridge

Cambridge station was a large and complex affair. The single main-line platform was on the down side, together with the station buildings. There were two bays at each end, whilst up through trains had to negotiate crossovers, either at the north end or in the centre of the station, to reach the platform. A great many rail routes radiated from Cambridge, apart from the main line. On the south side, trains could arrive via the Stour or Colne Valley lines from Mark's Tey and Colchester, from King's Cross and Hitchin via Royston, or via the LNWR — later LMS — route from Oxford and Bletchley. At the other end of the station trains left for Newmarket and Bury St Edmunds, the rural Mildenhall branch, which could also be reached via Newmarket, and the St Ives line, which also led to Ely and Huntingdon. Main-line trains generally used the through platform, although if they had too many coaches they might foul the central crossover and so cause severe congestion and some delays. Other services used the bays, so that LNWR trains usually ran from No 1, at the south end, which together with No 2 bay was also used by Liverpool Street stoppers, Haverhill branch services and some of the King's Cross buffet car expresses. The north end bays, Nos 5 and 6, were used by LMS trains to Kettering, together with workings to Newmarket and Mildenhall, and slow trains to Ely and March. Any of them might use the main platforms at off-peak times, although in the mid-1930s the half hour between 3.50 and 4.20pm saw a train leave via every route radiating from the station.

The main station building was a fine structure of buff brick, with a colonnade of 15 arches with square brick columns, each decorated with the coat of arms of a college. Its provenance is uncertain, and although Francis Thompson has been quoted, Sancton Wood and Henry Hunt were also involved. In the early days of the station vehicles and pedestrians could enter the colonnade from each end, although it was later blocked in and an awning built on the front of the station. The enclosed space was then used for functions such as the booking hall. In the 1980s British Rail carried out a great deal of refurbishment work and removed the awning, returning the building at least partly to its former appearance. The high ceilings in the booking hall retain their elegant appearance and can be fully enjoyed by passengers today. Various other buildings have gradually been added over the years, including the locomotive depot to the north and the coal yard (actually a goods yard) to the south. Spillers' factory was immediately to the west of the station. There were many private sidings on a number of sites, the proliferation encouraged by the fact that four pre-Grouping companies served the station, each having its own depot. The Great Northern had the Upper Yard (which became the coal yard), the London & North Western the yard to the west of Hills Road, the Midland was to the north of the station and locomotive depot, whilst the Great

Below: A view of the exterior of Cambridge station in GER days, featuring a fine collection of road vehicles, both motorised and horse-drawn. *Lens of Sutton Association*

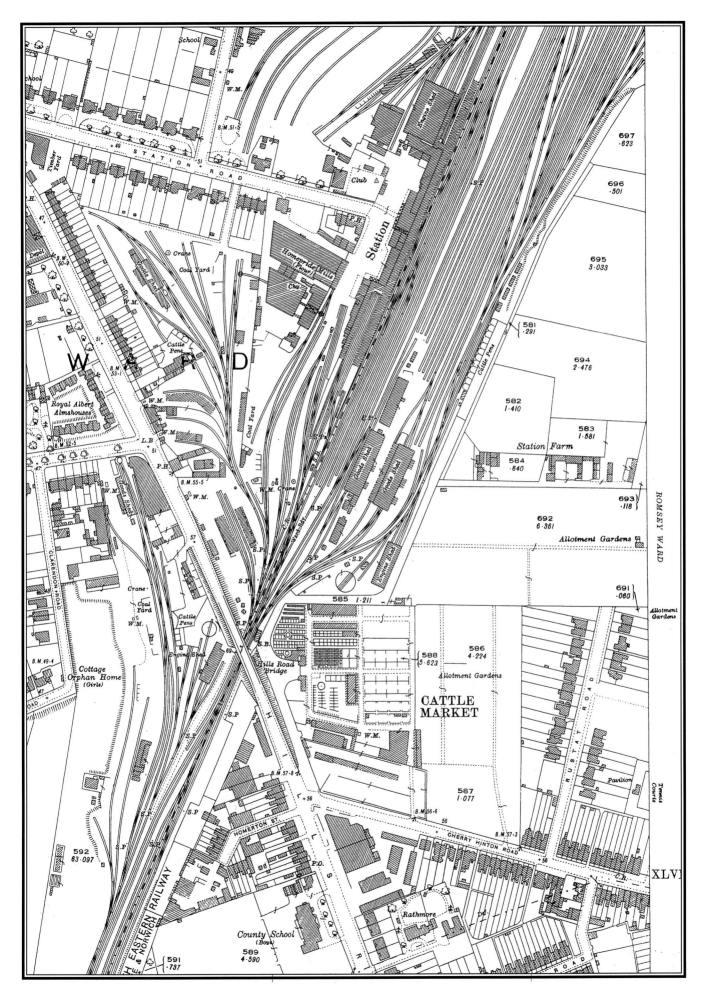

School

W.M.

B.M.51.5

STATION ROAD

Timber Yard

Club

L.P.H.

Station

Homepride Mills Flour

C.W.

697 ·623

696 ·501

695 3·033

Depot

B.M. 50·9

W.M.

Crane

Coal Yard

Cattle Pens

581 ·291

Cattle Pens

W A R D

W.M.

B.M. 53·1

Coal Yard

694 2·476

Royal Albert Almshouses

W.M.

W.M.

L.B.

P.H.

B.M.52·5

B.M.55·5

W.M. Crane

582 1·410

583 1·581

Station Farm

584 ·640

Goods Shed

Goods Shed

S.P.

Goods Shed

S.P.

S.P.

693 ·118

692 6·361

Allotment Gardens

ROMSEY WARD

Allotment Gardens

CLARENDON ROAD

W.M.

Crane

Coal Yard

W.M.

S.P.

Goods Shed

585 1·211

691 ·060

S.P.

S.B.

588 5·623

586 4·224

Cottage Orphan Home (Girls)

B.M. 49·4

Engine Shed

Hills Road Bridge

Allotment Gardens

CATTLE MARKET

RUSTAT ROAD

Pavilion

Tennis Courts

S.P.

B.M.57·8

+ 56

W.M.

587 1·077

B.M.56·6

B.M. 57·3

HOMERTON ST.

CHERRY HINTON ROAD

C.R.

XLVI

592 63·097

S.P.

S.P.

P.O.

Rathmore

GREAT EASTERN & NORWICH RAILWAY

County School (Boys)

589 4·590

591 ·737

ROAD

Above: This fine view of the exterior of Cambridge station was recorded on Christmas Day 1995, which explains the unnatural lack of people and traffic. The main building has been refurbished, and the original layout can still be appreciated. *Chris Burton*

Eastern itself occupied the very extensive yard on the east side of the station and main line. The locomotive depot took up considerable space immediately to the north of the passenger station, and although each of the pre-Grouping companies had its own facilities, in later years it provided motive power for all routes.

There was much discussion over the years about the need for a second platform at Cambridge, or indeed about the existence of one in the very early days. Cecil J. Allen asserted that when opened in 1845 the station was an island, with all the buildings on it, and connected to the 'mainland' by a footbridge for passengers and a tunnel for luggage. This, he said, led to much congestion, especially at the beginning and end of the university terms, so when the new station — essentially the present one — was opened in 1863 it had the present layout of a single long platform. This was certainly not the case, and in its edition of 23 August 1845 the *Cambridge Chronicle* inveighed against 'the single line of rails within the station itself', complaining that up and down trains arrived at the station together, so that they were sometimes held within sight of the station for up to a quarter of an hour. According to the Rev R. B. Fellows, quoted in *The Railway Magazine* in November 1935, it seems that the Eastern Counties had provided another island platform in 1850, replacing an earlier temporary construction. This was reached from the main station by a footbridge, and there was also a luggage tunnel. This was swept away in the Great Eastern's improvements of 1863, when the main platform was extended to 400 yards in length, with a new booking office located where the former entrance and luggage tunnel had been.

By the end of the 19th century the Great Eastern had decided greatly to extend the station. Traffic to and from Newmarket in connection with the races was very heavy — and growing — and, because horse traffic arrived by any of the lines, required a great deal of shunting. The Newmarket line was reached by a tightly curved track crossing all through roads immediately at the end of the north-facing bay platforms (which were much shorter than they are now), access being possible to the bays and up and down main lines, as well as the up-side sidings. The first move in improving the station was to relocate the Newmarket line completely, so that the junction moved nearly half a mile north, to Coldham Lane. This was located at Coldham's Lane Crossing, later replaced by a bridge, Coldham's Lane Junction already existing a quarter of a mile to the south. The new line rejoined the old about half a mile from the junction, and was opened in May 1896. Note that the railway always referred to it as 'Coldham' whilst Ordnance Survey and other maps call it 'Coldham's'.

In 1906 the Great Eastern decided to extend the platform by some 270ft, widen it by 11ft, and to raise it to the standard height. The platform widening was achieved by removing the down main line and extending the platform into the space created, with consequent track realignments elsewhere. From the platform these became the two passenger running lines — up and down, two continuous carriage sidings, two through goods roads, and two separate up and down goods reception roads. New sidings were provided at Mill Road and Coldham Lane junctions. Re-signalling was proposed, but did not take place until the 1920s.

The booking hall, waiting rooms and parcels offices were enlarged, and new awnings erected over the widened platform. It took some time to complete the work, and it was not finished until 1909. The Great Northern had its own offices, waiting rooms and entrance from the road, and used the south-facing bay nearest the road, now Platform 3. The London & North Western used the adjacent platform (now No 2) and together with the Midland used the Great Eastern's passenger facilities at the station. Note that the bays were previously numbered 1 and 2.

A significant event at Cambridge in 1922 involved the construction of an entire temporary

Left: A pair of ex-Great Eastern 2-4-0s wait to leave Cambridge for Newmarket in April 1952. No 62786 pilots 62788 on the 10.30am departure from Platform 5. *W. Temple*

Left: The GER station at Cambridge. An up train is at the main platform, and the two south-facing bays are also occupied. *Lens of Sutton Association*

Left: Passengers wait for a train at the south end of Cambridge station in the late 19th century. *Lens of Sutton Association*

Right: The centre of Cambridge station, showing the crossover and signalbox. Note the luggage and the conical milk churns on the trolleys. *Lens of Sutton Association*

Below: Class 47 No 1579 leaves Cambridge with a Summer Saturday train to Birmingham New Street in July 1972. The goods yards remain busy with a variety of traffic. *I. J. Hodson*

station in connection with the Royal Agricultural Show. The showground was located close to the Trumpington Long Lane level crossing, and the station was built between the Great Eastern and LNWR lines. A reception road on the up side was extended and given a 500ft side platform, whilst on the down side a platform was also built alongside an extended reception road, but this time 45ft wide and with another siding laid on its other face. This platform was connected to Long Road, and the whole controlled by Trumpington 'box. Temporary intermediate block signalboxes were provided between Shepreth Branch Junction and Trumpington, and between Chesterton Junction and Waterbeach, signalling being provided by men under the instruction of the signalmen. Many special trains were run by all the companies serving Cambridge — GER, Great Northern, Midland and LNWR. Livestock trains immediately before and after the show required careful timetabling, and included 25 trains on Saturday 1 July and 22 on the Sunday, coming from all parts of the country. Another 17 specials ran on the Monday, and the show was open to the public from Tuesday 4 July to Saturday 8 July. Return fares at single prices were on offer from stations up to 60 miles away, and at single plus a third from further afield. To cater for the evening attractions in Cambridge, including fêtes at St John's and Trinity colleges, a river pageant, water sports and flower shows, late evening trains were also laid on.

Major resignalling work was undertaken in 1926 by the LNER in the Cambridge area. What was described as an 'all-electric dynamic indication power signalling installation' was brought into use between 20 June and 19 September. It consisted of two new signalboxes (Cambridge North and Cambridge South) which replaced five earlier mechanical 'boxes. North, by

Below: Class 31 No D5522 passes through a forest of semaphore signals as it leaves Cambridge with an up freight on 3 April 1970. *J. H. Cooper-Smith*

Above: 'D15' 4-4-0 No 8896
and 'E4' 2-4-0 No 7490
stand at Cambridge on
12 September 1936.
E. R. Wethersett collection

the Mill Road bridge and exit from the locomotive depot, had 72 levers and South, by the Hills Road bridge, had 128. The new installation was based on the British Power Signalling Co's system, powered by 110V accumulator batteries. Both 'boxes featured miniature levers with the electrical interlocking housed below the operating floor. Both had 'doll's eye' track diagrams. The single platform with scissors crossover halfway along made the interlocking arrangements between the two cabins particularly complex, and colour light signals were used under the awnings on the platforms, being felt to be more convenient. Prior to this there had been signalboxes at each end of the platform, North End and South End, the platform stretching the entire distance between them of 22 chains — just over a quarter of a mile.

Behind Platform 6 was the locomotive depot, the end of which was a high wall; this is still there today, while in the car park can be seen the bricked-up doorways. There were seven roads, of which No 7 still exists. The depot was always busy with men coming on and off duty to and from the stores and so on. There were about 100 locomotives allocated, plus the inevitable 'visitors' — March locomotives were often 'borrowed', especially at weekends if they had worked in on goods trains.

Alongside the shed was the 'new' admin block containing offices, mess rooms and so on. From

the country end were the shedmaster's office, list clerk's office and running foreman's office, with mess rooms beyond these. Lastly was the lobby where the men had to go to sign on and read the notices. Inside the lobby door were two rows of desks with sloping tops, with a double-sided board for notices, including water notices, between them. Speed restrictions, engineering work etc were in the weekly notices book. There were also two windows in the lobby: one, on the left, into the office used by the foreman and his assistant, and the other, on the right, for the timekeeper.

The crew then had to find their locomotive. The fireman would go to the oil store and draw four pints of engine oil, two pints of black oil, a can of paraffin for the lamps and a can of red oil for the gauge lamp — unlike paraffin this didn't catch fire. The black oil went in the lubricator or the sight-feed if steam lubrication were in use.

Cambridge had a hot-water washout plant, which was mostly worked by Poles, who wore clogs because of the hot water. At the far (station) end was the office used by the fitter/foreman and also the firebox man; he re-riveted stays, renewed brick arches if necessary and cleaned the tube plate. Then there was the cleaners' foreman, who also had a loft with cleaning materials, including cloths, scrapers and paraffin. The Pay Office was part of the Locomotive General office block, and was at the front of the shed near the station. There was also a large office opposite for Cambridge

Above: Having stopped for water at Cambridge, Class B12 No 61572 gets underway again with its schools special to Liverpool Street in May 1961.
G. D. King

control, whose windows and doors were protected by steel blast doors which had been installed in wartime. Below ground level was a furnace which heated the mess rooms and may also have served the hot-water washout plant. Another old locomotive boiler and firebox was used for sand-drying. Water at Cambridge was piped from Chesterton Junction, and there was a tank near Mill Road Bridge. Locomotives left the shed by way of a headshunt which stopped just short of the North signalbox, and then reversed into the station. The points for this were released from the 'box, and the hand lever was pulled by the fireman. Locomotives coming into the depot could go to either of the disposal pits or, to avoid them, around the 'half moon' (which was near the sand bin and dryer), taking water at the column there, and thence as instructed.

Tenison Field was a goods yard to the west of the shed, with a number of traffic sources including coal, timber and tiles. There were also bike sheds here. A train of empties was regularly sent from here, made of various small lots, and often extended across the unofficial walking route to and from the shed, so great care had to be taken if ducking under it, which was against the rules. There was a footbridge — the official route — and this was used by older men who couldn't duck under the couplings.

The up and down goods yards were both to the east of the station. Both had reception roads and were used by trains depending on the direction from which they came. The down was nearer to the passenger station, and there was one exchange road between the two yards. Through goods trains simply used the goods roads. Behind Platform 3 were the 'coal fields', which — despite their name — handled general goods traffic, although this included some coal. The name probably came from a much earlier yard.

There were many pilots. The up and down yards each had one, as did the coal fields. The Trumpington pilot handled mostly North Western traffic, but in British Railways days this had become a Cambridge job. There was a Tenison Field and ashpit pilot, which also kept the coaling tower coaled, and took the empties away. Ash was thrown out into wagons in a sunken road, and it could then be difficult to pull them out: a 'J20' was often used, to give the extra power. There were three carriage pilots (north end, south end and middle), which were mostly 'E4s', although occasionally a 'Claud' was used, especially at the north end. Other pilots included 'J69s' Nos 8530 and 8645 and, later, Nos 8600 and 8609, which came from Thaxted after the branch closed. All pilot engines had to go into the shed for 'requirements' and would thus be absent from their duties for 45 minutes or so, during which time they took coal and water. It was a long way to go for the 'coal field' or Trumpington pilot.

Train Services

The railways out of Liverpool Street carried a wide variety of services, not forgetting the goods trains via the East London line. The London terminus has always been noted for the intensity of its suburban workings, and the story of the 'Jazz' trains has been recounted many times. Much had been done to encourage workmen's trains by offering low fares, and later tram competition drove this further. Suffice it to say here that the Great Eastern was not one of the country's most prosperous concerns, and although electrification was considered it was not implemented. Perhaps some of the blame must be laid at the door of James Holden, the company's locomotive superintendent from 1885 to 1907, who designed the famous (or possibly infamous) 'Decapod' 0-10-0 locomotive, of prodigious power and axle loading, in a successful attempt to persuade his directors that anything electric traction could do, steam could do better. The GER thus ran a suburban service of great intensity at very tight headways and using diminutive steam locomotives, and which necessitated the use of the Westinghouse system in order to give the braking characteristics demanded for the rapid station stops. This was retained by the LNER, even though it made the vacuum brake standard elsewhere after the 1923 Grouping. The LNER did make a start on electrification in the late 1930s, but this was interrupted by war, and was not inaugurated until the British Railways era. The wires spread slowly, finally reaching Norwich and King's Lynn, although diesel trains were still working regularly into the terminus at the start of 2009.

Trains initially operated from a temporary station at Mile End, extended to the terminus at Shoreditch in 1840, and itself replaced in stages by Liverpool Street. The line was extended from Bethnal Green to Bishopsgate Low Level on 4 November 1872, on to Liverpool Street for suburban services on 2 February 1874, and the terminus was finally opened to all traffic on 1 November 1875. It was extended in 1894, when the east-side station was added on a 6-acre site, bringing the number of platforms to 18. It was extensively rebuilt in the 1980s and '90s, with platforms extended, the roof reglazed and new trainsheds built to match the old. At the same time the old Broad Street terminus of the North London Railway was demolished, but unfortunately the opportunity to provide extra tracks to Bethnal Green was not taken.

Great Eastern services had never been among the real flyers, and there were many rude remarks about the lines going right back to Eastern Counties days: that company was a favourite target of local newspapers and *Punch*, among others. After the vicissitudes of the Eastern Counties' era, the Great Eastern gradually established a solid reputation for reliability. By 1887 the suburban services as far as Chelmsford had settled into a pattern of stopping trains as far as Romford or Brentwood, usually all stations including Globe Road and Coborn Road, with those calling at Chelmsford usually having fewer stops at the inner stations, and giving a roughly hourly service. There remained a very few trains from Fenchurch Street, such as the 10.30am and 5.35pm all-stations to Romford, with corresponding up trains. There was also a frequent GER service from Fenchurch Street to Forest Gate and Ilford. Shenfield & Hutton was not yet a junction, of course, the line to Wickford not opening until 19 November 1888, and on to Southend Victoria on 1 October 1889.

Chelmsford was served by longer-distance trains, of course, although trains that called at few stations nearer to London often turned into stoppers the further away they went. The 5.10am from Liverpool Street made its first call at Chelmsford at 5.55am , then Colchester (6.26am), Manningtree, Ipswich and most stations to Norwich. There were relatively few very fast trains: the 10.0am called at Chelmsford, Colchester, Ipswich, Stowmarket, Tivetshall (not Diss), Forncett and Trowse before reaching Norwich Thorpe at 1.15pm, whilst the 10.25am ran fast to Ipswich, then to Beccles where it divided for Lowestoft and Yarmouth South Town. The 4.0pm called only at Colchester *en route* to Ipswich, where it divided, with one portion going fast to Beccles, where it again divided for Yarmouth (7.15pm) and Lowestoft (7.10pm), and the other calling at principal stations to Lowestoft, arriving at 7.50pm. Some long-distance trains still served Norwich Victoria, including the 9.3 from Liverpool Street, which was semi-fast to Ipswich, and then Needham and all stations, arriving at 1.3pm. The Victoria service was generally stopping trains from Ipswich, or from Beccles via the Waveney Valley line and Tivetshall.

By the dawn of the 20th century the Great Eastern had established a schedule of express services over both its main lines, and these included trains to and from St Pancras as well as Liverpool Street. The route for the former was via Kentish Town and Highgate Road station onto the Tottenham & Hampstead Joint line and thence via

Tottenham West and North junctions to Tottenham and the former Northern & Eastern route. Even at this stage, the Norwich trains were generally much faster via Ipswich, because they made frequent stops at stations between Ely and Norwich on the Cambridge route. Trains to Yarmouth and Lowestoft via the East Suffolk were notorious for the difficulties of working via that line because of its severe gradients, and it was always regarded as the hardest section of the Great Eastern.

By 1910 — often regarded as the golden age of rail travel — matters had not changed greatly. The 'East Anglian' was advertised as a 'Luncheon Car' train to Yarmouth South Town; timed to leave Liverpool Street at 11.45am, it arrived at Yarmouth at 4.12pm and included a portion for Norwich Victoria, reached at 3.43pm. The up 'Dining Car' train left South Town at 6.5am, the Norwich portion being from Thorpe at 6.22am, and reached London at 9.25am. The 2.22pm from Liverpool Street called at Stratford, Chelmsford, Witham, Kelvedon, Mark's Tey and Colchester (4.40pm), where it joined with the 3.20pm non-stop from Liverpool Street to go forward to Norwich Thorpe (5.57pm) but with portions for the East Suffolk as well. The restaurant-car service between Cromer and London was well established, the 4.55pm down (Cromer at 8.48pm) and 8.0am up (Liverpool Street at 11.25am) being examples; the latter conveyed a Bury portion from Ipswich. The Continental trains to and from the Harwich branch also carried prestigious American traffic including the Continental express from Antwerp and the Hook of Holland express, departing Parkeston Quay at 6.0am and 6.30am respectively, the latter including breakfast cars for the 90-minute journey.

Further in towards London the Southend trains provided a roughly hourly service to and from Shenfield, supplementing those to Chelmsford, which were much more frequent than in earlier years. On a few occasions inner stations were served by slip coaches, such as Shenfield, where the 4.18pm from Liverpool Street to Colchester slipped carriages at 4.56pm, and the 5.30pm to Colchester, which slipped coaches for Ingatestone at 6.10pm. There were a few trains for Woodford via Ilford and the Fairlop loop.

In March 1914 the Great Eastern appointed as its new General Manager Henry Thornton, previously General Superintendent of the Long Island Railroad. He replaced Walter Hyde, who had carried the can for the fact that the Midland Railway had purchased the London, Tilbury & Southend company from under the GER's nose. One of Thornton's first acts was to inaugurate the 'Radical Alterations' timetable on 4 October 1914, shortly after the outbreak of war in August. New fast mid-day services were introduced to Norwich and the coastal resorts of Lowestoft, Yarmouth and Cromer, which had previously only had such trains in the peak summer months. Timings were generally cut and speeds increased, and the allowances for station working, including attaching and detaching portions, drastically cut.

Some of the changes proved too ambitious, and the war certainly didn't help, but it was a bold attempt to make a step change, and its standards were not again reached by the LNER until nearly the outbreak of World War 2.

In LNER days it was the East Coast main line that stole the timetable thunder, and it was accorded the honour of occupying Table 1 in the company's book of passenger services. The Great Central line out of Marylebone ranked second, in Table 2, with the Great Eastern lines to Norwich via Ipswich as Table 3, and Norwich via Cambridge Table 4. The Great Eastern itself had run much further afield with its services from Liverpool Street to Doncaster and York, using the Great Northern & Great Eastern Joint line, and there were also the long-distance boat trains serving Harwich, the last of which — the 'European' — lasted well into British Railways days.

Electrification for the suburban services was again considered in the years preceding World War 2 but was postponed through lack of finance and the outbreak of hostilities. The first part was finally implemented on 9 November 1949, when the resignalling of Liverpool Street was finished; the regular-interval electric service to Gidea Park and Shenfield had been introduced on 26 September. The opening ceremony had been performed by Alfred Barnes, the Minister of Transport, who first cut the ceremonial ribbon across one of the entries of one of the new sliding-door electric sets (later designated Class 306) and then drove the unit. The ceremony did not go without incident, as Gerard Fiennes related in *I Tried to Run a Railway*. He was then District Superintendent and was charged on the day with showing the Minister the controls. Having got him seated in the driver's cab he was 'halfway through the instruction when Alfred said "Do you mean like this?" and notched up the controller. Off we went, all doors still open; half the party was still on the platform. Luckily we had throughout control of the doors.' Those left behind from this inaugural trip had an extra hour in the bar, and were apparently not too upset!

The electrification system adopted at this time was 1,500V DC overhead, later converted to 25kV AC, with parts using 6.25kV where clearances could not easily be obtained for the higher voltage. Subsequently the whole system was converted to the 25kV standard, partly in the light of the experience gained with the experimental work on the Clacton and Walton lines. The new electric trains were an immediate success, and with tight diagramming and good passenger loadings became among the most profitable on the Eastern Region. The off-peak service pattern for the electrics was to run all-stations from Liverpool Street to Gidea Park at 10, 30 and 50 minutes past each hour, with Shenfield trains (calling at Stratford, Ilford, Romford, then all stations) at 5, 25 and 45 minutes past the hour. This varied in the peaks, of course, and between 5.0pm and 5.59pm in the winter 1951 timetable there were 18 electric departures scheduled from Liverpool Street.

In 1955 a £2½ million scheme to electrify the lines from Shenfield to Chelmsford and Southend Victoria was inaugurated. The 9-mile section on the main line saw the opening ceremonies on Friday 8 June 1956, with a special train from Chelmsford to Shenfield and back on which travelled Sir Reginald Wilson, the Eastern Region General Manager, and members of his board, together with Assistant General Manager A. J. White, the Bishop of Chelmsford, the Mayor of Chelmsford, the Vice-Lieutenant of Essex and the High Sheriff of Essex. The Mayor drove the train for part of the way on the return journey. It is interesting to note that the party also had a run — from Chelmsford to Hatfield Peverel and back — in one of the new Metropolitan-Cammell diesel multiple-units which were about to be introduced to replace certain local steam-hauled services between Chelmsford and Colchester. Suburban services on the other ex-Great Eastern lines from Liverpool Street, including Chingford, Enfield, Hertford East and Bishop's Stortford had to wait much longer for electrification, not being wired until 1960.

The electrification to Chelmsford extended 22 trains from Shenfield, thus providing through services with Ilford, Romford and so on. The pattern of off-peak electric trains from Liverpool Street at this time was something like this:

Every 20 minutes — all stations to Gidea Park

Hourly to Stratford, Ilford, Romford and all stations to Chelmsford

Hourly to Shenfield and stations to Southend

Twice an hour to Stratford, Ilford, Romford and all stations to Southend

There were various peak-hour extras, and certain stations continued to be served by longer-distance steam trains, such as some of the express services to Norwich and beyond which called at Chelmsford. The Clacton 'interval' expresses called at Shenfield and Chelmsford, thus providing the former with one of its few refreshment car services. This service had begun with the summer timetable for 1950, when regular hourly expresses had started running throughout the day, each conveying a buffet car and taking between 106 and 126 minutes for the journey. Prior to this, in the 1946 summer timetable, for example, portions of the first through train left Walton and Clacton (the former including a buffet car and running via Frinton and Kirby Cross) at 7.53am and 8.0am respectively, combining at Thorpe-le-Soken; the train arrived at Liverpool Street at 9.41am, having called intermediately only at Chelmsford. The next was at 9.8am from Clacton and called at all stations, including St Botolphs, to Colchester North, taking over three hours for the journey. And that was it for the through service to London!

The interval service revolutionised matters, and even though the trains ran at about three-hourly intervals in the winter timetable this was a vast improvement on what had gone before. They also called at Marks Tey, connecting there for the Cambridge and Bury St Edmunds lines, and sometimes at other intermediate points such as Witham. They were usually limited to nine or even eight bogies, and would be hauled by a 4-6-0 locomotive such as a 'B12'. In the 1955/6 winter timetable there were seven through trains in each direction on weekdays and two more on Saturdays, though these did not all include buffet cars; certainly the 11.15pm from Liverpool Street did not. The best time was 103 minutes, by the 7.40am up from Clacton.

Longer-distance services had taken some time to recover after the war. The 1946 summer timetable showed the service getting back to some semblance of normality, but more in terms of the numbers of trains rather than their scheduled speed, and the term 'express' may have caused one or two wry smiles. The 4.25am from Liverpool

---

REGULAR INTERVAL SERVICE
LONDON (Liverpool Street)
AND
CLACTON-ON-SEA

WEEKDAYS

DEPARTURES FROM

London (Liverpool Street)		Clacton-on-Sea	
MONDAYS TO FRIDAYS	SATURDAYS ONLY	MONDAYS TO FRIDAYS	SATURDAYS ONLY
am	am	am	am
8 43	8 36	8 14	8 16
9 A41	9 36	8 A55	9 0
10 36	10 36	9 54	10 0
11 H36	11 36	10 A54	11 0
		11 A56	noon
			12 0
pm	pm	pm	pm
12 36	12 40	12 54	1 0
1 A36	1 40	1 A54	2 0
2 A36	2 36	2 56	3 0
3 36	3 39	3 55	4 0
4 36	4 B36	5 A 0	5 0
5 40	5 36	6 0	6 0
6 36	6 36	6 H59	7 C 0
7 A36	7 36	8 A 0	8 0
9 A36	9 36		

A—23rd June to 5th September.

B—Not after 6th September.

C—28th June to 6th September.

H—Not after 5th September.

Buffet Car facilities are provided except on the following trains—

From **London (Liverpool Street)**

Mondays to Fridays 8 43 am, until **20th June** 11 H36 am and 9 A36 pm

Saturdays only 8 36 am, 9 36 pm

From **Clacton-on-Sea**

Mondays to Fridays 6 0 pm, 6 H59 pm and 8 A0 pm

Saturdays only 6 0 pm, 7 C0 pm and 8 0 pm

Seats are reservable in advance at London (Liverpool Street) and Clacton-on-Sea with certain exceptions. Fee 2s. 0d. per seat.

For further details of these and other services between London (Liverpool Street) and Clacton-on-Sea, Frinton-on-Sea and Walton-on-Naze, see Tables 5 and 27.

Street reached Norwich at 8.40am, although it did call at all 13 stations between Ipswich and Norwich; the first express from Liverpool Street was the 8.12am and called at Shenfield, Chelmsford, Witham, Colchester, Ipswich, Diss, Tivetshall and Norwich, where arrival was at 11.22am. The 10.00am was slightly faster and omitted Tivetshall but added Mark's Tey. The 12.30pm reached Norwich at 3.6pm, calling only at Ipswich; the 1.0pm was a through train to Holt, and carried a restaurant car to Norwich, arriving at 4.40pm. As well as the intermediate stops already mentioned it also called at Mellis. The 3.40pm called only at Ipswich on its way to Norwich and included a restaurant car as far as Cromer; the 4.18pm covered most of the main stations mentioned. The 5.6pm provided a similar service, reaching Norwich at 8.25pm, and was followed at 6.40pm by a restaurant car train to Ipswich and Norwich only. The last through train of the day was at 7.20pm and gave a more leisurely journey, calling also at Ingatestone and Hatfield Peverel.

The up service included expresses leaving Norwich at 7.50am, 8.45am, 10.10am, 11.50am, 2.15pm, 4.0pm and 6.45pm and offered the daunting possibility of catching the 7.20pm all-stations to Liverpool Street, where it was scheduled to arrive at 37 minutes past midnight! Departure at 11.35pm was also possible, connecting with the Postal from Peterborough at Haughley, and arriving in London at 4.5am. A similar journey was possible in the other direction. Generally speaking the service was handled by one or other of the 4-6-0 types then available — the '1500s' (the original Holden 'B12s'), the 'Sandringhams' (Gresley's 'B17s') or the 'Bongos' (the Thompson 'B1s').

Gerard Fiennes had been District Superintendent at Stratford since late in 1944, moving to Liverpool Street in 1948 as Assistant Superintendent; he had presided over the hugely successful new electric service out to Shenfield. He next turned his attention to the main lines had little in the way of improved schedules having been achieved since Thornton introduced the Great Eastern's 'Radical Alterations' of 1922. True, there had been the new 'East Anglian' just before the war, but that was just one train with limited load. Fiennes and his assistant Stuart Ward set about devising a timetable that would combine high speed, the minimum number of stops, and the maximum number of miles per locomotive and set of carriages. They soon realised that the existing locomotives were the limiting factor: they could climb Brentwood Bank at no more than 40mph. Salvation came in the shape of the proposed new Standard 4-6-2 locomotives, later to become known as 'Britannias', around which the new timetable was built.

The 1951/2 winter timetable showed the fruits of the new timings: the 8.30am down was scheduled to take only 2 hours 53 minutes. Named trains had reappeared some time before, such as the 'Norfolkman', which now left London at 9.30am and called only at Ipswich on its way to

Norwich, where arrival was at 11.40am. It then continued to North Walsham, whence the main train with restaurant car went to Cromer High, and the remainder to Sheringham via Mundesley. The train had been inaugurated on 27 September 1948 at Liverpool Street station, and as the *Eastern Region Magazine* commented: 'A unique feature of the inaugural ceremony of this train was that it was officially despatched from London by a provincial Mayor. Arrangements had been made for London's Lord Mayor to officiate and for the Mayor of Ipswich to travel with the train; also for the Lord Mayor of Norwich, Mr W. G. Cutbush, to meet the train on arrival at Norwich. At the last moment the Lord Mayor of London, Sir Frederick Wells, was unable to attend owing to an unfortunate indisposition, and the honour of giving the "Norfolkman" its inaugural "right away" at 10.0am fell to the Mayor of Ipswich, Alderman J. B. Cunningham.' The Eastern Region saw the train as complementing the recently reintroduced 'East Anglian'; it either gave a 'night

THE NORFOLKMAN

LONDON (Liverpool Street), IPSWICH, NORWICH, CROMER and SHERINGHAM

WEEKDAYS

	E	S		E	S
	am	am		pm	pm
London (Liverpool St.)..dep	9 30	9 30	Sheringham . .. ..dep	4 24	4 24
Ipswich .. ..arr	10 46	10 54	West Runton .. .. ,,	4 29	4 29
,, ...dep	10 49	10 57	Cromer (Beach) .. .. ,,	4 42	4 42
Norwich (Thorpe).. ..arr	11 40	11 47	North Walsham (Main).. ,,	5 5	5 5
Wroxham .. .. .. ,,	12 10	12 10	Worstead .. .. .. ,,	5 11	5 11
North Walsham (Main).. ,,	12 22	12 22	Wroxham .. .. .. ,,	5 19	5 19
Gunton .. .. ,,	12 33	12 33	Norwich (Thorpe) .. ,,	5 45	5 45
Cromer (Beach) .. .. ,,	12 47	12 47	Ipswich .. ..arr	6 36	6 38
West Runton .. .. ,,	1 2	1 2	,, ...dep	6 38	6 41
Sheringham .. .. .. ,,	1 6	1 6	London (Liverpool St.)..arr	7A55	8 6

A—On Fridays arrives 7 58 pm
E—Except Saturdays
S—Saturdays only

Restaurant Car available between London (Liverpool Street) and Sheringham.

Passengers travelling from London (Liverpool Street), Sheringham and Cromer (Beach), and also from Norwich (Thorpe) to Ipswich and London (Liverpool Street), by this service can reserve seats in advance on payment of a fee of 2s. 0d. per seat.

Above: The down 'East Anglian' on Brantham Bank, north of Manningtree, in the capable hands of 'Britannia' Pacific No 70006 *Robert Burns* on 6 June 1951. Marshalled immediately behind the locomotive (as it had been on the up working) is a dynamometer car, collecting data prior to the acceleration of services.
G. R. Mortimer

Below: A fine view of 'Britannia' Pacific No 70002 *Geoffrey Chaucer* on the viaduct near Mark's Tey with the down 'Norfolkman' on 11 June 1951. *C. W. Footer*

in London' or allowed London businessmen the chance to visit Ipswich or Norwich in a day, with reasonable time to conduct their business at either place. The return train left Norwich at 5.0pm and reached London at 7.20pm. It was then typically hauled by one of the 'Bongos' (Class B1 4-6-0s) and consisted of eight coaches, full reservation and restaurant facilities being available in both directions, and completed the journey to Norwich at an average speed of just over 51mph.

The rest of the 1951/2 winter express timetable had been similarly converted to departures at half-past the hour, and these were at 9.30am (the 'Norfolkman'), 10.30am, 12.30pm 1.30pm and 3.30pm to Cromer, the last being the 'Broadsman'. Like the 'Norfolkman', this went to Holt and Cromer High, the train dividing at North Walsham. The 11.30am Saturdays-only ran to Norwich, the 4.30pm was a Norwich train, and the 5.30pm a Cromer; the 7.30pm also terminated at Norwich. Between these, at 6.30pm, was the 'East Anglian', which had been inaugurated on 27 September 1937 to provide a Mondays-Friday service between London and Norwich at an

average speed of over 51mph. It had been suspended for seven years because of the war, being reintroduced on 7 October 1946, using the same six coaches that had been specially designed by Gresley and which had attracted so much interest when they first appeared. It was seen as a train for businessmen, the up departure being at 11.45am from Norwich. Morning meetings in Ipswich or Norwich could be followed by a meal on the train, afternoon meetings in the capital, and an evening meal on the return journey. Two of the 'Sandringham' (Class B17) 4-6-0s — Nos 2859 *East Anglian* and 2870 *City of London* (later Nos 61659 and 61670 respectively) — had been streamlined in 1935, prior to its introduction. This was a Norwich working, and each locomotive was allocated two regular crews working alternate duties.

In the up direction the service from Norwich had been similarly rearranged, the 'Broadsman' departing at 7.45am, Cromers at 8.45 and 9.45am, the 'East Anglian' at 11.45am, a Melton Constable at 1.45pm, Norwich at 2.45 and 3.45pm, Cromer at 4.45pm, the 'Norfolkman' at 5.45pm (arriving

in London at 7.55pm) and a Cromer at 6.45pm. The trains were now both heavier and faster, the fastest trains carrying nine or 10 coaches instead of eight, and taking exactly two hours for the journey. On the other hand the 7.23pm all-stations to Ipswich connected there for London, now arriving as early as 12.7am! Restaurant car facilities were offered on several trains, including most of the named expresses. In 1951 a full breakfast on the up 'Broadsman' would have cost 4s 6d, a plain one a mere half crown (2s 6d). A *table d'hôte* luncheon on the 12.30pm Cromer express would have set the businessman back 6s 0d, as would dinner on the 'East Anglian'. Afternoon tea could be taken for 2s 0d. One could, of course, have ordered a packed meal for 2s 6d or a deluxe version at 3s 6d. Unfortunately it was not normally possible to enjoy the restaurant car service on the Cambridge line, even the most prestigious trains — such as the 'Fenman' — offering only a buffet-car service.

The new electrification scheme had reached Southend at the end of 1956, the inaugural train running on 28 December, and public services starting on 31 December. Both of the new sections used the existing 1,500V DC system, though it was intended that they be converted to the 25kV AC system at a later date. The Colchester to Clacton and Walton lines had already been selected as the test-bed for the latter. When these schemes had been first announced, as part of the 1955 Modernisation Plan, it was expected that the electrification would be extended to include Ipswich, Clacton, and the Harwich and Felixstowe branches. Whilst it didn't take too long to get to Chelmsford or even Clacton, Ipswich was not finally reached until 1985 and Harwich in 1986; Felixstowe is yet to come! One other idea raised in the Eastern Region staff magazine for March 1955 makes interesting reading now: 'The possibilities of the use of atomic power have not been overlooked in the (modernisation) Plan. The experts advise that electricity drawn from atomic power stations is the likeliest development rather than locomotives carrying their own atomic power units.'

By the summer of 1959 the 'Britannias' had revolutionised the timings, being introduced onto the interval service at the start of the year. The down 'Essex Coast Express', leaving Liverpool Street at 5.27pm, arrived at Clacton only 86 minutes later, calling at Colchester (6.24pm) and Thorpe-le-Soken (6.44pm) only. A connecting stopping train left Colchester at 6.29pm, arriving at Clacton at 7.1pm; this was closely followed by another 'interval' service, the 5.40pm from London, which reached Clacton at 7.17pm. There were 13 interval expresses in that weekday timetable, all save the 6.53 and 7.59pm from Clacton including a buffet car; additionally there were other through trains onto the branch from both Liverpool Street and Romford. Incidentally, while steam still reigned on the Clacton and Walton express and local services, diesel multiple-units had taken over the Brightlingsea trains,

generally starting either from Wivenhoe or St Botolphs.

Harwich and Parkeston Quay provided another source of traffic. In the summer of 1946, with the Continental routes recovering after the war, the boat trains started running again, the 'Hook Continental' being reinstated in November 1945, but on a restricted basis. It ran in the down direction on Mondays, Wednesdays and Fridays, leaving Liverpool Street at 8.0pm and reaching Parkeston at 9.40pm, connecting with the 10.0pm sailing to the Hook of Holland, due there at 5.45am. In the up direction it left at 7.15am on Wednesdays and Fridays only, taking five minutes more for the journey; on Sundays, the up working left at 7.35am. All of them carried a restaurant car. The 'Scandinavian' left London at 3.55pm on Wednesdays and Saturdays and took 105 minutes for the journey; there was no corresponding train in the other direction. Otherwise, travellers for the branch had to change at Manningtree, except for the one through working from Peterborough North, which left at 3.58pm and arrived at Harwich Town at 7.53pm; the return working left at 1.0pm.

The 'Hook Continental' in its modern form had been introduced on Monday 10 October 1938, when a new Gresley-designed train entered service. Consisting of 11 coaches, it had seating accommodation for 84 First- and 240 Second-class passengers in vehicles 63ft 6in long and with a total weight of 459 tons; it was scheduled for 'B17' haulage. Some Open First saloons were provided, divided by partitions into sections seating four passengers in luxuriously upholstered swivelling armchairs, two each side of the gangway. Semi-open Firsts were also provided, half the accommodation being in compartments; Second-class passengers were also given the choice of open or compartment stock. Carpeting, silk brocade curtains, black ebony window

---

THE ESSEX COAST EXPRESS

CLACTON-ON-SEA,

WALTON-ON-NAZE, FRINTON-ON-SEA

AND

LONDON (Liverpool Street)

MONDAYS TO FRIDAYS INCLUSIVE

		am	am				pm	pm
Clacton-on-Sea .. dep	..		7 56	London (Liverpool St.) dep	5 27			..
Thorpe-le-Soken .. arr	..		8 3	Colchester .. .. { arr	6 22			..
Walton-on-Naze .. dep	7C50		..	{ dep	6 22			..
Frinton-on-Sea .. „	7C53		..	Thorpe-le-Soken .. arr	6D42			..
Kirby Cross .. .. „	7C56		..	Thorpe-le-Soken .. dep	..			6C47
Thorpe-le-Soken .. arr	8C 1		..	Kirby Cross .. .. arr	..			6C51
Thorpe-le-Soken .. dep	..		8 4	Frinton-on-Sea .. „	..			6C54
Chelmsford { arr	..		8 42	Walton-on-Naze .. „	..			6C59
{ dep	..		8 43	Clacton-on-Sea .. .. arr	6 53			..
London (Liverpool St.) arr	..		9 21					

C Connecting service   **D** Calls to set down passengers only

Buffet Car available between Clacton-on-Sea and Liverpool Street

---

HARWICH (Essex) from
Liverpool Street, 70¼ miles. Fares,
14/10a, 8/11c. R. T. for two months,
29/3a, 17/10c. Pop. 13,046.
Map Square 19.

L PL.ST.	HARWICH	HARWICH	L'PL.ST.
AM 5. 0	7.38	AM 7. 0	9.33
6.50	10. 5	8.45	10.58
8.45	11.35	9.55	12.39
10.26	12.56	PM12.10	3.13
11.30d	1.50	12.37d	3.42
11.56er	2.25	3. 2	5.48
PM 2.15	4.53	4.17	6.32
3.20	5.49	5.27	7.46
5.42d	7.41	7.40e	10.10
5.42e	7.45	7.50d	10.10
6.39e	9.10	—	—
7.42r	9.43	—	—
8.40r	10.19	—	—

Sunday Trains.

AM 9.20r	11.48	AM 9. 4	11.43
PM 4.40r	6.44	PM 4.51	7.10
7.40	10.19	6. 5	8.58
—	—		

d Saturdays only.
e Saturdays excepted.
r Refreshment Car.

Right: The up 'Hook Continental', with LNER Class B1 4-6-0 No 1149 at its head, calls at Parkeston Quay on 17 July 1947. The locomotive has been repainted in the revived green livery. *C. C. B. Herbert*

Below: LNER 'B1' No 1149 passes Wrabness on 17 July 1947 with the up 'Hook Continental'. *C. C. B. Herbert*

Right: Two LNER Class B12s — the leading locomotive being No 1565, in green livery — head the down 'Scandinavian' boat train near Wrabness on 9 July 1947. *C. C. B. Herbert*

Left: Class B1 4-6-0 No 61192, minus headboard, near Wrabness with the up 'Scandinavian' on 8 July 1950.
G. R. Mortimer

Below: The 'Scandinavian', in the charge of 'B1' 4-6-0 No 61264, stands at Harwich Parkeston Quay on 16 August 1950.
British Railways

Left: Stratford 'Britannia' No 70005 *John Milton* heading the up 'Scandinavian' near Mistley on 30 June 1951.
G. R. Mortimer

frames, individual lights and extensive sound-proofing were provided, together with full air-conditioning. The Eastern Region regarded the train as a valuable dollar-earner, such was the number of American passengers carried; needless to say, it ran in several portions in the summer. By 1951 timings had improved somewhat, the train now leaving Liverpool Street at 8.0pm (7.30pm until 8 October) and running daily, its time cut to 90 minutes; the balancing working left Parkeston daily at 7.15am.

During the winter of 1950/1 the 'Scandinavian' was due out of Liverpool Street at 10.5am, reaching Parkeston at 11.45am, connecting with the United Steamship Co's sailing to Esbjerg at 12.30pm. The incoming boat was due in at 1.0pm, the train leaving as soon as possible, and taking some 2½hours to Liverpool Street. The 'Scandinavian' ran in the summer timetable on weekdays, except Mondays, leaving Liverpool Street at 2.40pm. This changed to 3.10pm in 1951 and later, from 17 September until 5 October, ran on Mondays, Wednesdays, Fridays and Saturdays. After this the 'Day Continental' started on 8 October, leaving at 9.30am, being itself replaced in the following May by the 'Scandinavian'.

The normal formation of the 'Scandinavian' was nine coaches, accommodating 138 First- and 208 Third-class passengers, hauled by a 'B1' or 'B17'. The formation of the 'Day Continental' was very similar. The Peterborough train was much as before, but another through working had appeared from Liverpool Central, leaving there at 12.50pm and arriving at Harwich Town at 8.55pm. It conveyed a buffet car, and the return left Parkeston at 8.0am. The latter working affected the main line in that it was routed via the north curve at Manningtree, and called at Ipswich before running via March and Spalding. It is interesting to note that services such as these called only at Ipswich before setting out across country; nowadays it would be unthinkable to omit Stowmarket and Bury St Edmunds.

On the subject of named trains, there were occasions when the Eastern Region put on a special for a particular event. One such was on 27 October 1950, when the 'Oyster Special' ran from Liverpool Street to Colchester, the Class B1 locomotive being adorned with a headboard bearing a picture of Lewis Carroll's famous Walrus and Carpenter characters. Life-size cut-outs of these were also placed by the barrier at Liverpool Street! The occasion was auspicious because it marked the rebuilding of the oyster fisheries which had been ravaged by the war, and the 1950 Colchester Oyster Feast was intended to mark the restoration of the industry's former healthy production and trading situation. The guest list was distinguished indeed and included R. A. Butler and Ernest Bevin, as well as Lord Jowitt (the Lord Chancellor) and C. K. Bird, Chief Regional Officer. The driver was A. Dunabin, the fireman W. A. Lewis.

Ipswich was also the destination for a number of stopping trains from the south. Some services ran through from Liverpool Street and called at almost all stations: the 6.50am in the 1946 timetable was one such, finally arriving at 9.43am. There were faster ways to travel, of course, and the 8.12pm Norwich express arrived at Ipswich only 20 minutes behind it. In this way, the minor stations such as Ardleigh and Bentley were served, and given connections for onward travel. As the years progressed, the need for feats of endurance such as the 6.50 were lessened, and such trains had many of the stops at the London end cut out. Local services then tended to be Colchester to Ipswich, but at irregular intervals, and with many variations. For instance, the celebrated Colchester–York train, which during the winter of 1951/2 left at 5.15pm, covered the local stops to Ipswich and then called at Stowmarket, Bury and Ely.

Trains radiated from Ipswich in all directions. Quite apart from the Norwich line, services left for

Below: The best-laid plans... On Sunday 4 April 1954 'N7' 0-6-2T No 69713 pilots a 'B1' 4-6-0 between Takeley and Hockerill Halt on the Dunmow–Bishop's Stortford line. This had closed to passenger traffic two years earlier but was being used because of engineering work between Ingatestone and Chelmsford. It was hardly the fastest way for passengers on the 'Scandinavian' to reach London. *Ian Allan Library*

Left: The 'Day Continental' to Harwich Parkeston Quay, as reintroduced by British Railways. Class B1 4-6-0 No 61361 has charge of the train at Liverpool Street on 1 July 1950. *British Railways*

Left: Having recently arrived at the head of the 'Hook Continental', 'Britannia' Pacific No 70013 *Oliver Cromwell* stands on the turntable at Liverpool Street. *R. Cooke*

the East Suffolk (often through coaches detached from a Norwich train), the Felixstowe branch and the Ely and Cambridge routes. With a considerable concentration of freight traffic to add to things it was a bustling place indeed. In 1951 the 1.30pm from Liverpool Street would arrive at Platform 3 at 3.11pm, and the rear portion would be detached. The front portion, with the buffet car, would be worked forward to Cromer, calling at Stowmarket, Finningham, Mellis, Diss, Burston (Saturdays only), Tivetshall and Norwich, whilst the rear was taken forward at 3.24pm for principal stations to Yarmouth South Town. This particular train connected at Stowmarket for Bury. The 3.33pm, on the other hand, was fast to Ipswich, arriving at 5.2pm, where coaches for Felixstowe were detached, leaving at 5.15pm and reaching the Beach station at 6.3pm. The main train went forward to Yarmouth, calling only at Saxmundham and Beccles, where it divided again for Lowestoft. There was a connecting service for all stations to Norwich at 5.25pm, and another for

most stations to Yarmouth at 5.27pm.

By the summer of 1957 the division of trains had largely finished at Ipswich, the practice then being to provide connecting services. Clearly this was not possible with the 'Easterling', which left Liverpool Street at 11.3am, with a 'Britannia' and nine coaches, and whose first and only stop *en route* to Yarmouth South Town was Beccles, where the Lowestoft portion was detached. The 3.0pm (Saturdays only) from Liverpool Street to Yarmouth South Town via Gorleston was another such train, its first stop being at Lowestoft Central where it reversed. It was most unusual to run through Ipswich: the 8.20am Norwich, 9.30am Sheringham, 12.30pm Melton Constable, 3.30pm Sheringham, 3.33pm Yarmouth South Town and 6.30pm Norwich all made it their first stop, with many others calling there after Chelmsford or Colchester. The 3.30pm (arrive 4.43pm) had a connection for Cambridge, calling at all stations except Needham to Haughley, whilst the 3.33pm (arrive Ipswich 5.1pm) had a connection at

MELLIS	(Suffolk)	from

Liverpool Street, 91¼ miles. Fares, 19/4 *t*, 11/7*c*. R.T. for two months, 33/8*a*. Pop. 390.
Map Square 19.

L'PL. ST.	MELLIS	MELLIS	L'PL. ST.
AM 5. 0	7.42	AM 7.40*r*	10.30
10. 0*r*	1. 0	9.41	12.39
11 *ser* 3. 8		11.20*r*	2. 3
PM12.25*dr* 3. 8		PM 2. 7*r*	4.58
3.15*hr*	5.50	4.48	7.46
3.15*kr*	5.50	5.40*dr*	9.27
5.18*dr* 8. 1		—	—
5.18*er* 8. 4		—	—

Sunday Trains.

AM 9.20*r*	12.24	AM 8.12	11.43
PM 4.40*r*	7.17	PM 7.17*l*	10.15
—	—	7.20*t*	10.15

d Saturdays only.
e Saturdays excepted.
h Fridays only.
k Fridays excepted.
l Commences October 24.
r Refreshment Car.
t Not after October 17.

Right: Seen in the late 1950s, Class B12 No 61564 has just arrived at Ipswich with an up train from Yarmouth South Town as 'Britannia' Pacific No 70012 *John of Gaunt* waits to take the train on to Liverpool Street. *Author's collection*

Below: An immaculate No 70012 *John of Gaunt* waits at Ipswich to take a Yarmouth train forward to Liverpool Street. *Author's collection*

Right: The up mail, the 6.45pm from Norwich Thorpe to Liverpool Street, ready to leave Ipswich behind 'Britannia' No 70008 *Black Prince*. The leading vehicle is an LNER bogie van, the rest of the train consisting of Mk 1 stock in carmine and cream. *Author's collection*

5.25pm for all stations to Norwich. A Felixstowe Town all-stations left at 5.15pm, and a stopper to Yarmouth and Lowestoft at 5.30pm; this in turn connected for Aldeburgh and Gorleston.

Further along the main line towards Norwich, the service was dominated by the expresses already mentioned, though the line was shared as far as Haughley with the Cambridge and Ely services. The latter tended to provide much of the stopping service, as they still do today, though there were more stations open: Bramford, Claydon and Haughley Junction itself. The first two were omitted by many trains, and most main-line workings all of them. In the 1946 timetable there were a number of all-stations workings between Ipswich and Norwich, such as the 6.33am and 9.0am in the morning, supplemented by the occasional stopper to Haughley; the first-mentioned was in fact the 4.25am from Liverpool Street. The corresponding up workings left Norwich at 9.25am and 10.50am. Things had changed very little in 1951, but by 1957 Bramford (2 May 1955 to all traffic) and Swainsthorpe (5 July 1954 to passengers) had closed, and the 9.2am started back from Chelmsford at 7.50am, calling at all stations from there, and formed by one of the new diesel multiple-units.

In the 1959 timetable the 4.35am from Liverpool Street now omitted Claydon, Haughley and Burston, but a DMU working at 7.15am from Ipswich called at all stations to Norwich. The other morning train was now the 7.45am from Bury St Edmunds, a DMU calling at all stations to Norwich via Long Melford and Marks Tey, leaving Ipswich at 9.35am.

The main line via Cambridge was the first to offer train services between London and Norwich. It opened in July 1845, although the link to Thorpe station via Trowse swing bridge was not completed until December. The Norfolk Railway advertised a service between Yarmouth and London right away (the missing link doesn't seem to have worried it), with trains leaving Shoreditch at 8.0 and 11.30am, 8.15pm and the mail at 8.40pm. In the other direction trains were advertised as leaving Yarmouth for London at 5.30am, 9.30am, 3.15pm, and the mail at 10.17pm. In addition there were up trains from Yarmouth to Norwich at mid-day, and to Ely at 7.0pm. Third-class passengers could travel in covered carriages by the 7.50pm down train from Ely, which had left London at 2.15pm, and the 5.30am up from Yarmouth, which reached London at 2.30pm. There were five trains to and from Yarmouth on Sundays, two of which were to or from London, including the mail.

Nearer to the capital, the Eastern Counties offered other trains. From Shoreditch these included the 9.0am and 8.30pm to Broxbourne, the 9.30am and 7.0pm to Hertford and Cambridge, and trains to Hertford at noon, 3.20pm and 4.30pm. The up services were similar, the first being the 7.50am from Broxbourne, and the last the 7.20pm from Hertford, although the Yarmouth train followed this. A total of four trains ran each

---

THE EASTERLING

LONDON (Liverpool Street)

AND

LOWESTOFT AND YARMOUTH

WEEKDAYS
28th June to 6th September inclusive

	S am	E am			pm
London (Liverpool St.) .dep	10 33	11 3	Yarmouth (South Town) . ..dep		7 17
	pm	pm			
Beccles .. ..arr	12 51	1 16	Lowestoft (Central) .. .. „		7 18
Lowestoft (Central).. „	1 16	1 41	Beccles . .. . „		7 42
Yarmouth (South Town) „	1 13	1 38	London (Liverpool Street) ..arr		10 0

E—Except Saturdays.

S—Saturdays only.

Buffet Car available between London (Liverpool Street) and Yarmouth (South Town).

Passengers travelling from London (Liverpool Street), Lowestoft (Central) and Yarmouth (South Town) by this service can reserve seats in advance on payment of a fee of 2s. 0d. per seat.

---

way on Sundays, each with Third-class carriages attached.

In June 1883 the Great Northern put on a noon up express from Cambridge, calling only at Hitchin *en route* to King's Cross, which was reached at 1.15pm. The rapid insertion of a stop at Royston eased the timing to 77 minutes, which lasted for many years. The best Great Eastern trains at the time were 76 minutes to Liverpool Street and 77 minutes from St Pancras, although the new 4.32pm Liverpool Street–Doncaster later reached Cambridge in only 75 minutes.

By 1887 the service had evolved to a regular pattern. Local services out of Liverpool Street went to Hertford via Stratford and Lea Bridge, although some did use the newer route via Hackney Downs. St Pancras also saw a fair amount of Great Eastern passenger traffic. Slip coaches provided some services to Broxbourne, Bishop's Stortford and Audley End. A few trains combined *en route*, such as the 11.55am and

BISHOP'S STORT-

FORD (Herts) from *Liverpool Street*, 30½ miles. Fares, 6/6a, 3/11c. R. T. for two months, 13/0a, 7/10c. Pop. 8,857.

Map Square 24.

L'PL. ST.	B. STORT.	B. STORT.	L'PL. ST.
AM 5. 5	5.47	AM 1.40g	2.50
5.50	7. 2	1.40f	3. 0
7.18	8.44	6.57	8.18
8.30r	9.19	7.30	8.49
9.10	10.36	7.40	8.57
10. 5	10.56	8.33	9.27
10.34	12.26	8.54	9.48
11.50r	12.35	9.28	10.17
PM12.29d	1.21	9.42r	10.23
12.40d	1.50	9.50	10.59
12.48e	2.13	10.43	11.27
1.19d	2.26	10.52	12.15
2. 0d	3. 8	11.54	12.37
2.34	3.18	PM12.55	2. 7
2.48	4. 2	1.40r	2.21
4.15	5. 4	2.14d	3.18
4.45	5.28	3.38	5. 9
5.10	6.18	4.32r	5.17
5.49r	6.35	5.26r	6.10
6. 0e	7. 1	5.43	7.19
6.30	7.17	6.41	7.58
7.10r	7.55	7.47er	8.33
7.41d	8.49	7.52dr	8.33
7.41e	8.52	8. 4	9.33
8.22	9.10	10. 0	11.13
9.14	10.35	—	—
10.12	10.57	—	—
11.50k	12.31	—	—
11.50h	12.56	—	—
—	—		

Sunday Trains.

AM 8.12	9.18	AM 1.40	2.50
9.25r	10.13	7.48	9.33
PM 1.50	3.27	10. 4	11.27
3.25	4.12	PM 5.58	6.40
4.50	6.18	6.32	7.26
7.15	8.24	6.57	7.40
9.12	10.35	7.48	9.10
—	—	9.18	10.40

d Saturdays only.
e Saturdays excepted.
f Mondays only.
g Mondays excepted.
h Wednesdays and Saturdays only.
k Thursdays only.
r Refreshment Car.

Chequers Hotel. Family and. Commercial. Highly recommended. Centre of Town. Moderate. No extras. Bus meets trains. Motor Carriages. Garage. Tel. 20.
J. BRAZIER, Proprietor.

The George Hotel. Leading First Class Family and Commercial. Terms moderate. Omnibus meets all trains. Telephone 42.
F. C. LITTLE, Proprietress.

12.05pm departures from Liverpool Street and St Pancras respectively. The former called at Bishop's Stortford, Cambridge and Waterbeach before reaching Ely at 1.45pm, whilst the St Pancras service called only at Cambridge, arriving at Ely at 1.51pm. The combined train left at 1.58pm, calling only at Norwich Thorpe on its way to Reedham, where it divided for Lowestoft and Yarmouth. Trains via the GN&GE Joint line to Lincoln and Doncaster were mixed in with the rest of the service, and included the 11.0am from Liverpool Street, which ran fast to Cambridge and slipped a coach for Broxbourne, and then to Ely, March, Spalding, Lincoln and Doncaster. The 2.8pm from Doncaster called at just about everywhere on its way to March, picked up a portion from Lynn at Ely, and then made its way to Norwich Trowse and Thorpe before going on to Yarmouth.

The peak of the service, as regards timings and speeds, was probably 1905, when Liverpool Street and St Pancras trains were booked to reach Cambridge in 72 and 71 minutes respectively. These timings were not bettered for many years, and although the October 1914 timetable showed faster nominal journeys they had a proviso attached that they could be altered or cancelled without notice because of the war conditions. Of course, carriages became heavier and trains longer, so the work to be done in keeping these schedules was much greater.

Hunstanton was regarded as an important destination by the Great Eastern and LNER, and both developed the facilities at the terminus. However, it did not have the same size or status of the seaside towns served by the Ipswich line and its branches, and through services, apart from excursions, were generally provided by coaches detached from other trains. In the summer of 1911 there was an up breakfast-car express from Hunstanton at 7.45am, which called at all stations to Lynn, then Downham, Littleport, Ely and Cambridge and non-stop to Liverpool Street, reached at 10.56am. In the other direction the 5.12pm down from Liverpool Street had dining cars included from 1906, and reached Hunstanton at 9.5pm. Otherwise the 11.5am York express detached a portion at Ely for Hunstanton; other trains with through carriages included the 8.40am (Norwich) and 4.30pm (York).

By 1922 times had come down to under four hours between Liverpool Street and Norwich. The 8.30am stopped at Broxbourne, Bishop's Stortford and Audley End on its way to Cambridge and Ely. It then called at almost all stations to Norwich Thorpe, omitting only Roudham Junction and Eccles Road, even calling at Harling Road on Wednesdays and Saturdays. The 11.50am was a much better bet, calling only at Brandon, Thetford and Wymondham between Ely and Norwich, reaching the latter at 3.19pm. The 11.20am from St Pancras was a restaurant-car train to King's Lynn, although it was a summer dated train, starting on 24 July. In the other direction the July timetable offered First- and Third-class Pullman

cars to Liverpool Street on the 7.50am departure, and again on the 12.52pm from Cambridge. This train started from Norwich at 10.30am, whose passengers had to cope with a mere restaurant car. The 9.50am Lowestoft–York also offered a restaurant car, and used the avoiding line at Ely, as did the 12.10pm from Yarmouth Vauxhall. This acquired a portion from Lowestoft at Reedham and called at Trowse rather than Thorpe in Norwich.

Fast passenger-train workings in the 1930s tended to be in the hands of 'B12' and 'B17' 4-6-0s and seemed to be livened up by rebuilding of the former with round-topped fireboxes. However, it was not unknown for goods locomotives to be pressed into service to cover failures, and on one occasion 'J39' No 2726 was observed passing Great Chesterford only 4 minutes down whilst in charge of the 1.58pm restaurant car express from Norwich to Liverpool Street, due off Cambridge at 3.52pm and calling only at Bishop's Stortford on its way to London.

The 'Britannia' timetable devised by Gerard Fiennes marked a major change and introduced regular interval trains, although the pattern was more obvious on the Ipswich route. The Cambridge line trains tended to leave Liverpool Street at 24 minutes past the hour, with the Ipswich workings at half past. Some, such as the 1.24 and 3.24pm, worked only as far as Cambridge, and others were multi-portion offerings. The times to Norwich were slower than via Ipswich (typically 3 hours 10-20 minutes), but although fast to Cambridge and Ely these trains then served most stations to Norwich. The 8.24pm in the 1955/6 winter timetable offered a restaurant car as far as Ely, where it divided for Hunstanton and Yarmouth. The 'Fenman', 4.30pm from Liverpool Street and calling at Audley End, Cambridge, Ely and King's Lynn, provided a restaurant car through to Hunstanton, and also carried through coaches for March and Wisbech. This did not run on Saturdays, but was replaced by a similar train at 4.27pm, without the March and Wisbech coaches. The 4.36pm from Liverpool Street, unofficially the 'Bury Fenman', provided a restaurant-car service to Newmarket and Bury St Edmunds via Cambridge on Mondays to Fridays. Local services operated over other parts of the route, among them the 2.35pm (2.38 Saturdays only) from Cambridge to Lowestoft. The fast Cambridge service was provided by the King's Cross trains, many running as 'Cambridge Buffet Expresses' and taking about 80 minutes for the journey.

The 'Fenman' was a business train, and ran up from Cambridge at 8.48am Mondays-Fridays, and called only at Audley End *en route* to Liverpool Street. The down train changed locomotives at Cambridge, from where a 'Claud' took it on to Lynn. A related diagram saw a Stratford crew work from Liverpool Street to Ipswich, then a local to Bury St Edmunds. They picked up the main-line train at Bury at around 8.00am, which

222

Left: The 7.7pm express to Liverpool Street, headed by Class B1 4-6-0 61271, pulls out of one of the south-end bay platforms at Cambridge on 10 June 1962.
F. R. Hebron

formed the 'Bury Fenman' (no headboard) at 9.00am from Cambridge. It called at Audley End, Bishop's Stortford, Broxbourne and Liverpool Street, and loaded to nine or 10 coaches. The down service was worked by a Cambridge crew, with the locomotive going through to Bury. The usual motive power for both trains was a 'B1' or a 'B17'.

The major locomotive depots for Cambridge-line services were Stratford, Cambridge and Norwich, although most significant stations such as King's Lynn also played their part. Prior to the introduction of the 'Britannias' both Cambridge and Ipswich had had much of the working of the Norwich services: afterwards, they were handled almost exclusively by Stratford and Norwich. Cambridge was a very large and important depot and remained central to traffic working, of course. For example, the 6.30am stopper from Cambridge to Norwich was a return working for the crew who had relieved the newspaper train in the morning. The 4.20am newspapers from Liverpool Street called at Bishop's Stortford, Audley End and all stations to Cambridge, after which they had all been unloaded; this train then worked to Norwich, calling all stations, arriving at 6.30am, and was a Class D, in other words two-thirds fitted.

Service personnel provided considerable traffic in the area. Brandon was used by service personnel from Lakenheath, although traffic from Mildenhall came into Cambridge via the branch. Trains sometimes ran from Brandon through to London on Saturdays for this purpose.

Men in the express links at Cambridge worked rush-hour trains from St Ives, King's Lynn and Ely through to London. It was not a big link, and there were lots of short jobs between Cambridge and Liverpool Street, and in the rush hour it was very busy, with many trains in rapid succession. After dieselisation the through service from Liverpool Street to Norwich via Cambridge was largely withdrawn, and Cambridge–Norwich became railcar only. Prior to this express trains split at Ely, with the front six coaches going to

Norwich with the train engine (usually a 'Britannia') and the rear four to King's Lynn, with a 'Claud' backing on. Under the new arrangements the main service became Liverpool Street–King's Lynn. Cambridge men would work from Cambridge to Liverpool Street, back to Lynn and then back up to Cambridge.

Change, as always, was in the air. Table 4 in the LNER's summer timetable for 1946 showed the service between Liverpool Street and Norwich via Cambridge. Services as far as Broxbourne & Hoddesdon were shown in the suburban booklet, whilst King's Cross services appeared in Table 11. King's Lynn and Hunstanton appeared in Table 40, whilst services to March and Peterborough came under Table 38. Many parts of these showed strong similarities with earlier years. The 4.30am from Liverpool Street called at Bishop's Stortford, Audley End and Whittlesford, and then all stations to Norwich, reached at 8.51am. The 5.35am was rather slower, making its first call at Broxbourne and then all stations to Norwich, arriving at 10.37am. On weekdays the 8.20am down was a buffet-car express to Hunstanton (12.20pm), dividing at Ely for Norwich (also 12.20pm). The 10.0am departure was a through train to Peterborough East. There were a few semi-fast trains to Cambridge, plus the buffet-car expresses; the 2.20pm ran as a buffet-car express to Yarmouth Mondays-Fridays. The 'Bury Fenman' left Liverpool Street at 4.40pm and arrived at Bury St Edmunds at 7.7pm. The last express of the day was one of the best: the 7.15pm from Liverpool Street to Norwich Thorpe included a buffet car Mondays-Fridays and after its Ely stop called only at Lakenheath, Brandon, Thetford, Attleborough and Wymondham.

In the up direction the 'Fenman' left Hunstanton at 6.45am, collected the Bury portion at Cambridge at 8.48 and reached Liverpool Street at 10.3am. The 8.32am from Norwich picked up a buffet car at Ely, whilst the 2.20pm conveyed one throughout. It was followed into London by the 2.30pm from Norwich, which had joined with the

CAMBRIDGE from *Liverpool Street*, 55¼ miles. Fares, 11/6a, 6/11c. R. T. for two months, 23/0a. Pop. 59,262.
Map Square 18.

L'PL. ST.	CAMBDG.	CAMBDG.	L'PL. ST.
AM 5. 5	6.28	AM12.55g	2.50
5.50	8. 1	12.55f	3. 0
7.18	9.45	6.40	8.57
8.30r	9.58	7.47	9.27
10. 5	11.38	7.58	9.47
11.50r	1.17	8.30	10.17
PM12.29d	2.18	9. 5r	10.23
12.48e	3.16	10. 3	11.27
1.19d	3.25	11.14	12.37
2.34	3.58	11.53	2. 7
2.48	5. 3	PM 1. 0r	2.21
4.15	5.50	1.12d	3.18
4.45	6. 4	2.25	5. 9
5.49r	7.14	3.52r	5.17
6.30	8.13	4.42r	6.10
7.10r	8.35	5.36	7.58
8.22	9.50	7. 0d	8.22
10.12	11.42	7. 7er	8.33
11.50h	1. 0	7.10dlr	8.33
—	—	8.58	11.13
—	—	—	—

Sunday Trains.

AM 8.12	10.16	AM12.55	2.50
9.25	10.55	9. 5	11.27
PM 1.50	4.29	PM 5.17	6.40
3.25	4.50	5.29	7.26
9.12	11.26	6.12	7.40
—	—	8.27r	9.42
—	—	—	—
—	—	—	—
—	—	—	—
—	—	—	—

  d Saturdays only.
  e Saturdays excepted.
  f Mondays only.
  g Mondays excepted.
  h Thursdays only.
  r Refreshment Car.

ANOTHER ROUTE from *King's Cross*, 58 miles. Fares as above.

KING'S+	CAMBGE.	CAMBGE.	KING'S+
AM 7.10	9.34	AM 7.33	9.34
8.45	10.41	8.26	9.56
11.30	1.42	9.18	11.15
PM12.40d	2.21	10. 0	11.25
3. 0	4.45	11. 2	1.25
5. 0	6.25	PM 1.35	3.55
6.15	7.57	4. 3	5.58
6.55	9. 0	6.20	8. 8
—	—	7.30	10.14
—	—	—	—
—	—	—	—
—	—	—	—
—	—	—	—
—	—	—	—
—	—	—	—
—	—	—	—

Sunday Trains.

AM 8.30	10.52	AM 7.20	9.56
PM 6.50	8.56	PM 5.33	7.50
—	—	—	—
—	—	—	—
—	—	—	—

  d Saturdays only.
  k Fridays only.
  l Fridays only.

The Bull Hotel. Patronised by Royalty. Leading Family Hotel. Sixty rooms. Centre of principal Colleges. Terms moderate. Excellent Garage on the premises. Telephone No. 341. *See* advt. p. **128.**

ELY (Cambridge) from *Liverpool Street*, 70¼ miles. Fares,14/10a, 8/11c. R. T. for two months 29/8a. Pop. 7,690. *Map Square* 19.

L'POOL ST.	ELY	ELY	L'POOL ST.
AM 5. 5	6.58	AM12.23*g*	2.50
5.50	8.35	12.23*f*	3. 0
8.30*r*	10.25	7.16	9.27
10. 5	12.9	8.40*r*	10.23
11.50*r*	1.43	9.54	11.27
PM12.48*e*	3.54	10.41	12.37
1.19*d*	3.54	11.25	2. 7
2.34	4.22	PM12.32*r*	2.21
4.15	6.19	1.45	5. 9
4.45	6.28	3.25*r*	5.17
5.49*r*	7.45	4.14*r*	6.10
7.10*r*	9. 1	4.55	7.58
10.12	12.10	6.34*d*	8.22
—	—	6.39*er*	8.33
—	—	6.45*dr*	8.33
—	—	7.48	11.13

Sunday Trains.

AM 8.12	10.46	AM12.23	2.50
9.25	11.48	8.35	11.27
PM 1.50	5. 3	PM 4.32	6.40
3.25	5.24	5.36	7.40
9.12	12. 0	7.57*r*	9.42

d Saturdays only.
e Saturdays excepted.
f Mondays only.
g Mondays excepted.
r Refreshment Car.

2.40pm from Hunstanton at Ely, the latter including a buffet car throughout. None of this catering was available on Saturdays. Meanwhile the cross-country services from Norwich were represented by the 7.4am, which had started at both Lowestoft Central (5.45am) and Yarmouth Vauxhall (6.0pm), used the avoiding line at Ely and travelled via Peterborough East and North to Rugby Midland, where it arrived at 11.38am. The 11.10am from Norwich similarly included through coaches from Lowestoft and Yarmouth and went to York via Spalding. The seasonal weekend holiday trains were already picking up after the dark days of the war: on summer Saturdays (6 July to14 September inclusive) trains left Yarmouth and Lowestoft in quick succession for Manchester and Leeds, the first via Norwich and the second not, both also travelling via the GN&GE Joint line. There were several other such workings. There also continued to be a number of all-stations workings between Norwich and Cambridge. The 2.55pm from Cromer called only at North Walsham and Wroxham before taking the Wensum Curve and calling next at Ely (4.56pm), Cambridge (5.26pm) and Liverpool Street, reached at 6.55pm. The 1951/2 winter timetable showed many similarities with that of 1946. The 4.20am down from Liverpool Street had actually been slowed by 10 minutes, although the 5.50am was a bit faster. There were a number of tweaks to the service, and some solid improvements, such as the reintroduction of the 'Fenman' at 4.30pm, with through coaches to Bury. The 4.36pm turned into a restaurant-car service to Ely, with through coaches going to March and Wisbech.

By 1958 the express service had been fully established, although the 4.20am and 5.54am were largely unchanged in calling pattern and timings. The 8.24am down continued to divide at Ely, where the buffet car came off, Norwich being reached nearly 40 minutes earlier than 10 years previously. Trains such as the 12.24 and 2.24pm, dividing at Ely for Hunstanton and Norwich, had

appeared, establishing the pattern of trains alternating with the xx.30 departures for Norwich via Ipswich. The timetable had been speeded up overall, although the pattern of departures from Norwich to Liverpool Street was not regular. There were some interesting workings, such as the 10.2am from Norwich which had started from Yarmouth Vauxhall at 9.0am, and picked up the Hunstanton portion at Ely, plus a buffet car. The 'Fenman' continued to leave from Hunstanton at 6.50am, with a buffet car throughout, and carried through coaches from Wisbech and March, joined at Ely. The 8.0am from Norwich had a buffet car from Ely, and also carried through coaches from Hunstanton, and reached Liverpool Street at 11.20am; the 10.2am was similar, but called at all stations between Norwich and Ely. The 12.43 Ely–Liverpool Street, which included a buffet car, started from Brandon on Saturdays and called at Lakenheath and Shippea Hill, being aimed at service personnel from the nearby air bases. Other through trains included the 1.32pm, 2.42pm, 5.10pm and 1.45pm Norwich–Liverpool Street, all except the last with a buffet car throughout. Cross-country services continued to use the GN&GE Joint line, such as the 10.5am Yarmouth Vauxhall to York (summer Saturdays only) and the 10.0am buffet-car train from Lowestoft–York, which carried through coaches from Yarmouth. The 7.50am from Norwich to Birmingham New Street was routed via Peterborough East, Market Harborough and Rugby Midland, reaching its destination at 12.51pm.

Stopping services on the main line between Cambridge and Liverpool Street were hardly inspiring, trains running roughly hourly from Bishop's Stortford all stations to Broxbourne and then fast to London, some calling at Waltham Cross or Tottenham. Services between Broxbourne and Liverpool Street were covered by the local trains to Hertford East, mostly running via Clapton, and also the roughly hourly Stratford–Hertford East service. The Buntingford branch also offered a few through services in the peak hours. Help was at hand, as the less-romantic suburban services were progressively changed by electrification from 1960 onwards. Prior to this the Liverpool Street–Enfield Town service provided a half-hourly off-peak frequency, taking 39 minutes and calling at all stations. The electric service speeded these considerably, to 29 minutes for the all-stations trains, and trebled the frequency, some trains omitting some stations and cutting the journey time to 25 minutes. The new service of electric trains to Bishop's Stortford via the Southbury loop gave a half-hourly service, calling at Lower Edmonton and then all stations, and essentially combined these with the Hertford East service: trains divided and joined at Broxbourne. The time between Liverpool Street and Bishop's Stortford by these trains was 56 minutes. Some diesel workings necessarily remained, these comprising mostly stoppers to Cheshunt and also Stratford–Cheshunt trains, as these ran via the main line, which had not yet been wired.

THE FENMAN
KING'S LYNN, ELY, CAMBRIDGE
AND
LONDON (Liverpool Street)

WEEKDAYS

	am			pm
King's Lynn ..dep	7 46	London (Liverpool Street) ..dep		4 36
Downham ,,	8 3	Audley End ,,		5 26
Ely ..arr	8 24	Cambridge ..arr		5 46
,, ..dep	8 26	,, ..dep		5 49
Cambridge ..arr	8 45	Ely ..arr		6 6
,, ..dep	8 48	,, ..dep		6 10
London (Liverpool Street) ..arr	9 58	Littleport ,,		6 19
		Downham ,,		6 33
		Magdalen Road ,,		6 43
		King's Lynn ..arr		6 54

Buffet Car available

Passengers travelling from Liverpool Street by this service, can reserve seats in advance on payment of a fee of 2s. 0d. per seat.

224

The gap was finally plugged in 1969, the electric service on the main line starting on 5 May. From this date trains ceased to divide at Broxbourne. The Chingford service was reduced to take account of the opening of the Victoria Line, and this released electric units and paths into Liverpool Street, so that no extra rolling stock was required. The goods lines between Picketts Lock, south of Brimsdown, and South Tottenham Junction were completely removed: they had run round the east of each intermediate station.

The beginning of the end for steam came in 1958, when the first 2,000hp Type 4 diesel-electric locomotives (better known in later years as Class 40s) were delivered by English Electric. The very first, No D200, made its demonstration run from Liverpool Street to Ipswich and Norwich on 18 April 1958 in the capable hands of Driver G. S. Marle, the train also carrying Eastern Region General Manager H. C. Johnson. Ten of the new locomotives were allocated to the Eastern Region and were to be used on a proportion of the main Norwich trains, allowing the 'Britannias' to be released for the Clacton service. One interesting feature of the new locomotives was that they were fitted with an 800gal water tank and pick-up apparatus, needed to supply the train-heating boiler. Making tea was a rather different matter compared with the footplate of a steamer, and at night it was easy enough to accidentally switch off the locomotive lamps when brewing up! In steam days a driver could be pulled up by a signalman and told that he had 'both eyes shut', the oil lamps having blown out; these had then to be sent to the stores for examination, and if they were found to be defective the driver would be in trouble, their maintenance being his responsibility.

For the long-distance services the changeover from steam to diesel represented an enormous undertaking, and it speaks volumes for the management and men that it was achieved with relatively little trouble; the accounts of R. H. N. Hardy in his books *Steam in the Blood* and *Railways in the Blood* are well worth reading. Suffice it to say here that Stratford, once the largest steam depot in the country, went diesel within three years, and East Anglia became one of the first areas to convert entirely to the new form of traction.

By the summer of 1964 steam had disappeared for all practical purposes, but the 4.30am once again stopped at all stations between Ipswich and Norwich. However, Claydon had closed to passengers with effect from 17 June 1963. The 9.30am all-stations from Ipswich to Norwich still ran, but the writing was on the wall for the local trains. The axe fell on Flordon, Forncett, Tivetshall, Burston, Mellis and Finningham on 7 November 1966, when they were closed to passengers; Haughley and Needham survived only until 2 January 1967. The latter reopened as Needham Market on 6 December 1971, though now unstaffed. Feeder lines closed all over East Anglia, the East Suffolk between Beccles and Yarmouth South Town going in November 1959 and the Hunstanton branch in 1964. Many other secondary routes and smaller branches succumbed, so that it was no longer possible to travel by rail between Colchester and Cambridge along the Stour Valley after 1967, or between Norwich and King's Lynn via Dereham and Swaffham after 1968. Although no passenger stations closed on the Liverpool Street–Cambridge line, many between Ely and King's Lynn were culled. Hilgay and Stow Bardolph closed for passengers on 4 November 1963 and for goods on 13 July 1964, and Denver (which had closed to passengers in 1930, when the Stoke

Below: Electrification underway at Colchester on 22 April 1958, as Class J19 No 64651 leaves the Clacton line and passes the shed (left) with an engineers' train. *Author's collection*

Above: A British Railways publicity photograph for the new electric service between Colchester and Clacton, featuring a '25kV AC multiple-unit train on the up road between Wivenhoe and Colchester'. It was taken on 17 July 1959. *British Railways*

Right: A brand-new 'Clacton Electric' unit, in its smart maroon livery, stands at Liverpool Street in February 1963. These units revolutionised passenger perceptions of the service. *D. L. Percival*

Right: Yarmouth Vauxhall was the terminus for many cross-country services from Peterborough and beyond and also for those from London, especially following closure of Yarmouth South Town. This photograph, taken on 11 May 1975, features the signalbox overlooking the former locomotive shed, closed in January 1959. *David Pearce*

Ferry branch lost its service) finally lost its goods service in 1964. Magdalen Road closed to goods on 19 April 1965 and to passengers on 9 September 1968, although it was reopened in 1975 and renamed Watlington in 1989.

The diesels did not enjoy a long reign on the main lines. Electric trains had reached Chelmsford in 1956, and the Clacton and Walton branches, chosen as a testbed for the new 25kV overhead system, were wired in 1959; new services were inaugurated on 13 April, although electric units had been introduced to the existing times from 16 March. Through trains to and from London continued to be steam- or diesel-operated, and the Brightlingsea branch became an outpost of DMU operation. Resignalling between Colchester Junction and Clacton was effected at the same time.

It was a little while before the gap between Chelmsford and Colchester was plugged, the new service starting on 17 June 1963, when the newly built 'Clacton Electrics', in their smart maroon livery, took over. These had a high power-to-weight ratio and offered consistent 90mph running to achieve 85-minute timings on the fastest trains, such as the 'Essex Coast Express' — the 7.56am from Clacton, Mondays to Fridays, calling only at Thorpe-le-Soken. The down train, the 5.27pm from Liverpool Street, did call at Colchester, taking an extra minute. Both offered a restaurant/buffet service, and in terms of timings they represented a considerable improvement over the steam service they replaced.

There was then a considerable pause before further progress. In the late 1960s Liverpool Street–Ipswich–Norwich services settled down to regular Class 47 haulage. Off-peak they were hourly, generally xx.30 from London, most with a restaurant car, alternate trains calling intermediately at Ipswich and Colchester, or additionally at Diss, Stowmarket, Manningtree and Chelmsford, taking 1hr 55min for the faster journeys and 2hr 12min for the slower. There were several peak-hour extras. Several morning trains

started from Yarmouth Vauxhall, and evening trains terminated there, the stock being serviced at Yarmouth carriage sidings.

The next significant change to the Cambridge service came in the 1970s. During 1976 the Great Northern electrification scheme saw the gradual introduction of inner-suburban electric services, culminating in their introduction between Moorgate and Welwyn Garden City and Hertford North on 8 November. Outer-suburbans followed on 3 October 1977, which date saw the commencement of the electric service between King's Cross, Hitchin and Royston, worked by new Class 312/0 units. More were brought into use until all 26 sets were in service and all services operated by them. The consequence for Cambridge was the withdrawal of the through service from King's Cross, which did not occur until the timetable changes of 6 February 1978, after which passengers had to change at Royston, where refurbished Class 101 DMUs provided the connections. Through hauled trains from London to Cambridge ran from Liverpool Street only, extra workings being provided, and buffet cars continuing on the principal services.

On the Ipswich main line the Braintree branch was wired in 1977, although a dispute with the rail unions delayed the introduction of through trains.

In the 1980s a scheme was devised to extend electrification in East Anglia to Norwich and Cambridge. Both represented extensions of existing electrified areas, although that to Cambridge via Royston was part of the Great Northern scheme. Published on 11 February 1981, a joint report by the British Railways Board and the Department of Transport concluded that a programme of main-line electrification covering services carrying 83% of passengers would show an 11% return. East Anglian schemes included Colchester to Norwich and Harwich, Bishop's Stortford to Cambridge and Royston to Cambridge. Early in 1982 the scheme from Colchester to Harwich, Ipswich and Norwich was approved, the estimated cost being around £30

Above: Formed of a Class 101 Metro-Cammell DMU, the 12.30 from Yarmouth to Norwich via Acle passes the carriage sidings at Yarmouth, where the empty stock for the 13.00 to Liverpool Street is waiting. The latter, along with Class 86/2 No 86 246 *Royal Anglian Regiment,* had arrived behind '47/4' No 47 458, which then propelled the train into the sidings for servicing before running round. *David Pearce*

Right: Electrification work in progress: mast bases being prepared on the Harwich branch on 6 June 1983.
G. R. Mortimer

Below right: Much of the work involved with electrification is concerned with the need to increase bridge clearances. Here Bridge 235, north of Bentley, has been closed, and a temporary pedestrian replacement provided. The photograph was taken on 2 February 1983.
G. R. Mortimer

Below: Work in progress on 18 February on Bridge 235: the old arch and parapets have been removed, while the abutments are strengthened to receive the new structure.
G. R. Mortimer

Below right: By 8 March the new arch was in place, giving increased clearances for the overhead lines.
G. R. Mortimer

million. The other schemes remained under consideration, as did Copper Mill Junction to Stratford. Resignalling was to be undertaken at the same time, extending to Norwich, Harwich and Westerfield, on the East Suffolk line.

On the Norwich route the section from Colchester to Ipswich and Stowmarket was the first to be electrified, the working being carried out in conjunction with wiring the North London line between Stratford and Willesden. Preparatory work included taking an electric multiple-unit to Ipswich for crew training, and driver instruction with two Class 86/0 and two Class 86/3 locomotives started in October 1983. Wiring trains were based at the former locomotive depot at Ipswich. At Stowmarket the old footbridges had to be removed to give sufficient clearance for the overhead line, and both were preserved. Both platforms were doubled in length, and careful refurbishment was undertaken on the canopies and the Grade II-listed station buildings. Track in Ipswich tunnel was relaid using a continuous concrete slab to improve drainage and help give extra clearances for container trains. Ironically it was the same trains, now required to carry 9ft 6in containers, that necessitated closure for eight weeks in the summer of 2004 to increase clearances still further.

The new timetable which took effect on 13 May 1985 saw the introduction of electric haulage between Liverpool Street and Ipswich, where Class 86s handed over to Class 47 diesels. Seven minutes were allowed for the changeover, and whilst journey times were speeded up for passengers south of Ipswich, the delays onward to Norwich remained. For a while Stowmarket was given its own through electric service from Liverpool Street, at 17.20, which even called at the newly extended platforms at Needham Market; it ran up in the mornings at 07.03. Both trains ran Mondays-Fridays only, the up service surviving until May 1990, the down — running as a Network Express — lasting a further year.

Along the Harwich branch the wires were first energised on 24 March 1986, introduction of the full passenger service being scheduled to coincide with the timetable change on 12 May. Prior to this the 'Day Continental', non-stop at 09.40 from Liverpool Street, and the 'Hook Continental', likewise at 19.40, were the only remaining through services, returning at 18.00 and 07.40 respectively from Harwich Parkeston Quay. The 'European', outward from Parkeston Quay at 07.17 and due back at 21.10, was the only remnant of the cross-country service, taking a circuitous route to Glasgow and Edinburgh. Local trains connected Manningtree at irregular and infrequent intervals off peak, with an occasional working around the north curve to Ipswich. When introduced the electric trains were integrated with the main-line services and were generally hourly throughout the day, although there were still some gaps, and most ran to and from Liverpool Street. The 'Day Continental' and 'Hook Continental' continued much as before, but were joined by the 'Essex Continental', at 09.10 and 19.15 from Liverpool Street, calling at Shenfield, Chelmsford, Colchester and Manningtree before terminating at Harwich Parkeston Quay.

Work continued between Stowmarket and Norwich. On the long weekend of 28-31 March 1986 the throat at Norwich was completely remodelled. Thorpe station was closed, although the booking office and travel centre remained open. Trowse station reopened for the operation, its up platform having been rebuilt, and a bus shuttle was provided onward to Thorpe. Trowse swing bridge had to be replaced, and this was done with a single-track structure where the overhead wire — actually a rigid bar — swung with the bridge. It had proved impossible to monitor the River Wensum remotely, so it was provided with its own signalbox, working with Colchester power 'box, which controlled the remainder of the line. The new bridge was commissioned between 23.00 on Friday 13 February and 16.00 on Sunday 15 February, again necessitating replacement bus services and the use of Trowse station.

Left: Pictured soon after the start of electrified services to Ipswich, Class 86/2 No 86 217 *Comet* runs into Platform 4 with the 10.30 Liverpool Street–Norwich on 7 July 1985. *John C. Baker*

Right: A mixed message at Colchester as Network SouthEast Class 47/4 *Great Eastern* heads a Norwich–Liverpool Street service on 22 November 1986. *Rev G. B. Wise*

Above: Before electric trains were extended from Ipswich to Norwich, Stowmarket was the terminus for an electric service from Liverpool Street, which then survived for several years. Here Nos 309 614 and 309 606, in the brown and orange 'Jaffa cake' livery, approach the station with the 18.00 Saturdays-excepted service from Liverpool Street on 24 June 1987. *John C. Baker*

The new service started with the timetable change on 11 May 1987. Off-peak services were hourly in each direction between Liverpool Street and Norwich, generally down from London at xx.30, and up from Norwich at xx.55, calling at Colchester, Manningtree, Ipswich, Stowmarket, Diss and Norwich, with a few also calling at Chelmsford. The boat trains had inexplicably needed a change of name, the 09.40 to Harwich Parkeston Quay becoming the 'Admiraal de Ruyter', and the 19.50 the 'Benjamin Britten'. There were a few peak-hour electric-multiple-unit services to Ipswich, including the 08.04 from Liverpool Street which divided at Colchester, the leading unit going on to Clacton. The InterCity services were operated by Class 86 locomotives, initially hauled in both directions, with a turnround locomotive waiting to come on the back of the train when it reached the terminus.

After a while this system was replaced by fixed formations with the locomotive always at the London end, and driven in the other direction from a Driving Brake Second Open (DBSO) converted from Mk 2 Brake vehicles. Speeds not exceeding 100mph anywhere on the route, it was permissible for passengers to travel in these vehicles.

On the Cambridge route electrification continued to advance, albeit slowly and in fits and starts, the wires finally being extended from Bishop's Stortford to Cambridge in 1987. The first train had been scheduled for Saturday 17 January, although severe weather conditions forced postponement. Regular electric services started on 19 January, the full timetable coming into operation on 11 May. Prior to this there had been a roughly hourly service from Liverpool Street to Cambridge, alternate trains continuing to King's Lynn. Most of the latter offered at least a buffet service, including the 'Fenman' at 16.35; the 07.50 up from Lynn and the 12.35 down, Mondays to Fridays, also offered 'hot dishes to order'. This service was supplemented by stopping trains roughly hourly between Bishop's Stortford and Cambridge, while the 18.05 from Liverpool Street still continued to Norwich. The new service offered a stopping train to Cambridge every hour off-peak, plus the hourly buffet-car trains, alternately extended through to King's Lynn; the 17.35 from London still ran through to Norwich. One other innovation was the appearance of new 'Sprinter' DMUs on the line between Cambridge and Ely, some going to Peterborough and others continuing to Birmingham New Street. The buffet-car trains were worked by Class 86 locomotives from Liverpool Street to Cambridge, there changing to diesel haulage for the remainder of the journey.

On 23 March 1987 Cambridge was the destination of a special train comprising seven coaches (including a buffet car) and hauled by Class 86/4 No 86 401, the whole in Network SouthEast livery; upon its arrival the first works train for the electrification of the 'missing link' to Royston, hauled by Class 47/4 No 47 576, was ceremonially despatched. Wiring to Cambridge had been included in the original scheme to electrify the Great Northern services, but the Government considered that this depressed the returns, and it was dropped. It was finally authorised after the GE line, and the gap — a mere 10¼ miles — was duly filled in time for the commencement of the 1988 summer timetable, on 16 May, whereupon through services between King's Cross and Cambridge resumed after a break of more than 10 years. Initially hourly off-peak, they called at Finsbury Park, Stevenage and then all stations; the Liverpool Street service of hauled trains to Cambridge and King's Lynn continued as before.

Meanwhile the through service via Cambridge from Liverpool Street to Norwich had started to wither. The 1983/4 timetable had shown such trains leaving the capital at 12.35 (with full restaurant service), 18.05 and 19.35, while in the up direction they left Norwich at 06.37 (Saturdays excepted), 08.32, 11.34 and 15.36 (the last also with a full restaurant service); by the following year only the 18.05 down and 06.29 up remained, and these came off with the change of timetable on 3 October 1988. Services continued to operate between Norwich and Ely and across to Peterborough and beyond, although the GN&GE Joint line between March and Spalding had closed on 27 November 1982. With the introduction of 'Sprinters', from the 1988 summer timetable, cross-country trains called at Ely and reversed *en route* to Peterborough, and the reduced use of the avoiding line paved the way for its singling as part of the rationalisation accompanying the electrification to King's Lynn.

The continuing rise of air travel saw a spur to Stansted Airport opened in 1991, the first trains

running on 29 January, and the half-hourly service from Liverpool Street starting on 19 March. The connection facing London was double-track, the north curve, towards Cambridge, single, with a 40mph speed restriction.

Planning was in progress to extend electrification further, West Norfolk Borough Council campaigning strongly to get the wires as far as King's Lynn. On 28 July 1992 HM Queen Elizabeth The Queen Mother unveiled a plaque at King's Lynn station and the name *King's Lynn Festival* on EMU No 317 361, although it had not been permitted to work under its own power from Cambridge, work on the overhead lines not yet being complete. The wires went live on 11 August. The new timetable from 24 August saw the fastest time between King's Cross and King's Lynn come down to 100 minutes, and from that date 35 through trains daily used the route, operated by Hornsey-based Class 317 units. The new timetable also saw the withdrawal of the DMUs which had provided the service between Cambridge and King's Lynn while the electrification work was in progress. Sunday

Above: On the first day of the summer timetable, 12 May 1986, Class 312/1 EMU No 312 783 waits to depart as the 10.02 from Harwich Town to Manningtree. *Michael J. Collins*

Below: Headed by Class 86/2 No 86 249 *County of Merseyside,* the 'Day Continental' passes Wrabness on 12 May 1986, the first day of public electric operation on the Harwich line. *John Rickard*

morning services continued to be provided by buses until work needed to make the line driver-only was completed.

There had, of course, been an effect on the Liverpool Street service. Until May 1989 this had continued more or less unchanged, but with the introduction of the summer timetable on 15 May it was severely pared back. Whilst the stoppers and semi-fasts remained much the same, most of the through trains to King's Lynn were withdrawn, replaced by an hourly DMU from Cambridge. The only exceptions were, in the up direction, the 07.00 'Fenman' and unnamed 07.45, both still with a buffet car, and in the down the 16.32 'Fenman' and the 18.35, all four being branded as Network Expresses. From October 1989 services between Ely and King's Lynn were replaced in the middle of the day and on Sunday mornings by buses, and this continued until January 1991. With the timetable change in May 1990 the through trains finally came off. They reappeared with electrification in 1992, although London services were now operated entirely by electric multiple-units.

Below: Like its train in InterCity livery, Class 86/2 No 86 220 *The Round Tabler* passes Wrabness with the 18.45 Harwich Parkeston Quay–Liverpool Street on 4 July 1989. *Chris Shaw*

Right: Electrification is almost complete at Diss on 6 April 1987, as a test train formed of Class 309 EMUs Nos 309 622 and 309 601 passes *en route* from Norwich to Stowmarket. *G. R. Mortimer*

Left: The electrification to Cambridge was completed ahead of schedule, at the start of 1987. However, the use of elderley Class 305 units did not go down well with commuters on the route, who had been used to hauled coaching stock. Here No 305 508 accelerates away from Newport with a Cambridge–Bishop's Stortford service on 10 April *Michael J. Collins*

Left: In May 1987 Class 86 electric locomotives took over the haulage of express trains between Cambridge and Liverpool Street. Here No 86 221 *BBC Look East* leaves with the 11.05 up service. *I. J. Hodson*

Below: The Travelling Post Office is now a thing of the past. Here the working for Peterborough, Crewe and Carlisle leaves Cambridge on 5 May 1993, headed by Class 47/4 No 47 537. The following evening the set worked the Carlisle–Newcastle–King's Cross TPO, arriving back in Cambridge as empty stock the next morning. *Chris Burton*

M&GN services

The only competition for trains to East Anglia had been from the Midland & Great Northern and its parent companies. The Great Northern operated between King's Cross and Cromer, and also from some of its lines in Lincolnshire, whilst the Midland provided trains from places such as Leicester and Birmingham.

With its long single-track sections and meandering routes the M&GN was never really a main line, and it was only ever busy on a few summer Saturdays. Before the Great Eastern reached it in 1906 Sheringham was the only important resort in East Anglia served only by the M&GN, although at Cromer the latter enjoyed an advantage from the convenient siting of its Beach station, which was much closer to the town and beaches than was the GER's Cromer High.

In April 1910 the Great Eastern offered a restaurant-car service from Sheringham to Liverpool Street at 7.34am (Cromer 8.0am), arriving at 11.35am after some complex combining of portions at Ipswich. This new service had started in the summer of 1906 with three through services daily, the 1.30pm from Liverpool Street and the 12.36pm from Sheringham being non-stop south of North Walsham, the up train taking 3hr 19min, the down 3hr 13min. The Great Northern offered the 3.0pm from King's Cross, which reached Cromer Beach at 7.7pm, travelling via Peterborough, Wisbech and South Lynn. This was still running in 1938, albeit taking somewhat longer to reach Cromer and including portions for Yarmouth Beach and Norwich City.

It was in its cross-country services that the M&GN came into its own, and the July 1938 timetable showed a Monday-Friday express from Leicester London Road (at 8.52am) to Norwich and Cromer (arriving at 12.18 and 12.21pm respectively), and, on Saturdays, a succession of trains — some from as far afield as Manchester — to Yarmouth and Cromer, as well as one from Bedford, Leicester and Nottingham to Hunstanton.

Below: M&GN Beyer-Peacock 4-4-0 No 29 leaves Cromer for Peterborough. *Ian Allan Library*

Right: Ex-Great Northern 4-4-0 No 4321 approaches Sheringham with an excursion to Cromer Beach on 5 September 1937. *The Rev A. W. V. Mace*

However, local services were generally sparse. There were, for example, only five stopping services between Peterborough and Sutton Bridge on weekdays, an extra from Wisbech to South Lynn running on Saturday evenings. The long single-track sections also meant that the service was slow and timekeeping often poor, especially on summer Saturdays.

After 1936, when the LNER assumed full responsibility for all aspects of the M&GN's operations, the motivation for the LMS to send traffic that way diminished. British Railways increasingly tried to remove what it saw as surplus capacity and duplicated routes, and the M&GN became the first system (as opposed to a branch line) to be axed. Closure came on 28 February 1959, and although a few sections remained open for goods traffic, only the stretch from Cromer to Melton Constable retained a passenger service, operated as an extension of that from Norwich Thorpe to Sheringham via North Walsham. Norfolk & Suffolk Joint services between Lowestoft and Yarmouth South Town remained, as did the branch from North Walsham to Mundesley. The latter eventually closed in 1964, although the former continued until 1970.

Above: LNER Class D16/2 No 2543 heads an M&GN express at South Lynn on 15 April 1947. *H. C. Casserley*

Left: On 17 May 1948 Class D16/3 4-4-0 No 2592 departs North Walsham Town with the 1.30pm Melton Constable–Yarmouth Beach, which originated as the 10.35am from Peterborough North. *W. A. Camwell*

Below: Class D16/3 4-4-0 No 62597 hurries the delayed 2.29pm Saturdays-only Cromer Beach–Melton Constable near Melton Constable Junction on 30 August 1958. *G. R. Mortimer*

Goods services

Goods services on the Great Eastern had depended very much upon the agricultural traffic from rural East Anglia into London, and on the flow of coal arriving via the Great Northern & Great Eastern Joint line to keep the capital in fuel. There was other traffic, of course, notably fish from ports such as Lowestoft and Yarmouth, but this paled in comparison with the first-mentioned. The problem was that the Great Eastern had no indigenous coalfields or other minerals, nor did it serve any areas of heavy industry, so was not guaranteed the heavy baseload traffic of concerns such as the North Eastern. Much of the traffic into London arrived via the Great Northern & Great Eastern Joint line and Whitemoor (March), and so missed the Liverpool Street–Norwich route. However, coal was the *raison d'être* of many of the depots in the London area, such as Devonshire Street, and the railways were considerable consumers themselves.

Norwich was a focus for the local goods traffic, handling it at Thorpe, Trowse and Victoria. The latter two tended to deal more with bulk goods including coal, whilst Thorpe handled the smaller wagonload items as well. Trains would be despatched from Norwich to London, being destined principally for the yards at Goodmayes or Spitalfields, or possibly the terminus at Bishopsgate itself. Temple Mills later came to increased prominence with the redevelopment of the marshalling yards there, but tended to handle more of the traffic coming onto the Great Eastern section from other Regions such as the Southern or London Midland, or coming in via the docks.

In East Anglia, Lowestoft and Yarmouth were important fishing ports and despatched several trains per day towards London in the peak of the season; these would usually arrive on the main line via the East Suffolk. This was classed as passenger-rated traffic, and ran as Class C trains for the obvious reason that fresh fish — even packed in ice — really could not be left sweltering in a marshalling yard. Ipswich was a port of considerable importance and remains so, though now surpassed by Felixstowe and Harwich. It had an extensive system of dock railways on both sides of the Orwell, much of which was taken out of use only in the 1980s and '90s. The rise of Parkeston has been well documented, and although it has been better known in railway circles for its named boat trains, it has always been of the utmost importance for freight, and only lost its status as a train-ferry terminal in 1994. Other smaller ports have also been rail-served, among them Wivenhoe, Brightlingsea and Maldon, all contributing traffic to the main line.

The Norwich main line has suffered chronically from a shortage of track capacity, though it now appears worse than ever. Freight services have thus been much more prominent at night, and this has led to much of the unsocial nature of railwaymen's hours. Local goods traffic from the branches or the main line might be tripped in to one of the main centres during the day for remarshalling, long-distance trains leaving for London in the later afternoon or early evening.

As well as the main marshalling yards there were many smaller ones. Most stations had their own goods facilities, and there were innumerable private sidings. Devonshire Street depot was on two levels, to the west of the Grand Union Canal. There were sidings on the south side of the line at viaduct level. An incline was later built to a yard on the north side of the line at ground level, which also served canal wharves, and later still this was extended to include an area by the canal on the south side, the connection being by two very tightly curved tracks passing under the main line. It was the tightness of these curves and the extremely limited clearance under the main line in what almost amounted to tunnels that necessitated the use of the short-wheelbase, limited-loading-gauge 'Devonshire Street pots' for shunting the yard. A siding from the high level provided coal drops for the canal boats. Finally, just before World War 1 five long sidings were provided on the south side, extending north towards the Mile End Road.

TRAIN CLASSIFICATION
British Standard Headlamp/Disc Code
Class

A Express passenger, newspaper, or breakdown train; express diesel car; snow plough on duty; light engine proceeding to assist disabled train.

B Ordinary passenger, branch passenger or "mixed" train; rail motor (loaded or empty); ordinary passenger or parcels diesel car; breakdown train not on duty.

C Parcels, fish, fruit, livestock, milk or other perishable train composed entirely of vehicles conforming to coaching stock requirements; express freight, livestock, perishable or ballast train pipe-fitted throughout with the automatic vacuum brake operative on not less than half the vehicles piped to the engine; empty coaching stock (not specially authorised to carry Class A code).

D Express freight, livestock, perishable or ballast train with not less than one-third vacuum braked vehicles piped to the engine.

E Express freight, livestock, perishable or ballast train with not less than four vacuum braked vehicles piped to the engine; or express freight of **limited load** not fitted with continuous brake.

F Express freight, livestock, or ballast train not fitted with continuous brake.

G Light engine(s) with not more than two brake vans.

H Through freight or ballast trains not running under C, D, E or F conditions.

J Mineral or empty wagon train.

K Pick-up or branch freight, mineral or ballast train.

Left: An up Continental goods train heads through Wrabness on 8 July 1950, the traffic having come via the ferry from Zeebrugge. The locomotive is Class K1 2-6-0 No 62067.
G. R. Mortimer

The big yards worked round the clock, and there was much trip-working between them, keeping their respective pilots fully occupied. At the same time there were the smaller depots along the line to be served: a good example is shown in the summer 1955 timetable by the 2.45am Goodmayes to Brentwood, which arrived at Romford at 2.58am, departing at 3.45am, Gidea Park at 4.10am, Harold Wood at 4.40am and arriving at Brentwood at 4.55am. The 2.10am to Ipswich, on the other hand, made rather better time, passing Chadwell Heath at 2.14am, Shenfield at 2.48am and reaching Chelmsford at 3.12am, leaving again at 4.16am. The procession of freight along the main line was continuous: there had already been the 10.03pm Spitalfields–Wensum (Norwich), the 10.58am Spitalfields–Ipswich and the 11.45pm Goodmayes–Trowse. The next working was the 2.15am Goodmayes to Colchester; there was another to Ipswich at 5.5am. Much of the traffic carried on these trains would be raw materials imported via the London Docks (perhaps for the various provincial manufacturers), fruit and vegetables from the Continent and further afield and empty wagons being tripped back.

The Southend line also saw its fair share of freight traffic: the 4.48am Goodmayes–Southend Victoria was one such working. Meanwhile there were the overnight trips to be made to and from the Southern at New Cross Gate via the East London line. This involved working into Liverpool Street and reversing, trains going via East London Junction and Shoreditch station. The first of the night left Temple Mills at 8.20pm and was due at Liverpool Street at 10.00pm, while the last left New Cross Gate at 4.5am, being due at Liverpool Street at 4.40am. The constraints of working in and out of the terminus, with the need to reverse, clearly prohibited it being done at any other time. The usual motive power over the East London section was a 'J69', and the east-side pilot had a regular turn on this working. Another of these trips was the 11.8pm from New Cross Gate to Mile End (arriving 12.7am) which left Liverpool Street at 11.57pm. Working trains through the 'rat hole' was a Stratford duty, and locomotives had to be fitted with trip-cock apparatus. Conditions on the footplate for these crews were very poor, and on those occasions when double-heading was necessary only the second locomotive did any work when running through the tunnel itself, to avoid asphyxiating the crew.

In the meantime there were cross-London freights to be fitted in, such as those to and from Dagenham Dock or Acton. A good example was the 6.20pm from Poplar and West India Docks to Upper Holloway on the London Midland Region, via Limehouse Junction, Salmons Lane Junction, Gas Factory Junction, Bow Junction and Stratford. Numbers of trips — such as the 8.7pm — ran from Stratford to Ripple Lane, Barking, and there were various Class K trips to the many private sidings, such as Cook's or the Bryant & May's siding, both at Mile End. Daytime workings on the main line were fewer than those at night, but examples in the down direction were the 10.45am Goodmayes–Lowestoft and the 12.45pm unbraked goods to Ipswich. These required careful timetabling and operation to work them in with the rest of the service, as their low speed could easily have disrupted the faster passenger trains.

In the up direction the pattern of traffic looked much the same, with a concentration at night. Trains from country areas would depart in the early evening and arrive in London in the small hours. One of the earliest was the 3.10pm Class F Norwich–Spitalfields, which called at Goodmayes and Mile End, finally arriving at 12.17am; there was another Class F at 5.25pm from Ipswich to Goodmayes. The 9.54pm Class D from Norwich passed Chelmsford at 12.58am, arriving at Goodmayes at 1.33am, departing at 1.55am and finally reaching Spitalfields at 2.19am. The 8.40pm from Lowestoft Central passed Chelmsford at 1.21am, arrived at Goodmayes at 1.56am, left at 2.8am and arrived at Spitalfields at 2.30am. The 1.45am Southend

Above: Class B1 4-6-0
No 61104 heads an up van
train approaching
Colchester in June 1952.
Ian Allan Library

Victoria arrived at Goodmayes at 3.21am having called at Wickford if required, and there were a number of conditional trains from Parkeston, such as the 3.25am, due Goodmayes at 5.44am and Spitalfields at 6.09am.

The many Class J trips included the 2.18am Goodmayes–Stratford–Thames Wharf; the 2.35am Dagenham Dock–Goodmayes (which ran round Stratford East Curve between 3.15am and 3.34am), the 2.37am Goodmayes–Mile End–Spitalfields and the 1.45am Temple Mills–New Cross Gate. This last had a tortuous route, taking the goods lines to Loughton Branch Junction, then the carriage roads, the Cambridge-line carriage roads to Bow Junction and finally the electrified lines to Liverpool Street. The 4.00am Goodmayes–Acton transfer passed Stratford at 4.18am, and there was also a 5.15am from Goodmayes to Thames Wharf. Many of these trains had been worked as lodging turns — in other words, a Norwich crew might take a goods to Spitalfields one day, run light to Stratford and lodge there, returning the following night with a down working. The traffic in the mid-1950s was extensive, and a surprising amount was still carried in unbraked wagons which then required working back empty; coal empties in particular gave rise to a huge mileage. Coal, especially for the domestic market, was still in heavy demand and provided a substantial proportion of the railway's freight revenue.

Of the down services in the summer of 1956 many originated from Goodmayes, among them the 11.45pm Class F to Trowse, which called at Colchester and Ipswich for water and arrived at 4.22am, and the 12.25am Class F to Yarmouth South Town, which called at Colchester to take water and ran thence via Ipswich and the East Suffolk line. The procession from Goodmayes was continuous, comprising the 12.45am Class F to Colchester, the 1.5am (Mondays excepted) Class F to Colchester (if required), Manningtree and Ipswich, the 1.45am Class F (Mondays and Saturdays excepted) to Ipswich and Yarmouth South Town, the 2.10am Class E to Parkeston (which did not run when the 2.10am Mondays-

only to Chelmsford, Colchester, Manningtree and Ipswich ran), the 2.15am Mondays-excepted to Witham, Kelvedon and Colchester, the 5.0am Class E fast to Parkeston and the 5.10am Class H to Ingatestone, Chelmsford, Witham, Kelvedon, Colchester, Manningtree and Ipswich, where it finally arrived at 2.17pm, having shunted *en route* at all the locations listed.

The trains of unbraked coal empties working back to Whitemoor formed a procession along the Haughley–Bury line. There was a 9.32pm (Mondays and Saturdays excepted) from Stowmarket, and also a 9.32pm from Sproughton, just north of Ipswich, where the site of the yard is now obliterated by the A14. There was a train of unbraked empties from Colchester to Whitemoor at 12.1am, and on Mondays only this was followed at 3.6am by another from Sproughton. Much else focused on Whitemoor: the 9.32pm Class E from Ipswich and Stowmarket, the 11.7pm Class F from Witham and Colchester, the 11.32pm Class H from Ipswich, the 1.20am from Parkeston, not to mention others which had more restricted periods of operation.

Other trains, especially the Class K workings which called at every station and siding to pick up or drop off traffic, tended to run during daylight hours, when station staff were on duty and smaller signalboxes switched in. One such working left Manningtree at 6.25am for Brantham siding, which served the chemical works on the Ipswich side of the station, and the locomotive was allowed to propel its train. It returned at 7.4am. The 6.5am Class K from Ipswich called at Stowmarket, Finningham, Mellis, Diss and Tivetshall, arriving at Trowse at 12.58pm, having shunted at each station on the way. Intermediate stations between Ipswich and Stowmarket were covered by the 7.45am, which also called at Bramford siding, serving Fisons and Pryke Bros. The return working was the 1.40pm Class J all-stations to Ipswich, arriving at 5.38pm. The 5.10am from Goodmayes was a similar sort of train but Class H and called at Ingatestone, Chelmsford, Witham, Kelvedon, Colchester and Manningtree, reaching Ipswich at 2.17pm.

These Class K trains had been the lifeblood of local communities, although they had started to be supplanted by the motor lorry in the 1920s and '30s. Previously everything that was needed in a village arrived or left by train, and the railway had allowed those places it touched to prosper because of the agricultural produce that they could export, or the small works that could be rail-served and so cut the cost of materials and transport of the finished product. One or two illustrations of the sort of activity involved at the smaller stations on the main line in Norfolk and Suffolk are useful. Mellis and Tivetshall were near the top of the league for stations loading grain and flour on the LNER, and considerable tonnages were also on offer at Stowmarket and Needham. Stowmarket and Tivetshall loaded livestock; Needham and Haughley loaded vegetables, though in the latter case much of this was due to the nearby stations of Aspall, Brockford and Mendlesham on the Mid-Suffolk, which came under its jurisdiction. Stowmarket also saw traffic in ale and porter, whilst Tivetshall handled round timber. Several stations also saw considerable traffic in manure, and Bramford had enjoyed the dubious distinction of loading more than any other station on the LNER!

If the empties worked back to Whitemoor at night, the trains arrived loaded during the day, and not necessarily by the same route. The 10.40am Class H from Whitemoor to Colchester was routed via Long Melford and Mark's Tey, which had the advantage of not taking up valuable capacity on the main line, and the 4.55pm from Bury also arrived via the Stour Valley. Trains from Whitemoor might therefore arrive in Colchester from opposite directions. However, unbraked goods trains still ran along the main line and included the 12.45pm from Goodmayes, which called at Witham, Colchester and Manningtree, reaching Ipswich at 4.9pm. As with all of these workings, it shunted on its way and might be refuged or looped to let other trains pass. Not that all the daytime goods trains were as slow: the 2.0pm Goodmayes–Parkeston ran non-stop, as did the 4.18pm Spitalfields–Ipswich and the 5.2pm from Stowmarket to Trowse.

In the up direction, workings naturally balanced those in the down. The various local workings started early, such as the 4.40am Class K from Colchester to Haverhill via Mark's Tey, which was followed by the 5.16am Class J to Whitemoor. On the main line the 7.0am Class K from Colchester went as far as Witham, whilst a light engine (one of many such workings) went from Colchester to Sudbury to work the 10.6am thence to Bury. The 7.28am worked to Bentley and then Hadleigh, returning to Bentley and thence via Keebles siding to Manningtree. The epitome of the local goods train was probably the 3.15am from Thorpe, which called and shunted at all stations to Mellis (in 1956 they were Trowse, Swainsthorpe, Flordon, Forncett, Tivetshall, Burston and Diss); it then left for Eye at 9.36am, returning to Mellis at 10.50am, and continuing via Finningham and

Haughley to Stowmarket, finally reached at 12.47pm. The Waveney Valley branch was served by a separate trip which left Wensum Junction, Norwich, at 8.4am, and which would be worked by a 'J15' or an 'E4'. One of the more specialised types of freight was illustrated by workings such as the Fridays-only cattle train from Chelmsford, in connection with the market there, which left at 5.40pm and arrived at Temple Mills at 6.41pm. This was complemented by the 4.21pm light-engine from Colchester to Chelmsford, and which could run as a freight train on Fridays for the conveyance of cattle. The locomotive then worked the 6.40pm back to Colchester. The 5.1pm light engine from Colchester was booked to call at Kelvedon and shunt if required, reaching Chelmsford at 6.34pm and working the 7.39pm back to Ipswich.

The long-distance trains from East Anglia would run from the early evening, such as the 9.0pm Class F from Thorpe and Trowse to Ipswich and Goodmayes and the 8.40pm from Lowestoft Central to Goodmayes and Spitalfields. Traffic out of Harwich Parkeston Quay was carried by trains such as the 10.30am SX Class D to Goodmayes, 12.17pm SX to Whitemoor, and the 2.16pm to Whitemoor, which also served Mistley. The 5.5pm SX Class J called at all branch stations (Wrabness as required) on its way to Colchester. There was much inbound traffic from Whitemoor and Goodmayes, and considerable empty stock working, much back to Whitemoor unbraked. Cross-country workings included the 9.12pm Class J Cambridge to Colchester via Haughley and the 8.55pm Whitemoor to Manningtree and Colchester, which changed crews at Stowmarket. There were many, many more: the main line was never quiet. Signalboxes were either open continuously — all those at Ipswich, for example — or switched out for only a part of Sunday, and even then they might be required to open for specials. However, there were very few goods trains on Sundays, and most of them were continuations of trains that had started out the previous day.

Other workings which are worthy of mention include some of those which now come under the general heading of 'parcels', which were passenger-rated Class C diagrams. The other example of this type (apart from empty coaching stock) were the fish trains, such as the summer 1957 3.53pm from Lowestoft to Stratford Market, which called only at East Suffolk Junction to change crews, and Witham to let the 4.24pm Sheringham–Liverpool Street express pass. In 1949 there were newspaper trains out of Liverpool Street: the 2.40am for Manningtree, Ipswich and Norwich, due in at 5.37am, was one of the fastest of the day and was converted to 'Britannia' haulage right from their introduction. The same locomotive had worked in with the 9.41pm Class D goods from Thorpe to Spitalfields, due at 2.19am, and which had been a notoriously poor timekeeper until 'Britannias' were introduced, which cured the problem. The 3.30am newspapers ran to Chelmsford, Witham, Colchester and Clacton, arriving at 5.44am. The 5.40am empty milk tanks ran from Channelsea Junction to Norwich, calling as required from Haughley to Tivetshall. The 6.59am parcels called at Brentwood, Shenfield and then all stations to Ipswich, and the 12.42pm similarly, replacing Brentwood and Shenfield with Stratford. The 3.0pm Ocean Mail special ran non-stop to Parkeston, arriving at 4.55pm, and there was an express parcels from Parkeston to Ipswich and March at 7.51pm.

By the 1959/60 timetable things were looking a great deal thinner in terms of goods workings, even though the wholesale withdrawal of services and the move out of sundries traffic of the Beeching era were still three years away. The effects of line closures were beginning to be seen: the East Suffolk had closed between Beccles and Yarmouth South Town on 2 November 1959, and the Midland & Great Northern in February. Parts of both were retained for local goods, but they were finished as through routes. Traffic was diverted onto the main line as a result: for example, the 12.7am Class D Goodmayes–Lowestoft Central now ran via Wensum Junction, the East Suffolk being closed at night, though the 4.17am Class D Spitalfields–Lowestoft empties (as required, Mondays excepted) did run via Beccles. Temple Mills naturally now played an even more important role in freight workings, and some of the longer-distance trains started there, such as the 11.54pm Class E to Goodmayes, Colchester (where it stopped for water only), Ipswich and Trowse. Unbraked trains such as this continued to be a feature of freight working, trips still including, amongst others, the 1.8am Goodmayes–Colchester, the 9.45am Sproughton–Whitemoor and the 10.50pm Ipswich–Whitemoor empties, but their number was slowly diminishing.

The general pattern of working was still very similar and showed trains such as the 7.35am Class K Ipswich and all stations to Stowmarket, those to Brantham siding from Manningtree, the Hadleigh goods and the leisurely return trip from Trowse to Tivetshall and Bungay. Traffic between Colchester and Cambridge could still run via the Stour Valley, and both Spitalfields and Bishopsgate were still open, though diminishing in the amount of traffic handled, the latter eventually burning down in 1964. It was a particularly rough place, where it seemed as though the men ran the management. When Dr Beeching tried to introduce the 'open terminal' concept whereby traders brought in their goods and loaded and unloaded wagons themselves, there was great opposition from the motor drivers who feared loss of work and employment.

A revealing picture of the pattern of contemporary goods traffic was painted in the *Eastern Region Magazine* in 1962, which printed maps of England and Wales, showing the density of passenger and freight traffic. As expected, the section between Shenfield and Liverpool Street was the busiest in the country for passengers,

though goods traffic in East Anglia showed a different picture. Between London and Haughley the main line carried between 10,000 and 50,000 tons per week, whilst the section between Haughley and Norwich managed only between 5,000 and 10,000 tons, the line to Parkeston Quay similar. Even so, the Beeching report showed Norwich Thorpe, Trowse and Victoria (and City as well) each generating over 25,000 tons per annum, as did Stowmarket, Ipswich, Colchester North and Hythe, Chelmsford and Brentwood. Others fed similar amounts onto the main line, including Yarmouth, Lowestoft Central, Clacton, Felixstowe, Braintree and Maldon, although it didn't stop them being proposed for closure. The only other routes in former Great Eastern territory carrying the larger amount of goods traffic were from London to Ely, Haughley to Ely, Norwich to Ely and Cambridge to King's Lynn via March and Wisbech. Norwich then, as now, saw most of its freight going in and out via Thetford; March continued to be the major centre.

In March 1963 Dr Richard Beeching, Chairman of the British Railways Board, published his report on the reshaping of the railway. Most of the country stations on the main line between Colchester and Norwich closed to all traffic by the end of 1965, leaving only a few to function as 'railheads'. The report observed that the railway system had grown to its full extent when the horse-and-cart jolting along an unmade road was the only competitor, so rail had penetrated deeply into the local distribution network. Consignment sizes were frequently small and the cost-effective long bulk hauls were few. As roads improved the advantage of rail disappeared rapidly: for example, 57% of stations open in 1962 contributed only 1% of parcels revenue, and 58% of them generated less than 1% of the minerals and merchandise traffic. Dr Beeching's answer was to concentrate on 'railhead depots' — Temple Mills, Witham, Ipswich and Norwich being scheduled for this purpose — and to develop 'liner trains'; only Ipswich and Norwich were to be so served. A service was proposed between the two along the main line, but the London–Norwich route was to be from King's Cross via Stevenage, Cambridge and Ipswich! The days of the Class K freight, calling at all stations and ambling along the branches to Eye or Hadleigh had gone, to be replaced by the block trains of today. When steam finished, the Felixstowe branch contributed almost nothing in freight terms to the main line; now it has the lion's share of the traffic by virtue of the relentless expansion of the port for containers.

An aspect that does not at first sight fit in with freight was empty carriage stock (ECS). Such workings were much more prominent in the London area, where Thornton Fields, Stratford and Ilford were the most important locations for the storage of stock, and its working was mostly in the hands of men in the goods links. Channelsea sidings, Thornton Fields, Woodford and Ilford were the main sidings for suburban stock, which was largely worked by the suburban tank engines as part of the day's diagram. A typical Stratford turn might have involved going light to Thornton Fields, ECS to the Street and then pick up the suburban service running. At the end of a shift, it might have been ECS from Liverpool Street to Ilford and then light-engine to Stratford. The ECS shifts that were mainly engaged in this work full-time were those that moved main-line express and intermediate rolling stock. This work was covered by crews drawn from either the suburban passenger or the main-line goods links.

The suburban crews would mainly use the locomotives of their own link, which were 'Buckjumpers', 'Gobblers' or 'N7s'. The jobs were not as easy as they sounded — with 10 coaches of corridor stock behind an 'F5' plenty of slipping was guaranteed. This was especially true going up to Liverpool Street, which was on a rising gradient until Bethnal Green. Another problem encountered when working ECS with tank engines was maintaining the brake. It was surprising how much steam and water were used in maintaining 21 inches of vacuum, and also in recreating it after brake applications. Although the brake apparatus was the same on the tank engines as on '1500s' or '2800s', the vital difference was in the steam pressure and boiler capacity, and the little old 'Buckjumper' would be blowing its boiler out to maintain 21in with a full head of steam. If a crew were having a rough run a drop in steam pressure would make the brakes start to drag. There was a lot of difference between boiler pressures of 160 and 210lb/sq in when using the vacuum brake, and with the steam-heating requirements on main-line stock in the winter a tank of water didn't go far!

An ECS crew would leave the Stratford carriage sidings via the carriage roads, which worked in with the goods roads as far as Bow Junction. They would then mainly stay on the up suburban until reaching Liverpool Street, where most of the main-line trains left from Platforms 7-11. After the train left empty stock would be worked back to Stratford from an inward main-line train, all of which took much more time than might be realised. Allowing for the preparation of the locomotive and travel to the siding as an hour, the crew would couple onto the train. Sometimes it would be necessary to shunt to put the stock into the correct order, after which the brakes were tested and the wheel examiners would have a final check, with the fitters attending to faulty brake cylinders and/or steam heaters. This could take up to half an hour. The haul to Liverpool Street could take another 30 minutes as ECS trains were fitted in between other traffic. Parcels traffic, mails and so on had to be loaded, so that the coaches could be at the platform for up to an hour before departure.

After release the ECS locomotive and crew would stand in a shunting spur and wait for the incoming main-line train, which then had to be unloaded. By the time it had been taken back to Stratford the crew would have worked six hours, and would then go light to the locomotive depot

and dispose of the locomotive. If they were under seven hours they would report to the locomotive foreman, who might be hard up for manpower in the disposal yards and give them a locomotive to dispose, thus making up their time. If not, they would sign off and be grateful for a short shift for once.

Empty stock working was not confined to the London area, of course. Each of the major stations had its own carriage sidings, and there were pilots on hand to cover the workings to and from these. Norwich Thorpe had its own carriage pilot, whose duties might include ECS workings, and the addition or removal of passenger-rated stock such as horseboxes. Cambridge had three carriage pilots (north end, south end and middle), which were mostly 'Intermediates' ('E4s'), although occasionally a 'Claud' was used, especially at the north end. There were also trips along the length of the line which were needed for stock balancing purposes. Examples from the 1957 summer timetable included the 1.20am Thornton Fields–Colchester (2.5am Mondays only), which was required for an early-morning Ipswich–Yarmouth trip. Another ran from Thornton Fields to Ipswich at 5.10am (3.20am on Mondays), and another at 9.53am on Fridays only, which worked back as the 2.45pm from Ipswich to Liverpool Street. Summer extras generated even more ECS working: the 6.43pm up from Walton worked back from Liverpool Street to Colchester at 9.39pm, arriving at 11.7pm. These trains would be in the charge of the normal express locomotives, and were timed at normal express speeds, although there were restrictions if running tender-first. Regulations were that locomotives travelling tender-first could only move at 75% of their timetabled speed, but even so this could result in doing 45mph out on the road, with the hazards of flying coal dust and difficulties with sighting. Considerable light-engine mileage was also associated with this type of working.

The Cambridge line was very busy indeed with goods traffic. Much of the work from Cambridge itself involved re-manning of Temple Mills–Whitemoor workings in both directions, using 'K1s', 'K3s' and 'WDs'. This was mostly coal for Becton, West Ham and Brimsdown, where it would have to be backed round the curve into the yard. Some went to Broxbourne power station or Angel Road gas works, and the locomotive could then run light to Stratford. The train could be taken to Temple Mills West Yard, thus avoiding the hump, and a local engine would then take it the rest of the way. Cambridge men did sometimes use the hump, and such trains went on the main line via Picketts Lock, Tottenham and Northumberland Park on the goods lines. These were very busy, and were worked on the permissive block system with no distants, so there was much calling-on. At night it could be like rush hour — trains block to block, and it was quite possible to get shunted for a Class D fast goods to pass.

One job involved the empties from Northumberland Park to Niddrie. Sometimes after taking a train of coal up, or possibly travelling on the cushions, the Cambridge crew would go to Ponders End to pick up empties. Other times they would go to Stratford to see whether there were any jobs, and would leave their locomotive on the shed and collect a different one. Work was often kept for Stratford men, where promotion came very early because of the local pressure on jobs. There were Stratford men who were drivers at 21, whereas it was nearer 30 at Cambridge or Ipswich, which caused some jealousy.

To work trains in the other direction, up to three sets of men could go up to Broxbourne 'on the cushions' on, for example, the 9.15pm to Liverpool Street. They would then get a local to Lea Bridge and walk through the goods yard to Temple Mills North, where there was an old black carriage, with the foreman's office at one end of it. There would be a bucket of water for washing. The Cambridge crews would reman trains on the goods roads for Whitemoor, usually with a 'K3'. These were good steamers if the coal were good but very hard work if it were poor. These trains were allowed 45 wagons loaded or 70 empties going back, the latter figure being dictated by the length of loops and refuges such as Spelbrook, where there was also water. It was not unknown for a crew to 'stop for water' if they really needed a blow-up. One of the Cambridge main-line goods workings was for South Wales via Yarnton (north of Oxford), with a 'J20'. Cambridge crews worked this as far as Bletchley, the locomotive working right through and returning the next day with another load of 'greenhouse' coal for the Lea Valley nurseries. There were two trainloads of this coal per day via this route.

Goods traffic on the Cambridge line was always dominated by the coal coming in via the GN&GE Joint line, which the Great Eastern had fought so hard to establish. This dictated that much of the working was via Whitemoor, with crews from elsewhere changing over with men from March. At the other end of the line the marshalling yards at Temple Mills were always very busy, and there were many destinations in London, including Spitalfields and Bishopsgate, and much traffic to and from the docks. There were also the workings over the East London line to and from the Southern.

The timetable for the summer of 1913 shows the down services starting with the 4.20am Mondays-excepted from Temple Mills, which ran via Lea Bridge and called at both Harlow and Sawbridgeworth to leave London goods and whose purpose otherwise was to drop off trucks for most stations to Cambridge, which was reached at 9.10am. About 20 minutes later it was pursued by the through goods, destined for Peterborough, which passed the earlier train at Bishop's Stortford, making its first stop at Whittlesford at 6.50am, and passing Cambridge without calling. Its next stop was at March between 8.35 and 8.45am, and it reached Peterborough at 9.20am. There had already been a number of earlier goods workings on the route

between Ely and Peterborough, such as the 8.15pm from Ipswich, Stowmarket and Bury St Edmunds, which reached March at 1.45am, and the 9.45pm from Temple Mills to Peterborough, which arrived at 4.30am.

The procession from Temple Mills continued with the 4.50 and 5.45am trains to Cambridge. The first ran Mondays-only and worked any traffic to Brimsdown, shunting as required. It then called at Elsenham, Audley End and Great Chesterford to pick up cattle, which were taken to Cambridge, reached at 9.35am. It then continued via St Ives to March, which it reached at 11.5am.The second did not run on Mondays, called at Brimsdown, Cheshunt, Broxbourne and Burnt Mill (as required) to leave London goods, before arriving at Harlow, where it shunted. It then continued to Peterborough via St Ives, calling at Whittlesford but not Cambridge, and March.

The 3.35am Temple Mills–March also called at Spitalfields and Stoke Newington. The 8.20am Saturdays-only Temple Mills to Cambridge was limited in its load, and forbidden to shunt at intermediate stations, being allowed only to attach or detach traffic. It called at most stations, many for 'brake goods' only, and also at Rochford's siding, which was between Broxbourne and Cheshunt, near Wormley, and which served the extensive greenhouses in the Lea Valley. The 8.55am Stratford–Doncaster was required for a Class A locomotive, and officially designated as 'Through Trucks'. It called at Ponders End to allow the 9.10am Liverpool Street–Norwich train to pass, then Whittlesford and Ely. If required to wait for other trains to pass at Ely North the locomotive could call for requirements — in this case, water; if nothing needed to pass there it had to call for requirements at Whitemoor. The 10.45am Mondays-excepted from Temple Mills to Cambridge called at Angel Road and just about everywhere else, apart from Roydon and Littlebury siding, finally reaching its destination at 6.45pm.

At the other end of the line goods tended to reach Norwich and stations from Ely via Whitemoor. The 5.40am from there ran via the avoiding line and called at Attleborough as required, Wymondham, Trowse and Thorpe. The 3.30am from Temple Mills called at Whittlesford and Ely , and then Shippea Hill and Two Mile Bottom as required, and all stations except Roudham Junction and Spooner Row to Norwich Thorpe, reached at 11.25am. Timekeeping was not good on this working, and much provision was made to allow for this. There was a 5.10am goods from King's Lynn, which travelled via Dereham to reach Wymondham at 8.40am, then on to Trowse and Thorpe. The 7.30am Mondays-excepted express goods from Peterborough travelled via the avoiding line at Ely and then called at Lakenheath as required, Brandon, Wymondham and Norwich, and was followed by the Mondays-excepted 8.20am from Cambridge, which called at most places including Roudham Junction, but not Hethersett or Trowse. There was a coal train at 10.45am from March via the Ely avoiding line, which again served almost all stations before running via the Wensum Curve to Crown Point sidings at Norwich.

Loaded coal trains arriving at Whitemoor via GN & GE Joint Line, 1913

Time	Onward destination	notes
1.35am	Norwich	
2.35am MX		
2.42am		
4.45am		
5.5am MX		
5.15am SX	Parkeston	
7.10am TuO		
8.35am		
9.2am		
9.35am MO		coal and goods
10.52am	Peterborough	
11.5am MX	Peterborough	
12.35pm		
1.15pm MX		
2.10pm		goods and coal
4.25pm		
8.10pm		goods and coal
8.30pm	Norwich	from March
9.10pm SX		
9.57pm	Cambridge	
9.54pm		goods and coal
10.0pm SX		
10.19pm		goods and coal
10.41pm SX		
11.2pm SX		

M - Monday
Tu - Tuesday
S - Saturday
X - Excepted
O - Only

Thus was East Anglia — and much of London — supplied with coal. This does not include much of the other goods traffic that came in via the Joint line, nor the relatively infrequent passenger service, although this included the Great Eastern's services to Lincoln, Doncaster and York. Trains were, of course, loaded heading south and run as empties ('trucks') northbound.

Lesser lines such as the Hunstanton branch also had their share of goods services, although far less frequent, but reflecting the agricultural GER hinterland. There was a Tuesdays-only express cattle train from Wells at 5.45am, which ran via Hunstanton, and reached King's Lynn at 8.10am. The 4.45pm goods from Hunstanton reached Lynn at 6.5pm, and started from Wells at 3.7pm. There were also some workings between Hunstanton and Heacham and onto the Wells line. In the other direction empties ran from King's Lynn to Hunstanton, Docking and Wells on Tuesdays only at 5.0am, with the 7.37am down goods from Lynn calling at all stations. The 10.47 from King's Lynn also called at all stations except Hunstanton, going on to Wells from Heacham. The down express cattle train left King's Lynn on Tuesdays only at 3.53pm, reaching Wells at 6.40pm.

Much of the goods traffic at the southern end of the main line was carried over the goods lines between Copper Mill Junction and Waltham Cross. One working involved a Cambridge crew taking the 7.37am to Bletchley with a 'Claud' and bringing back the 10.8am freight from Bletchley with a 'Black Eight' (LMS Class 8F 2-8-0). This carried Welsh coal for the greenhouses in the Waltham Cross area and loaded to about 30 wagons. There were up and down goods loops at Wormley, Broxbourne, Roydon, Harlow and Spelbrook, while other locations to the north also had them, notably Whittlesford. Cambridge and Ely had 'goods independent' lines allowing goods trains to bypass the passenger stations; they were generally worked on the 'no block' system, which meant that, in effect, trains could move 'on sight' if it were safe to do so. The system failed on one occasion, on 7 January 1931 at Northumberland Park. A down goods, headed by 'J15' No 7649 was standing at the down goods starting signal when a light engine, 'J69' No 7364, running bunker-first, came to a stand to the rear of the train. A down special coal train, headed by 'J39' No 1265, was then allowed onto the same line, also in accordance with the rules, but failed to stop. The resultant collision drove the light engine into the brake van of the goods train, which in turn was pushed forward some 40 yards. Two tank wagons containing petrol, which had been marshalled next to the brake van of the goods train, were derailed, the leading one being thrown against the side of the light engine, the other coming to rest against the locomotive of the coal train. The petrol poured out and ignited immediately, and the guard of the goods train and the driver and fireman of the light engine lost their lives in the ensuing blaze. Much damage was done to the light engine and the rolling stock. Lt-Col E. P. Anderson, the inspecting officer for the Ministry of Transport, concluded that the fault lay with the driver of the coal train, who had considerably underestimated the speed and distance needed to stop his train. However, despite occasional such incidents, it is worth remembering just how safe the railways were (and are), and just how dedicated and conscientious their staff.

Above: A typical freight train of the later British Rail era: Class 47/0 No 47 052 passes Colchester with the Felixstowe–Garston Freightliner working on 19 June 1986.
Michael J. Collins

243

Motive Power

The Great Eastern Railway nurtured a number of distinguished locomotive engineers at its works at Stratford. Samuel Johnson, Locomotive Superintendent from 1866 to 1873, left to join the Midland Railway, William Adams went to the London & South Western, and T. W. Worsdell went to the North Eastern in 1885. The GER had inherited a number of locomotives of varying dimensions and reliability from its constituent companies, mostly from outside builders. These included some from Sharp Bros of Manchester, built for the Eastern Union. The original Eastern Counties' Romford factory was moved to Stratford, starting in 1848, and the first superintendent to work from there was John Viret Gooch. His designs included a number of 2-2-2 locomotives, both tank and tender. He resigned in 1856, to be succeeded by Robert Sinclair, who was in charge when the Great Eastern came into being in 1862. Among his most successful designs were the 'W'-class singles, built on contract by

outside firms, and they operated the express services on the GER for many years. When Johnson took over Neilson, Reid & Co supplied five 2-4-0s, which, together with an additional three similar locomotives built at Stratford, formed the basis for the 'Little Sharpies' supplied by Sharp, Stewart and Stratford Works between 1867 and 1872 and which were still at work in the far corners of Norfolk into the early 20th century.

Massey Bromley had a short spell in charge, which was noted for the 4-2-2 express locomotives which he designed and which were used on the principal trains. Four were based at Yarmouth, four at Norwich, and the other 12 at Stratford. Bromley's key move was to greatly increase the importance of Stratford in building Great Eastern locomotives, reducing the reliance on outside firms. Worsdell extended this, requiring all the company's locomotives to be built at Stratford. The Class Y14 (LNER 'J15') 0-6-0 was one of Worsdell's conspicuously successful

Below: Thetford Junction on 17 July 1909, with GER 2-4-0 No 114, the first of the 'Sharpies', on a Swaffham train. This locomotive was broken up *c*1912.
Ian Allan Library

Above: An immaculate Great Eastern Class P43 4-2-2, No 18, heads an up express away from Ipswich Tunnel. *Ian Allan Library*

Left: Class J15 0-6-0 No 65457 on station-pilot duty at Cambridge in September 1960. *John C. Baker*

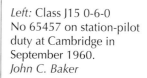

Left: The GER 2-4-0 Class T19s, designed by James Holden, were the mainstay of express work for many years. They survived through LNER days until the British Railways era as Class E4. Here No 7502 leaves King's Lynn with a stopping train for Cambridge. *F. R. Hebron*

Above: 'Claud Hamilton'
4-4-0 No 62586 prepares to
leave Platform 3 at Norwich
on a local working.
Ian Allan Library

designs and for many years formed the basis of the GER's goods working. Worsdell's other lasting contribution was the introduction of the royal-blue locomotive livery for which the GER became famous.

James Holden became Locomotive Superintendent in 1885. Among his designs were the Class T19 2-4-0s, which for many years were the mainstay of express services and which went through a number of rebuilds, ending up as LNER Class E4. The modifications included replacement of the leading axle with a bogie, provision of superheating, and the use of oil-burning. In 1900 Holden introduced the first of his new Class S46 4-4-0 bogie express locomotives, the first being numbered 1900 and named *Claud Hamilton*, after the GER Chairman. Shown at that year's Paris Exhibition, it was initially oil-fired and was fitted with a scoop for picking up water from troughs. By the end of 1911 some 111 examples had been built, these being joined in 1923 by a further 10 contructed by the newly formed LNER. They proved to be very long-lived, most surviving into the BR era, and the last examples, still based in their traditional operating area, remained in service until 1960. Their 'Claud' nickname was perpetuated on BR long after their demise and the end of steam generally. Having been displaced many years earlier from front-line duties, they had found employment on the various cross-country and other secondary services in East Anglia and could be seen working trains between Norwich

and King's Lynn via Dereham, or on the Wells line; as such they became the province of a peculiarly Great Eastern system whereby drivers who had been in the top links stepped down onto these less-demanding local trains — into the 'Claud link'.

The 'Clauds' were good-riding, free-steaming locomotives with 7ft driving wheels and were very sure-footed in dry conditions, although they would slip with a heavy load on a wet day. They had a long sloping firebox and needed a thin fire at the front of the box but thick at the back and sides; too much at the front would cause them to steam badly. Nevertheless, they developed tremendous power, and those with the larger-than-normal-diameter cylinders (10in instead of 8in) almost seemed to be bending the frames with each thrust of the pistons. They had a relatively low water capacity and when they had been the mainstay of the Norwich service had needed to take water twice, at both Tivetshall and Ipswich troughs, especially if running through to North Walsham and Cromer without calling at Norwich. In many ways taking water was easier with a 'Claud' than with later locomotives, as the Great Eastern had used the Westinghouse air brake. This meant that there was air pressure to operate the water scoops, and lowering or raising required only the 90°turn of a small tap to operate the valve.

Great Eastern drivers were very proud of the 'Clauds', and Dick Hardy, when Shedmaster at Ipswich, felt that there often seemed to be a

Above: The last surviving 'B12' 4-6-0, No 61572, backs onto its train at Norwich Thorpe in May 1961. *John C. Baker*

'Society for the Prevention of Cruelty to "Clauds"' in operation. On one occasion in the late 1930s they had been regularly rostered for the night mail, about 10.35pm from Liverpool Street. The General Post Office claimed that the train was regularly losing time, and two ex-Great Central Class D9s were drafted in for the job. The crews were not pleased by this and treated them with disdain, thrashing the daylights out of them. The regulator would be opened wide at the foot of Bethnal Green Bank and left there; they would need to take water both at Ipswich station and the troughs! They kept the 'Postal' to time, but the cost in coal and water was phenomenal, and the turn soon reverted to 'Clauds', which took it smoothly in their stride.

The appearance of the 'Clauds' was accompanied in 1900 by the Class F48 0-6-0 locomotives, essentially the goods version, and these also proved long-lived, surviving well in the British Railways era as Class J37. That distinction also belonged to Holden's 'Y14s', which he continued to build, later becoming Class J15. These locomotives also proved astonishingly long-lived, undergoing a series of rebuilds and undertaking a variety of work, both passenger and goods, that is almost unparalleled.

In 1907 James Holden was succeeded as Locomotive Superintendent by his son, Stephen. The increasing demands of faster and heavier trains meant that more-powerful locomotives were needed, and so the Class S69 4-6-0s appeared in 1911. Always known as the '1500s', they were classified by the LNER as 'B12s' and did sterling service on most parts of the main lines, including the boat trains to Harwich and the North Country expresses. The '1500s' followed the 'Clauds' and represented a significant advance in terms of power and adhesion, their nominal tractive effort of 21,969lb easily outclassing the earlier type's 17,096lb in final 'D16' form. Six-coupled, with 6ft 6in-diameter drivers, the '1500s' were also less prone to slipping. However, they required drivers to be familiar with them before handling them, and if belted along on full regulator they tended to run hot big or small ends. They were better run with a 'bit of lever' and in first port, in other words with the regulator not wide open. They could inspire a fierce pride in their regular drivers: in the 1930s, Bob King of Norwich shed would oil up No 8509 after he had finished his day's work if he knew that he was not working the following day, so that even if the next crew did no oiling at all, 'she would still be all right'. He recalled how his chest would swell with pride when passengers congratulated him on a right-time arrival at Liverpool Street. He also insisted on throwing out the smokebox ash himself, which could amount to as much as 20 or 30 barrowloads, so that he could be sure that the door seal was perfectly clean and airtight; otherwise air could be drawn in whilst running and thus cause overheating, and it was not unknown for '1500s' to arrive at Norwich with the smokebox door glowing red to the handles! Their appearance, along with that of 'Clauds' and 'T19s', was changed dramatically by the fitting of ACFI feedwater heaters in the 1930s, leading to the nickname of 'hikers'.

A. J. Hill became the GER's Locomotive Superintendent in 1912, and one of his main contributions was the 0-6-2T design that later became LNER Class N7. Few had actually been produced by the time of the Grouping in 1923, so many of the suburban services remained in the hands of the smaller Holden tanks.

H. N. Gresley took charge of the locomotive affairs of the new London & North Eastern Railway at its formation in 1923, and the next advance came with the 'Sandringhams' ('B17s' or '2800s'), introduced by him late in 1928. Developing a maximum tractive effort of 28,555lb, these in turn offered an increase in power over the '1500s' and had 6ft 8in driving wheels and three cylinders. It could be difficult to detect trouble with the middle big ends, and the solution adopted was to fit a glass container full of aniseed, which broke when they ran hot, revealing its presence by smell. They could reach 80mph but had a tendency to roll at speed, especially when 18 months or more out of the shops and with wear in the axleboxes. In 1935 two of the class, No 2859 *East Anglian* and No 2870 *City of London*, were streamlined to work the 'East Anglian' between Norwich and London. When introduced on 27 September 1937 this train was allowed 2hr 20min for the journey between Norwich and Liverpool Street, calling only at Ipswich. Although withdrawn for the duration of the war it was reintroduced in October 1946, but the streamlining was removed from the locomotives in 1951. Two crews were regularly allocated to each of these engines, which were based at Norwich, and No 2870 was always considered the faster of the two. This locomotive and its home depot achieved a remarkable feat during World War 2, after Driver George Ewles of Norwich noticed that the middle small end was using rather a lot of oil. The locomotive had almost completed 100,000 miles since last being 'shopped' and was thus due a major overhaul; it had not been stopped for repair once in that time, and shed staff hoped to get it past the magic 100,000 mark and achieve the record. On the trip in question Driver Ewles had to get underneath at Liverpool Street and oil it up, and the mileage was safely reached.

From 1945 some of the 'B17s' were rebuilt by Edward Thompson as two-cylinder locomotives, and these were redesignated 'B2'. The lack of pits for oiling-up at places such as Colchester gave them an advantage over the inside-cylinder machines, though they were not always liked by the crews. They were designed to replace the 'B12s' on the heaviest and fastest trains and did so successfully on the main Norwich services.

The next new type to appear was the 'B1', designed by Thompson. Officially known as the 'Antelope' class but invariably referred to as 'Bongos' (a nickname derived from No 1005 *Bongo*), these were 4-6-0s, with 6ft 2in-diameter

drivers. Developing a maximum tractive effort of 26,878lb, they ran well up to about 70mph but vibrated rather than rolled at 80mph. They could keep to 'Britannia' timings on occasion, but this caused problems with the boilermakers, as this sort of treatment caused the tubes to leak, after which they had to be re-rolled onto the tubeplate.

When Gerard Fiennes and Stuart Ward wanted to recast the main line timetable out of Liverpool Street after World War 2 they soon realised that the existing locomotives were the limiting factor: they could climb Brentwood Bank at no more than 40mph. Salvation came in the shape of the proposed new standard 4-6-2 locomotives, later to become the famous 'Britannias', with a tractive effort of 32,150lb, and around which the new timetable was built. Twenty-three were allocated to the Great Eastern for the new service, though a trial was first made with 'Battle of Britain' Light Pacifics — tractive effort 31,050lb — borrowed from the Southern Region.

Three of these locomotives were based at Stratford for a time, and they soon demonstrated their power. On the first trial, with 400 tons trailing, one of them was blowing off when it topped Brentwood Bank at 56mph. They were fast and strong but very heavy on coal, probably because of the reverser. They were fitted with an air-pressure type, controlled by a single lever, and it needed a quick and skilful movement to get the cut-off right: it was all too easy to go from 25% into backward gear when aiming for 15%, with a very obvious and nasty jolt for the train. Some of the LNER engines had the lever-type reverser, whilst others including the 'Britannias' had the screw-type. The Southern locomotives thus tended to be run at 25% cut-off, which pushed up the coal consumption.

At Norwich Bill Harvey was especially interested in the 'Britannias' for two reasons: they were the first examples of what he described as 'a new national type of locomotive', and they were coming to East Anglia. Nos 70000-5 went to Stratford, while the Norwich allocation arrived in May 1951, 10 of them staying 10 years. He realised that the spotlight was on Norwich: questions might even be asked in the House about these locomotives! He wanted to put on a good show, and he certainly succeeded handsomely, though in some ways this was fortuitous. The 'Britannias' developed 25% more power than the 'B1s', with a grate area 1½ times bigger, and could tolerate poor coal much better than the smaller locomotives they replaced; crews often objected when given back a smaller locomotive after a 'Britannia'. In other parts of the country 'Britannias' replaced LNER 'V2s', LMS 'Royal Scots', Southern 'Battle of Britains' and 'West Countries' and GWR 'Castles', all of which were of a similar power to the new Pacifics, and crews thus tended to take a poor view of the newcomers. This was especially true of the Great Western, which had been littled changed by the Grouping in 1923 and had thus enjoyed a continuity of practice not found elsewhere: Western men didn't

Above: One of the Thompson
'B17' rebuilds, Class B2
No 61671 *Royal Sovereign*
looks immaculate passing
Trumpington with the
4.10pm Cambridge–King's
Cross on 7 September 1954.
E. R. Wethersett collection

Left: No 70000 *Britannia*
heads an up excursion near
Chelmsford on 11 May
1951. *P. Ransome-Wallis*

take kindly to the essentially LMS-style overview at nationalisation. Cardiff Canton depot had an ex-LMS man in charge, and this was the only ex-GWR depot where the 'Britannias' performed well.

Locomotive rostering meant that the Norwich 'Britannias' travelled all over the country. Stratford was often in trouble with them, and, if one of its allocation failed, Bill Harvey had to supply one, which was returned only when a washout was needed. A typical Stratford 'Britannia' turn involved the North Country boat trains but might start with a freight from Goodmayes to Ipswich and another from Ipswich to Parkeston Quay, followed by the boat train to Sheffield; there the locomotive would have three hours' rest before returning to Harwich with the night boat train, finalling arriving back at Spitalfields on a freight. Eventually the situation at Stratford became so bad that the maintenance of East Anglia's entire allocation of 'Britannias'

(a total of 23 locomotives, reduced to 16 by the early 1960s) was concentrated at Norwich. Bill Harvey kept a close check on the movements of his 'Britannias', virtually becoming his own controller. He might find out from Control, for example, that one of his locomotives had been stopped at Sheffield, and would then be able to get it back quickly, and he thus kept their availability high.

The 'Britannias' averaged about 7,000 miles per month, though at one stage No 70012 did over 10,000 miles in successive months. A double London trip (via Colchester) was 460 miles per day; one return trip via Cambridge was 264 miles. The introduction of the 'Britannias' had revolutionised the train times, and they were popular with the locomotive crews. They were good riders and good steamers, but with their wide firebox they were heavy on coal. It was possible to burn 4½ tons each way between London and Norwich, though this could be reduced with careful driving. They were fitted with a rocking grate which could be rocked gently when the locomotive was in motion in order to keep the fire clean. They also had a steam-chest pressure gauge, which often didn't work but which, when it did, effectively measured the pressure of steam being supplied to the cylinders. It was useful to try to get this and the boiler pressure as close to equal as possible, which meant that the steam was being used as efficiently as possible. The 'Britannias' were not fitted from new with speedometers, but these appeared later.

An experienced driver would swap with his fireman and take a turn with the shovel: this kept him fit and allowed the fireman to learn the road, the signal placings and the techniques of driving, though an Inspector would reprimand the crew if he found them swapped over. A 'Britannia' could get 11 coaches from Norwich to Liverpool Street without trouble in two hours when the need arose, and although the trip could be done with one tank of water, it was customary to re-fill from the troughs at Ipswich. It was also common for a crew to work a train from Norwich out via Ipswich and back via Cambridge, or *vice versa*. Each locomotive was allocated to two drivers: from Norwich, one would take it to Liverpool Street and back in the morning, and the other in the afternoon. Later a pair of small hooks was fitted on the cab side, and each driver given an engraved nameplate to hang there, so that the public knew who was in charge. As Driver George Ewles of Norwich said, 'When a man reached this position he didn't think so much that he worked for the railway; he was so proud he thought he owned it!' The practice was perpetuated in the early days of the diesels but did not last long.

On one hair-raising occasion Driver Fred Shingles was on a 'Britannia' working the 8.30pm Liverpool Street–Norwich, due to call only at Ipswich. At Chadwell Heath the locomotive parted from its tender, leaving both crew on the former with a box full of 1½ tons of fire! All their tools were on the tender, except one bar for rocking the grate. The brake pipes having parted, the train would stop safely, but the problem was to stop the locomotive and get rid of the fire, since there was no water — it was all in the tender. They rocked the grate to get rid of the fire, igniting the sleepers in the process, and eventually managed to stop. It transpired that the cotter had been left out of the drawbar when the locomotive had last been in works.

Eventually the Norwich 'Britannias' were transferred to Immingham, where they replaced 'V2s', which were much better riders. Subsequently the performance of the 'Britannias' deteriorated markedly, prompting the Motive Power Superintendent, Mr Dixon, to visit Norwich. He suggested that the maintenance at Norwich must have been poor, but Bill Harvey pointed out that it had been excellent: there was a price to pay for performance. For example, they were prone to burn out superheater elements, which thus needed frequent renewal. The piston

and valve rings had a low life — seldom over 12,000 miles, and possibly as low as 6,000 miles, whilst the expectation for the BR Standards was 36,000 miles; on occasion they had to be renewed every shed day! It was a case of 'The brighter the light, the darker the shadow'. This is not to say that the older LNER locomotives did not have their defects, and it was sometimes necessary to carry out modifications when they arrived from the shops, making sure to remove them before return.

In the spring of 1958 BR's Eastern Region started to take delivery of 10 Type 4 diesel-electric locomotives ordered by the British Transport Commission from English Electric. They were finished in the standard dark-green livery with the later BR roundel and were numbered D200-9. Five were allocated to Stratford for working the main line via Ipswich. Rated at 2,000hp, they could work in multiple with a number of other types and were also to be used on freight duties, with availability for 22 out of every 24 hours envisaged. They were fitted with steam-heat boilers and an 800gal tank and water scoops. On 16 April 1958 No D200 undertook a demonstration trip between Liverpool Street and Norwich, carrying a headboard proclaiming:

FIRST 2,000hp DIESEL
LONDON–NORWICH
Progress by *GREAT EASTERN*

The introduction of these locomotives allowed the timetable to be reorganised from 5 January 1959, when they took over the principal trains to Norwich via Ipswich, with 20 'Britannias' being used interchangeably on services to Norwich, Yarmouth and Clacton, and local and stopping trains beyond the electrified areas being worked by DMUs. Express timings were all brought up to 'Britannia' standards, and the consequent tighter schedules allowed a more intensive use of rolling stock and thus a generally more frequent, regular-interval service.

Electrification gradually ensured that multiple-unit stock replaced locomotive haulage on services as far as Colchester and Clacton and ultimately on all trains to Cambridge and King's Lynn. First introduced in 1962, the Brush/Sulzer Type 4 diesel-electric locomotives (soon to become known as Class 47) had started to appear on services to Norwich via both routes by 1968. Although there were many variations and modifications within the class during their lifetime, they offered a considerable increase in power over their predecessors, to 2,750hp. Other, smaller locomotives continued to be used, notably Brush Type 2s (later Class 31) — and English Electric Type 3s (Class 37), both continuing in use for very many years on account of their high levels of reliability.

As electrification spread the diesels were finally replaced in the 1980s by Class 86s, of similar age, displaced from London Midland Region services on the West Coast main line. Norwich Crown Point depot gained 14 examples, initially used to

Left: Preserved Class 40 diesel No D200 runs round the 'Anglian Diesel Farewell' train at King's Lynn on 9 May 1987. Ironically, King's Lynn did not bid farewell to diesels for several more years. *A. C. Smallbone*

Left: A Cravens two-car DMU waits in the north-side bay at King's Lynn on 12 July 1986, having worked in from Cambridge and Ely. *Dr Iain C. Scotchman*

Left: A 'Clacton Electric' unit waits at the Essex terminus on 25 May 1963, resplendent in its lined maroon livery and showing the wraparound cab windows that characterised the class as built. *Brian Haresnape*

haul trains in both directions, with another locomotive backing on at Norwich or Liverpool Street, releasing the incomer for its next duty. In due course the TDM (Time Division Multiplex) system was developed which allowed the locomotive to be controlled from a DBSO (Driving Brake Standard Open), a coach modified with a cab at one end, and thus eliminating the need for attaching and detaching at termini. Class 86s were displaced from the Cambridge line when King's Lynn received its electrified services. Lacking electronics and computers, these locomotives have been described as 'electric steam engines', yet on the Ipswich route they lasted well into the privatised era of Anglia Railways, and Class 86s, usually in pairs, can still be seen on the line operating Freightliner services between Ipswich and Stratford.

Finally the newer Class 90, a familiar sight on freight trains in East Anglia, were first tried on the Ipswich line in July 2002, on hire from Freightliner and, later, English, Welsh & Scottish Railway, and, completely replaced the Class 86s after National Express took over the wider franchise in 2004, as 'one' Railway.

The diesel and electric fleets operating on the Ipswich line are based and maintained at Crown Point depot, opened in 1982. This carries out servicing and heavy maintenance and has about 140 staff (including around 50 maintenance staff and 50 cleaners), of whom about 20 are outbased. The depot has 3.6 miles of track and 26 sidings. The other major servicing and repair depot for both main lines is at Ilford, although much of the fleet was maintained at Hornsey when West Anglia Great Northern Railway operated services out of Liverpool Street on the Cambridge line. Time will tell what happens in the future: Network Rail's recent Rail Utilisation Study for the Great Eastern lines envisages electric-multiple-unit operation of all main-line services, including those to Norwich. There will continue to be much of interest.

Below: Before King's Lynn was electrified Network Expresses changed locomotives at Cambridge, where Class 86/2 No 86 246 *Royal Anglian Regiment* is seen at the head of the up 'Fenman'. *King's Lynn & West Norfolk Borough Council*

Left: Representing the DMU revolution of the 1980s, 'Sprinter' No 150 103 waits to depart Ipswich as the 15.43 to Sheffield on 7 January 1987. Did British Rail really run Class 150s that far? *Brian Morrison*

Below: Time moves on, and on 10 May 1989 Class 321 EMU No 321 330, in Network SouthEast livery, was recorded leaving Cambridge on the 10.25 service to Liverpool Street. *Chris Milner*

Index